TOO SMALL A WORLD

Mother Frances Xavier Cabrini

THEODORE MAYNARD

TOO SMALL
A WORLD

The Life of Mother
Frances Cabrini

With a foreword by
Timothy Cardinal Dolan

IGNATIUS PRESS   SAN FRANCISCO

Cover art montage:
Restored photo of Mother Cabrini,
© CatholicArtAndJewelry.com;
New York City background, © Adobe Stock.

Cover design by Paweł Cetlinski

Published in 2024 by Ignatius Press
All rights reserved
ISBN 978-1-62164-704-1 (PB)
ISBN 978-1-64229-314-2 (eBook)
Library of Congress Control Number 2024931065
Printed in the United States of America ∞

To Padraic Colum

CONTENTS

PART III
GOD'S GYPSY

Though we drift apart, we are always near one another, since we are here in the tiny space of this small world that to us—with our small, narrow minds—sometimes seems so huge.

Saint Frances Xavier Cabrini

FOREWORD

Timothy Cardinal Dolan
Archbishop of New York

The name Theodore Maynard is indeed enshrined in the Cooperstown of U.S. historians of the Catholic Church. One of his best works was his acclaimed 1945 biography *Too Small a World*, a life of Mother Frances Cabrini, whom the Church has since canonized as a saint. Thanks to Ignatius Press, we've got this gem available again.

Maynard had that talent of keeping his historical works scholarly yet readable, accurate yet inspirational. While a serious academic, he never felt the need to deny the supernatural, the power of the invisible in the lives of those he studied.

The life of Mother Cabrini is especially welcome today. In a culture tempted to demonize immigrant and refugee, we behold a woman who exhausted herself embracing them. In an atmosphere that characterizes the Church as antifeminine, we behold a strong, courageous, independent woman before whom prelates trembled. For those who think the rejection of pious, traditional faith is essential for a liberated life of fulfillment, we have a powerful portrait of a woman who believed humble obedience the key to power and success.

And Mother Cabrini helps us recover the sense of "catholic" as one of the four marks of the Church. Proudly Italian, she longed to serve in China, ended up in the United States where she gratefully became a citizen, and traveled extensively on missions throughout Central and South America. She belonged to everybody, and she embraced them all, earning the title given to her for all time: Mother.

The welcome reappearance of Maynard's biography, and that of the film *Cabrini* from Angel Studios, promises a renewal of devotion to this small, fragile woman who to this day walks tall on the streets of New York, Chicago, Seattle, Denver, New Orleans, and beyond. We venerate her here in New York, seeking her intersession not just to find parking spaces, but to find a spot for Jesus in our hearts, a place for the poor, the sick, and the immigrant in our embrace.

INTRODUCTION

Not many years ago, in Milan, a frail-looking nun came to consult a noted and scholarly priest on some business affairs. The interview over, the churchman called his old housekeeper: "Did you see that little nun?" he said. "She has crossed the Atlantic Ocean more than twenty times, she has founded many institutions in Europe and America. A great missionary, yes—and a saint! And what have *we* done for the glory of God during our whole lifetime?"

The frail little nun was Mother Cabrini and the scholarly churchman, Achille Ratti, Prefect of the Ambrosian Library, who later, as Pope Pius XI, raised her to the honors of the altar, proclaiming her *Beata*, only twenty-one years after her death.

Yet, the reader must not conclude that the mere casual acquaintance of the future pontiff with the Servant of God can account for the record speed of Mother Cabrini's beatification. Without the required miracles and the incontestable proof of heroic virtue, as evidenced during a long and tedious process of investigation, no servant of God ever reaches the honor of beatification. Thus the test of Mother Cabrini's cause lasted ten years, while witnesses were examined in many countries by the ecclesiastical tribunals in various dioceses in Europe and America.

Heroes in our armed forces are rewarded with the Distinguished Service Cross or with the Medal of Honor for having acquitted themselves exceptionally on battle fields, in the air, or on the seas by some heroic act "beyond and above the call of duty". In the Church, men and women who have practised in a heroic degree, not occasionally but habitually, all the Christian virtues and whose lives thus stand out conspicuously above what we might call a normally good life are raised to the altars and officially declared saints. To this, moreover, must be added the indubitable evidence of fully attested miracles.

Saints are as diverse one from another "as star differeth from star in glory", but all are identically one in their Christ-life. "I live," says Saint Paul, "now not I, but Christ liveth in me"; meaning: In the eyes of God, it is only Christ's life that He sees reproduced in them. Thus God is glorified in His saints. They are held up for our encouragement, proposed to us as our models and as the objects of our veneration. Their lives are written for our study that we may see in them, displayed at its finest and best, the example of those virtues, qualities, and motives that made them what they were during their mortal career.

The halo of canonized saints may at times dazzle rather than illuminate us when we compare them with ourselves. Then, too, some saints are so distant from us in point of time that they are almost lost in the dim light of history. We are so embroiled in the battle of life that their voice reaches us from afar, muffled and indistinct, owing to the noise and confusion of this bustling age.

Mother Cabrini, whose life story is told in these pages, lived in our times and moved in our midst. Many who knew her and were closely associated with her are still alive. She died a few years ago only, not in a distant land, but in one of our busiest cities, Chicago; and her mortal remains have been laid to rest in New York. Born in Lombardy, she adopted America for her country and was a citizen of these United States during the last ten years of her life.

At the very moment when this world seemed to have been enlarged beyond all limits by nationalistic ambitions, she declared it to be *too small* for her zeal. Charitable institutions were opened by her in Europe, in the United States, in South and Central America—institutions where the Sacred Heart of Jesus is known, praised, and loved day and night, through all the year. At her death, sixty-seven such houses had been set in operation over all the world.

Speaking of some modern saints who by their penitential lives have sounded the call to repentance, we have heard scoffers dismiss them with a shrug of the shoulders, saying: "But this is the twentieth century." Yes, unfortunately the twentieth century has been our undoing. Two world wars in a single generation have disillusioned even the most enthusiastic regarding our boasted modern progress.

Mother Cabrini can be called in all truth a twentieth-century saint: what is best in this century she represents. What message, then, has she for us moderns?

In her exterior life there was nothing extraordinary that cannot be imitated by the average man—save only her ceaseless activity. What, then, does her life teach us? *Practical Catholic action!* In obedience to her ecclesiastical superior, she dedicated her life to a special phase of missionary work. When she wanted to be a simple and an obscure nun in some existing community, she was told by her bishop to found a new missionary institute. When she longed to go to China, Pope Leo XIII pointed to America. In childlike obedience, instantly, she followed the immigrants to America. In search of them, she went into places where even the police were afraid to go. That was her apostolate. To her countrymen she dedicated her own life and the labors of the congregation that she founded. Wherever her people went, she followed. To quote Cardinal Mundelein's radio address at her beatification:

When we contemplate this frail little woman, in the short space of two score years, recruiting an army of 4000 women under the banner of the Sacred Heart of Jesus, dedicated to a life of poverty and self-sacrifice, fired by the enthusiasm of the crusaders of old, burning with the love of their fellow-men, crossing the seas, penetrating into unknown lands, teaching peoples and their children by word and example to become good Christians and law-abiding citizens, befriending the poor, instructing the ignorant, watching the sick, all without hope of reward or recompense here below—tell me, does not all this fulfill the concept of Catholic Action, practised by a modern saint?

It is the same old story of Divine Providence. From the helpless little family of Bethlehem it is no far cry to Mother Cabrini. "The weak things of the world has God chosen to put to shame the strong" (1 Cor 1:27).

Many good Christians are content to look after their own salvation, believing they are thus fulfilling their mission on earth. But Mother Cabrini saw in the poor, wretched creatures of the slums the suffering members of Christ's Mystical Body. To helping them by corporal and spiritual works of mercy she dedicated her life. Well she knew that Christ needs no one to carry on His work in the world. He can convert sinners, as Saint Paul was converted on the road to Damascus. He can cure the sick and maimed, as He healed the lepers and paralytics in Galilee. He can feed the hungry as He fed the multitude in the desert. Yet, to keep the Mystical Body alive, healthy, and growing, He wants our efforts, no matter how poor and insignificant they may be. Christ is *incomplete* without us, in the sense that Saint Paul says, the Church is "His fulness".

It is not an easy task to write Mother Cabrini's life and to paint her portrait in the true perspective. The Church declared her a saint, not for what she did, impressive as were her phenomenal activities and achievements, but for what she was. About her interior life we know little or nothing. She so jealously guarded the interior sanctuary of her soul that even those she loved best were not allowed to get a glimpse of her mystical relations with her Creator. The *Arcanum Regis* remained her secret to the end.

In the whole Catholic hagiography there is probably no other life of a saint in which we find such marvelous exterior activity and so few signs of mystical experiences. And yet we know she prayed continuously. Obvious to all was her constant recollection, even when traveling and overwhelmed with business cares. Her attention to the minutest details of foundation and government regarding her many houses did not distract her in the least from her habitual union with God. Hence her calm and peaceful countenance, her quiet and subdued voice. This, indeed, was Mother Cabrini's secret.

In undertaking, therefore, the writing of her biography, as here offered to the reader, Theodore Maynard well knew the difficulties awaiting him. But every facility was accorded him, and he had free access to the apostolic process of beatification and other private documents. The result has been a laudable and fine piece of work.

May this book achieve what the author intended—the glory of God, who is wonderful in His saints. May it inspire many to work with greater confidence for their personal sanctification and to serve Christ in His Mystical Body, by adopting as their own the words of Saint Paul, Mother Cabrini's *leit-motif*: "I can do all things in Him Who strengthens me."

ARISTEO V. SIMONI
Vice-Postulator of Mother Cabrini's Cause

PROLOGUE

The Arrival

The last day of March 1889 was one of dull gloom. The ship as it came into the harbor of New York might have met gusty weather or snow or even a high, gleaming sky. Instead, there was nothing but a thin rain turning into fog. March was not going out either as a lion or a lamb. Perhaps it was like a jellyfish—cold, damp, inert, with a sting hidden somewhere.

The fifteen hundred immigrants—mostly Italians—crowded into the steerage quarters of the *Bourgogne* could not have enjoyed the eight days of their voyage from Le Havre even had the weather been better or the ship more comfortable. For most of them, the bare thought of the sea had had such terrors that they were ill from the moment they left the wharf. Some of them had become seasick as soon as they put foot on the as yet steady deck. Not least was this true of the seven young nuns who had left their quiet convent in Lombardy to work among the neglected Italians of New York. Of one alone was it not true. That one was not only the leader of the band but no less a personage than the General and foundress of a new religious congregation.

She was even more of a personage than that. By becoming naturalized as a citizen of the United States, she was to be the first American to be canonized. Her name was Francesca Cabrini.

To her name she had added, because of the missionary
enthusiasm that had possessed her since she was a child,
the distinctive name of Xavier, Italianized as Saverio. Now
that her ambition was about to be fulfilled and her life-
work begun, her heart soared. For her even those dreary
skies were gilded.

Since early morning she had been on deck trying
to make out what she could of the low shores of Long
Island. A few of her companions had been courageous
enough to crawl out of the berths where they had huddled in misery all the way across the dreadful Atlantic.
Even to see dry land might be a restorative. As they could
see very little that foggy morning, they soon wanted to
crawl back into their berths. There they pulled the blankets over their heads again and said the rosary. It would
be time enough to get up when the ship berthed by
its pier.

One of them stayed by Mother Cabrini, her affection
overcoming her strong desire to lie down. To cheer her,
Francesca cried, "Ah see! That beautiful gull. Don't you
think it's like our guardian angel coming to look after us?"

The poor Sister smiled wanly and shook her head. She
was too miserable to see anything like that. "No, Mother,"
she confessed, "To me, when coming out of the fog, it
looks more like a ghost. Or perhaps ..."

"Perhaps like what, Sister?"

"Worse than a ghost—a lost soul or a devil."

Francesca took a swift look at the young nun's white
face. "Sister," she said, "you are not feeling well. Hadn't
you better go to the cabin with the others?"

The tiny fragile-looking woman—she seemed hardly
more than a little girl dressed as a nun, though she was

nearing forty—was left alone on deck, staring out into the fog. There she remained all that day, except when she went to the dining-saloon or the Sisters' cabins. The young nuns, her daughters, still had to have their spirits kept up, for though the long-drawn-out fog-horn above their heads, and the answering hoots, were an assurance that they were really about to land soon, they were also rather frightening.

On deck, Francesca Cabrini stood trying to make out through the misty greyness anything that would indicate New York. But the boat went slowly, with several stops, and it was late in the afternoon before it slipped with a muffled bump or two beside its pier.

There had been little enough to see. An officer had stood beside Francesca a moment or two, and she had asked him in French, "Where is this famous Statue of Liberty?" It had been completed only a year or two before and was talked about more then than now.

His hand pointed in the direction. "Over there, Mother."

"But I cannot see it."

"No, you won't see it today."

The still more famous skyline of New York—famous even fifty years ago—was hardly to be made out at all. The large innocent blue eyes could not see much, though they were avid to see everything. Until she had founded her institute, it had been her habit to keep her eyes lowered, even though her head was always held erect, for Francesca was by nature a shy and retiring person. But for the last ten years or so, she had had to change all this: as General, she soon learned that she had to keep her eyes very wide open indeed.

It was a pity that she could put them to such very little use now. Here in New York, after all, was to be the start of her work. But though she could see so little, her

long, firm, smiling mouth moved in a continuous prayer
of thanks that she had at last arrived.

✦ ✦ ✦

Yet her coming to New York involved the renunciation
of a dream. As a child, she had wanted to go as a missionary to China, and China had been in her mind when
she founded her Institute of the Missionary Sisters of the
Sacred Heart. When Bishop Scalabrini of Piacenza had
first suggested that she go instead to work among the poor
Italian immigrants of New York, she had told him, "But
New York is too small a place for me."

He had smiled at that. "Well, what about the United
States, Mother Cabrini? You ought to find it large enough."

She in turn had smiled. "No, Monsignor. For me the
whole world is too small."

Not until she had knelt before Pope Leo XIII and had
unfolded her ambitions to him was her destiny fixed. The
old man in the white robe and the scarlet cape edged
with white fur put his hand on her head. She looked
up at his face—at once rugged and sensitive—and he
said very gently, "Not to the East, my daughter, but to
the West."

After that, there was no hesitation. Commissioned by
the pope himself, her work could not fail. It was he who
had paid her fare and the fares of the six nuns she had
brought with her. They were certainly better off than the
two Little Sisters of the Poor whom they had discovered
in the steerage. On their behalf, Francesca had spoken to
the captain—she was always bold enough when it was
a question of asking something for other people—and
they had been transferred to the cabin section. There
they had joined her own Sisters when they sang the *Ave
Maris Stella* at evening, on such evenings as any of them

felt well enough to come on deck. Had it not been for the pope's generosity, Francesca would have had to go steerage herself.

The most precious thing in the scanty baggage in her cabin was a packet of letters introducing her to the American bishops. The principal document was one drawn up by young Monsignor Giacomo Della Chiesa, who was to be her lifelong friend and eventually pope as Benedict XV. It was signed by Cardinal Simeoni, the prefect of Propaganda. She could hardly have had more impressive credentials.

Even so, the work she had undertaken would have dismayed anybody but herself. For though Archbishop Corrigan had invited her to New York to work among the Italians, and she had been given to understand that a convent was ready for their reception, she had no money, and she was invading the land of the fabulous dollar. Moreover, she knew hardly a word of English. Against the strenuous Americans she had nothing to pit except her faith in God and the strenuousness that, somewhat to her surprise, she was already beginning to discover in herself. At her capacity for work and her confident courage the Americans themselves were soon to gasp.

She felt these qualities rising in herself as something new, called forth by the new situation she had to meet. That she was going to grapple with difficulties uplifted her, strengthened her. It was out of obedience to the pope that she was going forward. But she knew that she would need all the strength she could muster. It was a small thing to have carried her six nuns across the ocean, almost literally on her own tiny back. They—good, honest girls from inland Lombardy—would, she was sure, be all right as soon as they felt the earth solid again under their feet. Perhaps it was fortunate for them that their seasickness disabled them from thinking about anything except their misery. They were all so accustomed to depend on her, confident that Mother would manage everything well. The difficulties she saw ahead had not so much as occurred to them. Their great comfort that day was that they would sleep that night in their own convent in New York.

❧ ❧ ❧

It was late in the afternoon that they got off the ship, and it was seven o'clock before their trunks and baggage received the chalk marks of the customs-inspector, little though there was to inspect. Father Morelli and another of the priests of the Congregation of Saint Charles Borromeo— the order her friend Bishop Scalabrini had founded to work among the Italian immigrants—met her at the pier and acted as interpreters. The Irish inspector passed her quickly with a "Say a prayer for me, Sister."

Father Morelli explained what he had said, and she smiled her eager, "*Sì! Sì!*" The good Irishman seemed to understand.

The nuns were at once carried off by the two priests to their rectory of Saint Joachim's Church at 26 Roosevelt Street. That was where their rectory was to be; while it was being got ready for occupancy, they were living in hired rooms nearby. But at least there was a real Italian dinner once more. How good it tasted! It helped to revive the Sisters, who had had so little to eat on the voyage. But their seasickness had been as much psychological as physical. Healthy young women, they were now hungry for food, and they ate heartily and thankfully.

Yet Francesca had a feeling all through dinner that these priests were ill at ease about something. Their welcome was cordial, and they were obviously delighted to have with them the nuns about whom Bishop Scalabrini had written; but their bursts of vivacious conversation, followed as they were by intervals of awkward silence, were slightly disturbing.

Francesca soon found out why. Almost the moment that the meal was over she said, "I am sure you Fathers will not mind if we don't stay any longer. The Sisters are very tired. If you will now be so good as to take us to our convent ..."

There came a moment of silence that was more than awkward. Then Father Morelli, shrugging his shoulders and using eloquent hands, murmured, "Of course, Mother—your convent ..." His voice trailed away into silence. It was his companion who had to come to the rescue, stammering lamely: "It is not our fault, Mother Cabrini; it really is not our fault."

Francesca looked at him in surprise. "What is not your fault?"

The shoulders and hands were eloquent again with embarrassment. Father Morelli had to explain. "Well, Mother, I'm sorry to tell you this, but the fact is that there *is* no convent."

The faces of the poor nuns went white with dismay. "No convent!" exclaimed Francesca. "But I was told that one was ready."

"There will be, perhaps later. The archbishop ... difficulties. It would take too long to tell. You will see the archbishop tomorrow. It is not our fault."

There was clearly no use in discussing the matter further just then, and the Fathers appeared to know nothing except the appalling bare fact. They could give no idea as to whether or not a house had been taken as a convent or (supposing this had happened) when it would be ready.

"But what are we to do for tonight?" Francesca asked.

Father Morelli vaguely suggested a hotel.

In 1889 the telephone existed, but very few people possessed one. The Fathers did not. There was therefore no way of getting rapidly into communication with hotels. For that matter, the money in Mother Cabrini's purse was so little that she shuddered at the idea of a hotel bill for even one night.

That gave Father Morelli a solution, of a kind. "We might find", he said, "a rooming house not very far away. Would that do?"

"Perfectly", Francesca agreed. "Tomorrow I will see Archbishop Corrigan. There must be some mistake. For one night missionary nuns can surely put up with a rooming house. If it is near here, so much the better. The Sisters want to go to bed."

❦ ❦ ❦

The rooming house was in the first of the many Little Italies Francesca was to see in the United States. That made it seem an appropriate place for her. She even thought that further appropriateness came from the circumstance that it was on the edge of Chinatown. They would at least see Chinamen, even though they had been unable to go to China as missionaries. The group of nuns accepted the rooms willingly, without even bothering to inspect them first. Sleep was what they needed at the moment.

When they got into their rooms, they soon discovered that sleep was about the last thing they were likely to obtain there. In the early days of the institute, they had often had to sleep on straw, like troopers, not finding it uncomfortable. But in these rooms, they could not bring themselves to stretch out on the naked boards of the floors, so horrible was the filth.

One of the nuns turned down a blanket and screamed, "Ah! Look at that—see they're crawling!"

Francesca looked. "I see", she said, drawing back dismayed. Dirt was bad enough, but this ...! The stinking sheets and blankets were alive with bedbugs. The convents from which they had come were bare enough, but immaculately clean. Poverty was one thing; this was another.

All the same she found an encouraging word for them, "My daughters," she said, "we are missionaries, and missionaries must be prepared for mishaps of this sort. It is a sign that God is going to bless us."

To get into the foul beds was out of the question. Yet so tired were they that, sitting in chairs and resting their heads on the table or against the wall, they snatched cat-naps, waking every now and then with a jerk to imagine that vermin were crawling all over them. Nor was this quite imaginary. Mice scuttered across the room in the darkness and a few bedbugs crawled up to them. Martyrdom would have been easier to endure by Italians accustomed to sticking mattresses and bed-coverings every morning through the open window for a thorough airing.

Francesca made no attempt to sleep, though she urged the Sisters to get what sleep they could. She had a special fastidiousness, and for mice she had her full share of feminine terror. Leaning against the head of one of the beds, she prayed all night.

In spite of everything, she felt a strange kind of joy. Already she had discovered by experience that difficulties and discouragements at the outset showed that success was to follow. It was not for her to say what sort of trial God should send; that this was of an unexpected variety did not disturb her confidence in the divine love. As the day that was to come would be sure to bring another trial—for what Father Morelli had said showed that something had gone wrong—all the more she needed the fortification of prayer. In what seemed a quiet, lucid dream, she stood all that night, leaning not so much against the bed as on the bosom of God.

Francesca and her nuns after their terrible night in the rooming house went very early to Mass and Communion at the Italian church on Centre Street. It had been a warehouse, and it still looked rather like one. But there they received the Bread of Heaven for which they felt all the more famished because of the long fast they had suffered during their voyage. With special fervor they received it, praying for a favorable outcome of their interview with the archbishop. That same morning, with the two Scalabriniani Fathers accompanying them, they called at the archbishop's house on Madison Avenue.

Michael Augustine Corrigan, though still only fifty, had been a bishop for sixteen years, first at Newark, where he was born, then as coadjutor to Cardinal McCloskey, before succeeding him in New York. He was a kindly man, and one who smiled a good deal. He smiled more than was necessary, because by doing so he could hide a slight malformation on one side of his mouth. This made him look somewhat sleek, and those who did not like him found for him the name of "Smiling Mickey".

When Francesca and the Sisters called on him, he did not smile at all at first. He was greatly surprised and a little annoyed to see them there. To one of the Sisters present, who many years later wrote her impressions of that interview, he seemed decidedly cold—*massima freddezza* was the phrase she used—though this probably was nothing more than the reserve of a man taken aback. To women in their predicament, with their sensitiveness sharpened by anxiety, anything less than effusive cordiality naturally seemed frigid.

At once he asked, "But did you not get my letter asking you not to come just yet?"

"No, Your Excellency", Francesca said. "No such letter reached me. It must have crossed the Atlantic while we were on our way. Bishop Scalabrini told me that everything was ready; and I find that nothing is."

The archbishop explained further. "But Mother, I did not know you would come so soon. You wrote to me in February to say that you might come in May."

"Or *before*, I think I said", she corrected him.

"Well, yes, I believe you did, now that you mention it. Even so, I had not counted on your getting here the last day of March. I see, Mother, that you must be one of those rare people whose performances outrun their promises."

At this this group of nuns, who had been very anxious in looks, for the first time allowed themselves a wan, half-hearted smile. On such occasions, sisters are accustomed to leave the conversation to their superior; had they spoken they could have answered for Francesca, "Our Mother is just that, Your Excellency. She moves like a flash of lightning."

The archbishop this time did not find it necessary to smile deliberately. But his smile was no more than a flicker, and it passed quickly; then he looked grave again. However it had happened, he was sorry for the misunderstanding—more than ever sorry when he looked at the circle of tired, pale, timid faces. But he saw also that Francesca's face shone with intensity and determination and that her eyes flashed whenever she spoke. He had already set her down in his mind as somebody very exceptional.

There was at least one advantage Francesca had in speaking with him; he had made his theological studies in Rome and so knew Italian. He needed it now, for he saw that it was necessary to make himself painfully plain.

At last he came to the point. "The situation", he told her, "is such that frankly I do not believe you can work to any profit here. It's most unfortunate that you've come. Now the best advice I can give you is that you and the rest of the Sisters get on the same ship by which you came and go back to Europe."

He was not meaning to be brutal. But he saw no use in not telling her just what he thought.

The group of nuns whitened at the words. Had they made that dreadful journey all for nothing? Were they now, just when they thought it was all over, to endure another such week on the sea? The mere prospect of it made them feel seasick again.

They need not have been alarmed. They had a redoubtable Mother to protect them. In her little high-pitched decisive voice, Francesca answered the archbishop.

"No, Your Excellency," she said, shaking her head slowly, "No. We cannot do that. I came to New York under obedience to the Holy Father. Here I shall remain."

The archbishop looked at her sharply. If this was so, it put a different aspect on everything. He could see that the diminutive nun before him was not intending the slightest disrespect, and he admired her courage. But he also knew that people sometimes imagine themselves to have authorizations which they do not actually possess—and especially so in ecclesiastical matters. He asked mildly: "I suppose you have some letters to show in proof of this."

She had. She laid her bundle of letters on the table before him. A glance at them showed what she said was correct. One of them, that signed by Cardinal Simeoni, the prefect of Propaganda, said that she had come "by order of this Sacred Congregation", which meant by order of the pope himself. In face of that not even the archbishop of New York could do anything. He saw that he would have to let her stay.

He found himself beginning to want to let her stay. Like so many people who looked into Francesca's large candid eyes, with their gleam of fire, he was suspecting that here was somebody who could not easily be refused. Her ardor impressed him. So did her calm determination.

Rising he said, "Well, of course, I cannot allow you to have another night like the last. I understood that Father Morelli was getting a place ready for you on Roosevelt Street. You must have taken him by surprise, too. Later on I shall need to explain things to you more in detail. But for the present I shall have to get you settled somewhere. If you will come with me ..."

He put on his high silk hat and led them one block up Madison Avenue. On the comer of Fifty-First Street, in the red brick building afterward occupied by Cathedral College, there was then a convent of the Sisters of Charity, the branch that had become diocesan. They conducted an orphanage, and their warm-hearted Irish superior, Mother Mary Martha, took instant pity on the homeless Italians.

"Why, of course, Monsignor," she said, "of course they may stay here. They will be very welcome."

❧ ❧ ❧

The explanation of the archbishop's attitude came out within the next day or two. Father Morelli, for one, had a great deal to say. "The archbishop," he told Francesca, "like all the American bishops, wants to do something for the Italians, but a good many of the clergy share the general prejudice against us. And our people do not understand many of the American customs. They don't like having to give a dime when they go into church. They never had to do that in Italy. That they resent it is resented by the priests. What happens? If they go to church, our poor Italians have to hear Mass in a basement apart from everybody else. So they stay away altogether. They are made to feel that they are strangers even in the House of the Lord. Now the Protestants are luring them away, buying them up. Most of these *contadini* have never so much as heard of Protestantism and don't know that they are doing any harm. No wonder we lose them!"

"Father," Francesca asked, "isn't that all the more reason why Italian priests and nuns should work among them?"

"Of course it is; or it should be. But perhaps this will help you to understand why Italians are looked down upon even by their fellow-Catholics. You cannot expect much help from them. And among our own people there's little unity. You will find all this out in time. I'm afraid you are going to encounter many difficulties."

"I expected difficulties", she returned serenely.

Further explanations came from the lady who had promised to provide Francesca with an orphanage. She was an American named Mary Reid who was married to Count Palma di Cesnola, an exile of the Risorgimento who had come to New York and was now director of the Metropolitan Museum of Art. She had taken a house for the Sisters at 43 East Fifty-Ninth Street, putting up some money herself and collecting more from her friends. The trouble was that the archbishop disapproved of the location.

The contessa urged Francesca to take possession of the house and so force the archbishop's hand. This she refused to do. "No," she said, "though I came at the order of the pope, I must have the archbishop's blessing. I shall wait."

To Francesca, when she saw the archbishop again, he said bluntly: "The contessa is quite absurd in wanting to locate you in that wealthy and fashionable district. I cannot permit you to go there."

"But Your Excellency," Francesca protested, "the contessa thinks that an orphanage established there would attract notice and obtain support."

"It would attract *too much* notice—not of the kind to do you any good. You must let me decide a matter of this sort. An Italian orphanage there would only arouse antagonism."

The archbishop had some reason for his objection. He knew how despised Italians were, and he was afraid of wakening again the smoldering American animosity against foreigners. It had but recently been directed against the Irish, his own race. The American Protective Association, which had been organized only two years previously, was pallid enough when compared with the Know Nothings of the past; all the same, the archbishop had no wish to give it something it might seize upon. He realized that, though Nativism had social and economic roots, it always flowered into anti-Catholicism.

"No," he told Francesca, "so long as the Italians keep to their Little Italies and remain out of sight, no harm will be done. But to bring them out swarming on Fifty-Ninth Street would be inviting disaster. If you can send some Sisters to teach at Saint Joachim's parish, that will be all right. And if you can find a place for an orphanage downtown, that will be all right, too. But I thoroughly disapprove of the Contessa Cesnola's scheme."

"But she has already rented the house and furnished it for me, Your Excellency."

"Yes—without my permission. As you are here, I suppose I can find something for you to do, though I cannot undertake any financial help. Schools, yes; that orphanage, no."

🌿 🌿 🌿

The most that Mother Cabrini could do was to get Archbishop Corrigan to consent to see the contessa. That she succeeded in this was a minor feat of tact, so far had relations become strained. This time, shifting his ground a little, the archbishop took the position that the material means to be put at the Sisters' disposal would be altogether inadequate. He mentioned this merely by way of giving himself a second and supplementary argument. Francesca quickly made of it the main issue.

"So it is a question of resources, Your Excellency?" she asked innocently.

"Not altogether that, Mother", he replied. "However, just to stick to this one point, how much money is it that you have, Contessa?"

"Five thousand dollars, Archbishop", she told him.

"Not nearly enough! Five thousand dollars—how long do you suppose that will last? It will all be spent at the end of a year. What then?"

The contessa also was a quick-witted woman, and an impulsive one. Fastening by instinct on this one point, she contrived to remove the objection to Fifty-Ninth Street as a location from the discussion. She went down on her knees. "Your Excellency," she exclaimed, "remember that in the Our Father we ask only for our *daily* bread—not bread for one year!"

Francesca did not kneel. She was disinclined for emotional scenes, so she stood there erect but a little puzzled, having no idea as to the meaning of the English words. The archbishop drew the contessa to her feet. There was no use in arguing with a woman, and by now he was more than half inclined to believe that if anybody could effect the impossible, it was this Italian nun. He gracefully gave in.

"All right, all right", he said. "As you have already rented that house, I'll let Mother Cabrini take possession of it."

The Sisters got in on April 21, just three weeks after their arrival. A pleasant surprise awaited them: they found at the door a statue of the Sacred Heart, a gift they knew they were going to receive; it had been left on the doorsteps because there was nobody in the house. On the base of the statue somebody had put a loaf of bread. It was an omen. "You see!" cried Francesca. "Providence is never going to desert our little orphans."

The following Sunday, which was Palm Sunday, the archbishop visited them, bearing with him the blessed palm he had received that morning in his cathedral at Mass. He gave it to Francesca, and she took it as her palm of triumph. It was the beginning of her great missionary career.

PART I

LIGHT OVER LOMBARDY

Chapter One

A CHILD AT PLAY

When Francesca Cabrini was a little girl, she often used to go from Sant' Angelo, her village near the town of Lodi on the Lombard plains, to stay with her uncle at Livagra a few miles away. He was Don Luigi Oldini, one of the local priests, a man so charitable that he was known to take the shoes off his feet and the blankets from his bed for the poor. "He is a thief of himself", was the saying there. Francesca loved him because he was so kind, but she also liked to visit Livagra because there she had opportunity for a game she had invented and could not play at home. The deep, rapid Venera that crossed the town was built up with canal walls, and these made its current all the more swift. This exactly suited it to be the widest ocean in her imagination. Making paper boats, she filled them with violets and sent them down the stream. These violets were the missionaries she dreamed of sending all over the world.

Francesca always played this game alone, perfectly happy with her fancies. She was a very shy child and felt instinctively that to let anyone share her game would be to spoil it. Now and then a couple of boys passed her on the towpath; they looked at her for a moment half in contempt and half in envy before muttering to one another, "What does a girl know about boats!" Even to the little girls who came up to ask what she was doing she did not explain. They saw the boats and they saw the violets; she did not tell them that the violets were her missionaries. Only Uncle Luigi got a hint of that. "Very nice, Cecchina", he would say with grave interest. "Only be careful not to fall in the water."

One day when she was about eight, she got a little too engrossed in this delightful game. Her blue eyes and her golden curls made her appear to be more ethereally delicate than she really was, but until that day nobody had seen any special danger in this launching of violet-laden ships. Then, leaning too far over the stone embankment, she fell into the canal. As a little way farther down it ran through a tunnel, she would have been drowned had she been drawn under it by the stream. But somebody pulled her out just in time, and she lay on the bank half dead from fright.

A boy who saw her there dripping wet rushed off at once to Don Luigi's house nearby shouting, "Come quick! Cecchina's drowned."

It was not as bad as that. She opened her eyes when her uncle knelt over her.

"Thank God you're all right!" he exclaimed. "But who pulled you out of the water?"

"I don't know, Uncle. I just found myself lying here."

Don Luigi pondered this. "Are you sure you don't know who pulled you out, Cecchina?"

She shook her head.

"Then *I* know", he said. "It must have been your guardian angel."

He took her up in his arms and carried her in. After his housekeeper had got her to bed, he went into her room and sat beside her.

"Listen, Cecchina", he said gently. "You must never play with your boats again. What would your mother have said had anything happened to you while you were staying with me?"

"Don't tell mother", she begged. "Say you won't tell mother, Uncle."

"I don't know whether I can keep this from your mother, child."

She was silent a long while. Then she whispered, "Well, tell mother if you like. Only make her promise not to tell Rose."

He was silent in his turn, thinking grimly. He knew why she said this, but he asked, "Why mustn't we let your sister know?"

"Rose would be very angry with me", she whispered again. "She thinks it silly of me to want to be a missionary."

"All right, naughty little missionary", Uncle Luigi said at last. "But you must promise me never again to go near the canal."

She was able to promise that with immense fervor. Nothing would ever again draw her to the banks of the Venera. She had acquired such a phobia about deep water that it would have put an end to all her missionary ambitions had they not been based on something more solid than dreams. The cold she caught that day soon went, but not for thirty years, when she was about to begin travels that would carry her over more of the earth than even her hero Saint Francis Xavier ever saw, did she quite recover from the shock. All the same, she continued to believe that she was to be a missionary.

❦ ❦ ❦

Yet Francesca came of a most unadventurous stock, one securely rooted in those quiet, flat Lombard pasturelands and rice fields. So very stay-at-home had her forebears been that once, when they received word that a rich relative had died at Rome and had left a legacy which they could collect only by going there in person, they set out—but came back a couple of hours later. Upon reaching a point in the plain from which they could no longer see the campanile of the church and the five flaming red brick towers of the castle built centuries ago by Regina Visconti della Scala, they got frightened. They looked at one another and, without a word, decided to drive home again.

Francesca herself was by nature as unadventurous as any of them. She was completely devoid of the desire to travel for the mere sake of travel. But she did get quite early a desire to travel in order to win souls for God.

This idea was implanted in her during the long winter evenings when the family sat round the large open fireplace in the house on the Borgo Santa Maria. While the logs crackled, she listened to her father read aloud from the *Annals of the Propagation of the Faith*. That missionary magazine set her mind on fire. There in the old-fashioned patriarchal kitchen that served as the living room—a large room with a kneading-trough, a kettle hanging from a chain, and a bucket of water with a ladle from which they all drank—Francesca's imagination was stirred. And when a missionary from the Orient arrived at Sant' Angelo Lodigiano and preached on his work, what he had to say aroused so much enthusiasm in the thirteen-year-old girl that she could not hold herself in. She confided in Rose, who was more than twice her age, "One day *I'm* going to be a missionary."

Rose was crushing in her scorn. "*You* a missionary!" she exclaimed. "One so small and ignorant as you a missionary!"

Rose had talked like that before, but the words, so far from smothering Francesca's ideas, only hardened her determination. Though, after that, she was careful to keep her dreams to herself, her sturdiness of character may, at least in part, be set down to the credit of Rose herself. What she had said—what she often said—was far from kind, but she had made Francesca able to bear such taunts by the severe training she had given her.

❦ ❦ ❦

The little girl had come as the last of thirteen children, and it fell upon Rose rather than their mother to bring her up. This she did in a stern, uncompromising fashion that does not make us like her, or make virtue appear very lovely in her case, but to which we may nevertheless attribute Francesca's resoluteness and perhaps even the extraordinary sweetness that balanced it. Closely as Francesca imitated Rose as a child, nobody could have resembled her much less as a woman.

Just why Rose did not herself become a nun is something of a mystery. Or it would be, were it not clear that her true vocation was that of training a nun. In this she may have been vicariously achieving her own ambition. It is more likely that she was acting without any design and merely exhibiting her prim old-maidishness toward her little sister. As the child's hair grew in beautiful curls, Rose did her best to prevent any youthful vanity by plastering down those curls on her head and trying to straighten them out.

"Stand still, can't you, Cecchina!"

"Yes, Rose."

"Bend your head down."

"Yes, Rose."

"*Lower*, child!"

She pressed the brush down until the stiff bristles brought tears into the little girl's eyes.

"There, that's better. I'm not going to have you looking like a silly simpering doll."

In her old age, Francesca used to say that there was no danger of her hair ever turning white; it had received too much oiling from Rose for that to happen.

From the day of Francesca's birth—two months before its due time and when her mother was fifty-two—there seemed to be a special seal upon her. It may have been merely a charming coincidence, though it was taken for something more, that that very morning, when her father was threshing grain in the courtyard of his farm, a flock of white doves descended. He tried to scare them away with his flail, but they kept returning, and at last one of them got entangled in the leather thongs. It was unhurt and Agostino Cabrini carried it indoors to show the children. They wanted to keep it, but he said, "No, no; let it join the others."

He opened the window and let it fly. That same morning of July 15, 1850, Francesca was born. A pretty story, kept in remembrance by the white doves now painted on the old house, though what it is supposed to signify is not very clear. But the family thought of her as a little white dove. They made her one by having her baptized the same day.

A dove or a lamb was what she seemed to be, this shy child who was to grow into a woman whose life, regarded from one angle, reads like a resounding success story. Nobody could have seen in her the great organizer and executive. What everybody did see was the *santina*, the little saint, even if some may have wondered whether so precocious a piety would last. It was only to be expected that she would

be pious when she had a mother who rose at dawn to pray
for an hour before going to Mass and who prayed another
hour before going to bed. The father, too, was admitted
on all hands to be a *Cristianone*, a genuine Christian. With
Rose to complete the process, Francesca could hardly
have grown up except as she did. Even her dolls were all
dressed as nuns, and she herself presided over them as a
Lady Abbess.

Children are always given to the imitation of their elders.
And Cecchina, as she was called in those days, set out to
model herself upon Rose. This extended even to the ges-
tures Rose made in church. Like her, Cecchina bowed her
head right down to the pew in front, looking out meanwhile through her fingers to see whether she could catch
any other hints regarding religious deportment. Now and
then the imitation was a trifle embarrassing, as on the day
the child followed the woman into the confessional. And
again, at six, Cecchina wanted to go to Communion.
Then Rose put her off with the explanation, 'But, Cecchina, you have no white veil."

The little girl looked at Rose in dubious silence.

Rose repeated, "You understand, Cecchina. Before
you can go to Communion you must have a white veil."

Cecchina's acceptance of this explanation was set down
by her elders to her beautiful simplicity. It may, however,
have been rather because she perceived there was no use in
arguing with grown-ups when they present children with
what purports to be a relation between cause and effect.
Many children have felt this, and Cecchina was, after all,
an unusually intelligent child.

Contrary to the custom prevailing today, she was confirmed before she made her First Communion. In fact

Confirmation, which was conferred on her on July 1, 1857, was the great experience of her childhood, the turning point of her life. For her there was no need of any conversion, but at her Confirmation she passed from the innocence of childhood to a conscious union with God, such as is the mark of sainthood. Years later when she spoke of this, she used to make a gesture which seemed to convey that the Holy Spirit had surrounded her with His light as with a cloak. Then she said, "The moment I was being anointed with the sacred chrism, I felt what I shall never be able to express ... I seemed no longer on earth. My heart was replete with a most pure joy. I cannot say what I felt, but I know it was the Holy Ghost." And in middle age, writing in a notebook she never supposed anybody would ever see, she addressed Christ, "You know that my heart has always been yours." That "always" is the key to her life.

Already little incidents had occurred to her in which the miraculous has been seen. Nor need the miracles be doubted by anyone who has been aware many times of a protecting hand. One day, having gone to pray, as she often did, in a retired spot, she chose a woodpile—which fell down the moment she left it. We can imagine that once more her guardian angel was looking after her. On the other hand, when she went, another day, to the parish church at a time when the doors were usually locked and found, upon pushing, that they opened to her, the incident may perhaps be adequately accounted for on the simple supposition that the sexton had forgotten to lock them. What is really more remarkable, as evidence of the growth of her character, is the self-control the child had already developed to a high degree. Once when an earthquake shook the village and when the terrified elders ran over to the house to save the "baby", they came across her sitting quietly in a corner saying her prayers quite undisturbed.

This self-control sometimes showed itself in quaint ways. As she was going to China as a missionary, and as she had somehow got it into her head that there was no candy in that country, she gave up eating candy, the better to prepare herself for an austere apostolic life. Yet she was normal enough to feel intense disappointment whenever her delicate health kept her from going out to join in a local *festa*. She found it hard to stay indoors when bands were playing in the streets and people were walking down them holding hands and singing.

She did not take that or any other disappointment as children usually do—sulking or in tears, so early had she begun to learn in the school of the saints. In the local priests she found simple, humble men who understood what was going on in her soul. The first of her spiritual directors was Don Melchisedecco Abrami, the curate of the parish; the second, into whose care she passed when she was fifteen, was the pastor, Don Bassano Dedè. Don Melchisedecco, who used to call her his little child because of her fragile build, permitted her to take a private vow of chastity when she was eleven, but, being a wise man, only for one year. Many years afterward he was to write that he had always considered her a saint. Not until she was nineteen was she permitted to make her vow permanent, though it still remained only of the private sort that could easily have been dispensed had she ever asked to be released.

Don Bassano was of a laconic temperament, and his advice when she took him her small problems was nearly always the same. After thinking in silence he would say, "Go and tell that to Jesus." He may well have considered that Cecchina stood in some danger of being cast in too rigid a mold by Rose and hoped to counteract this by encouraging a familiar and spontaneous intercourse with God. For her this was the best possible advice that could have been given. The circumstances of her later life made it impossible for her to have any regular spiritual direction. It was therefore good that she was so early led to trust herself completely to the divine promptings.

❦ ❦ ❦

There are times when one cannot but feel a little sorry for Cecchina, so often was she domineered over by her dry, sharp-spoken sister. Their mother had sometimes to intervene when she thought Rose was carrying things too far. "But she is hardly more than a baby, Rose!" she would protest. "You must not be so hard on her." Then for a while Rose would soften the regimen a little.

Cecchina herself never complained of Rose. So far from that, she took her as a kind of spiritual model, though fortunately this did not continue too long. And not only did Rose train her in religion, she was also Cecchina's first teacher, for as she had a normal-school certificate, she conducted a little private school in the town. She appears to have been a good teacher and was certainly a courageous one. For when the inspector pointed out that her classes in Christian doctrine were contrary to the prevailing law, she told him she meant to go on in the same way. As it was so very private and small a school, he did not think it worthwhile to raise any further objection.

From Rose she learned a little French and a deep appreciation of their Italian language. One feels from her letters—hastily written as they were and without the faintest idea that any of them would ever be published—that she might have become a writer had she cared to aim at that calling. Such things, however, were merely incidental to her; to have felt any ambition of that kind she would have had to be an entirely different woman. At this time the only study that really absorbed her was geography. By the hour she used to pore over the maps in her atlas. No longer did she send violets down the river in paper boats as missionaries, but her imagination was taking hold of something more concrete by learning facts about the various countries of the world.

❦ ❦ ❦

These years went by extremely quietly, the quietness deepening as the Cabrini family retired more and more into seclusion as politics grew more and more confused in Italy. The struggle for independence had begun, and in the spring of 1859 white-uniformed Austrians marched into the town, only to pass through it again in early summer—this time in disorderly retreat. But the nationalist movement was by now getting so entwined with an extraneous anticlericalism that it was not very easy for good Catholics—especially for those who wished for a peaceable life—to take sides. Nor did clarification come from the fact that Cecchina's father's cousin, Agostino Depretis—who was later to be prime minister of a united Italy—was already one of the nationalist leaders. General Garibaldi, with whom this cousin was now associated, himself arrived at Sant' Angelo one day in 1862 in his red shirt and made a speech there of a kind hardly calculated to please the pious Cabrinis. Distrustful of the revolutionary spirit, and essentially timid and conservative, they were careful to take no part in politics. But in later life Francesca came to believe that the quarrel between political Italy and the Church was for the most part adventitious. There was no greater patriot than herself.

It was from circles so still as almost to be called stagnant that Francesca was drawn forth to her masterful and exciting career.

❦ ❦ ❦

At thirteen, she was sent to a private school conducted by the Daughters of the Sacred Heart at nearby Arluno. This promised an even greater seclusion than she had known at home. There she remained for five years, taking the courses that would lead to a teacher's certificate, the *corsi magistrali*. From the frequency with which she quotes Latin in her letters—and without any books of reference at hand—it is evident that she learned that Latin thoroughly, though without bothering with more than she required for practical purposes. One may also infer that she had a good head for mathematics; she needed it for the big business deals she was to make in subsequent life.

In taking a teacher's certificate, she appears to have been again imitating Rose, for there was no obvious need for her to prepare herself to earn a living. Teaching was virtually the only "white-collar" job then open to women. As Rose was a teacher, Cecchina became one, too. Beyond that there could have been no definite plans, and though as a missionary she had to initiate many forms of charitable activity, with the training of young girls as the chief of them, Francesca herself was hardly if ever in the classroom. She remained a teacher, however, and she was one by natural endowment rather than by grace of the state examining board.

At eighteen, she obtained her teacher's certificate, rounding out her studies at Arluno with a course of lectures at the Lodi normal school. Her health was so precarious that it was feared that she would not be able to sit for her examinations. But she passed them *cum laude* and immediately afterward applied for admission into the community.

She was refused by the superior, Madre Giovanna Francesca Grassi. The nuns had all been vastly edified by her, but they did not believe she was strong enough for the religious life. There was nothing for it but to go home and settle down to the domestic routine.

Had Francesca been accepted by these Sisters, she would probably never have been heard of again by the world. But that she applied for admission is a little strange, in view of her missionary ambitions. Must one conclude that she had brought herself to believe that these were only a childish dream? Perhaps she thought that, as there was no such thing at that time as an order of missionary nuns, she had better reach out her hand to take what seemed more within her grasp. A sensible compromise—that was all that appeared to be possible. It was one that she was not permitted to make.

❦ ❦ ❦

Returning home that autumn of 1868, the young woman who still looked like a child made no effort to obtain a teaching position. Without a ripple, she slipped back into family life, helping her mother and Rose with the household duties, saying her fervent prayers, and doing little acts of unobtrusive charity. It looked like a life that might last indefinitely; she had no designs for herself beyond what the day brought forth. But she continued to believe that God had designs for her.

This life did not last long. There came a morning in the following February when her father was getting ready to go to church. Suddenly he slumped into a chair and said in a strange voice to his wife, "Stella, do you think you could stir the fire and warm some coffee for me?"

"What is the matter, Agostino?" she asked anxiously. "Are you ill?"

"It's nothing. I'm just cold. Very cold. Icy."

When the coffee was brought he found he could not swallow. The doctor was sent for. Agostino had had a stroke.

He lingered on for about a year and then died, telling his wife that they would soon be reunited in heaven. The words proved to be prophetic. Before the year was out Stella Cabrini, while dressing for Mass, felt death upon her. They got her into bed. Before the night fell, she was gone.

By now only four of the thirteen children were left, and of these one was a girl who had infantile paralysis. She also died before long. But Giovanni Baptista, the only brother left, was able to keep the farm going with hired help and a hand lent by Rose and Francesca. He was a brisk young man, and when he attended the local fairs he did not affect anything like his father's old-fashioned mantle lined with fur. But he had no great interest in the farm and was already planning to become a teacher. If he managed the little estate, this was only because there was for the moment nothing else to do.

They were certainly in no want, even though they lived, by habit, frugally. As of old they were still able to give to the poor. When a child, Cecchina had often got her father and mother to double the alms they gave at the door; now she and Rose made themselves responsible for the feeding of an old woman dying of cancer. It was a manner of existence that gave no hint as yet of what the future held.

🦋 🦋 🦋

A remarkable change had come over Rose with the death of her parents. The sternness that made her virtue not always attractive disappeared: to Francesca, to whom she used to be somewhat unnecessarily harsh, she now showed a beautiful tenderness. The very fact that there was no longer any mother to restrain her when she was being too severe with the "baby" made her put a restraint on herself. Now, nearing middle age, she knew that she would have to give up all idea of becoming a nun. Perhaps it was because she had looked upon herself as thwarted that she had been somewhat sharp and even bitter. With resignation came sweetness.

That she had actually known toward what development she had been leading Francesca cannot be supposed; she had simply been acting, according to her lights, as her mother's auxiliary. But by now she perceived that all she could do for Francesca had been done, though she could not have been wiser than everybody else as to what was her sister's destiny. If she had a share in developing Francesca, her methods, had they been applied to anybody else, might well have defeated their own purpose. As it was, Francesca always spoke of Rose gratefully.

The year 1871 went by placidly and uneventfully. But the spring of the new year brought an epidemic of smallpox to Sant' Angelo, and Francesca herself caught the infection while nursing those who were stricken. That she had a deep repugnance to the sight and smell of sores and wounds made her charity toward her cancer patient, as now toward those whom she nursed in smallpox, all the more heroic. The natural inclination of this notable founder of hospitals was very far removed from work among the sick.

Now that Francesca herself had smallpox, Rose had a chance to signalize her devotion. Not only did she carry Francesca safely through, she was so unsparing in her attention that no pockmarks were left. Constant anointings with

salves and washings in milk, without any thought for her
own safety, more than made up for all the cutting remarks
of earlier years.

It is our last glimpse of Rose, and it gives us the truest
idea of her. By severity she had molded Francesca's character, at the same time convincing her that severity is not
the best means for the purpose. An exquisite kindness and
affability were always marked in Francesca's disposition.
At the same time it would be less than just to Rose not
to admit that in the case of Francesca the methods were
successful and that, at the end, Rose became not unlike
Francesca herself. We hear of her going out some years
later to the Argentine to keep house for her brother when
he accepted a teaching position there. She had done her
work; Francesca was just about to begin her own.

Chapter Two

THE FALSE START

It is a common observation that many of those for whom
a great destiny is prepared have made a false start. Of no
one is this more true than of Francesca Cabrini. That is, if
it is true at all.

For eight years she appeared to be going farther and
farther away from what she had known, even as a child, to
be her missionary vocation. Then just when that vocation
seemed to be forever lost, she found that every step she had
taken had been leading her to it. When at last she was able,
upon a height, to turn and look back, she could trace the
whole of the devious road by which she had come. Then
she understood clearly that, had she not followed it, the
sudden and final resolution of her difficulties would never
have occurred. She had gone into the darkness, holding
the hand of God. From the hilltop where dawn broke she
saw that everything had been a preparation for the work
she was called to do.

❧ ❧ ❧

It all started when, just after she was out of bed barely
recovered from her attack of smallpox, Don Bassano Dedè,
the local priest, asked whether she would be willing to
substitute for a couple of weeks for the teacher at the public school at Vidardo, a mile and a half away. Otherwise,

he explained, the teacher, who was sick, might be permanently replaced.

As it was put to her in this way, Francesca could not refuse. As things turned out, she was to remain at Vidardo for two years; and there she met, in the rector of the parish, Don Antonio Serrati, the man who was to be her guide for years to come. That neither then nor later did he have any real idea as to her vocation, and that for all his sympathy and shrewdness he was acting blindly, does not alter the fact that his entry into Francesca's life determined its pattern.

Early morning now found the new teacher walking after Mass along the pleasant, narrow, tree-shaded road to Vidardo. At evening she walked home along the same road under the leafy or bare trees, with fields of green or fields of snow on either hand. On Saturdays, a child used to accompany her, as she stayed those nights to help with the catechism class on Sundays. But as soon as Francesca believed this little girl to be asleep, she used to get up and pray. Sometimes the child, on waking in the morning, found Francesca still on her knees.

But at the beginning, her position as teacher was not very happy. She had never taught before and felt rather shy and awkward. Perhaps for this reason, she tried to assume a stern manner modelled on Rose's. Natural teacher though she was, she was making a bad beginning.

For this she was criticized. At any rate, this was made the excuse for criticism. The fact that she was keeping the job open for a teacher who was sick shut the door against the application of a young woman who was very anxious to get that job. She and her friends thought it unfair that Francesca, who did not have to earn her own living and who was moreover an outsider, should be depriving one who needed the position. They forgot that what Francesca was doing was being done out of charity.

The criticism did not last long, however, or soon lost its point. Fortunately Francesca discovered that she was making a mistake in trying to be stiff and formal and so changed to that easy naturalness which was ever afterward to be one of her distinguishing characteristics. Not only were the mischievous children brought under control but their somewhat antagonistic parents were won over. Before she left Vidardo, she had even made a conquest of the mayor, Carlo Zanardi, an old anticlerical. He stretched things so far as not only to permit her to teach Christian doctrine but also to conduct special devotions during May. In the end, he went even farther than that; he himself returned to the practice of religion.

If Francesca's first somewhat stiff manner in the classroom was a mistake, she made what she afterward came to regard as another mistake. It is one common enough to religious enthusiasts in their youth: she applied to herself bodily mortifications of a sort that she afterward discarded in favor of those that were interior. Not of course that she would ever have said that great good cannot be derived from such practices, but she conformed with the trend of Catholic asceticism in attaching much less importance to these things than to others. But at this time we hear of her sleeping on a couple of boards instead of in bed, with the result that her already weak health nearly gave way. Her mature conclusion as the founder of a religious order was that the perfect observance of the Rule provided not only all the mortification anybody needed but the most thoroughgoing of all mortifications. During the Vidardo period, she was a little injudicious; she was only at the outset of her career, and she still had many discoveries to make.

At Vidardo, the eye of the parish priest, Antonio Serrati, was already upon her. He was an able man, at once laconic and perhaps a trifle addicted to managing other people's affairs for them. Though wholeheartedly loyal and forthright to the point of bluntness, he sometimes was somewhat devious in his methods. Thus when he discovered that Francesca was going to apply again to be admitted to the Daughters of the Sacred Heart, he did not argue against it; but so as to save her for his own pious projects, he privately recommended the superior to reject her. He stressed—what was a fact—that Francesca's health was delicate, and it was on this ground that she was refused. And when she offered herself to the Canossian Sisters at Crema—the attraction there was that they had a mission in China, to which she might get sent—they refused her, too, because Father Serrati advised it. This case—that of a young woman being kept out of a convent by the wire-pulling of her spiritual director—is probably unique in the lives of the saints. Francesca did not know until sometime afterward that it was her friend who had been secretly working against her.

He had what he considered good reasons for acting as he did. He was about to be transferred to Codogno, a much more important charge, and he had work there that he wanted Francesca to do.

In all this, Monsignor Serrati—he was now advanced in ecclesiastical dignity and was also provost of Codogno and technically a mitered abbot as well—was, in fact, actually working for the best, as time was to show. Yet the credit is due not so much to his foresight as to Francesca's spirit of humble obedience. What he was on the point of calling her to was the most difficult of all assignments. She had to try to bring sanity to a madhouse.

Codogno was a pretty little town situated where three rivers—the Po, the Lambro, and the Ticino—come together. It had at this time an orphanage founded in 1857

and known as the House of Providence, and this had got into a very bad way. What Monsignor Serrati proposed was that Francesca should go there and reform it.

The institution was headed by a woman named Antonia Tondini, and as she had given thirty thousand lire by way of endowment, it was not easy to get rid of her, unsuitable as she had proved herself to be. In the hope of effecting some improvement, the bishop of Lodi, Dominic Gelmini, managed to persuade the Tondini woman and her friend Teresa Calza who lived with her to become nuns, though he was well aware that they had little inclination for the religious life. They agreed to make a novitiate with the Sisters of Nazareth, but did not stay long, in spite of which Monsignor Serrati, believing that if they took vows they might possibly behave like nuns, gave them a six days' retreat and permitted their profession. At the same time, their cook, Giuseppa Alberici, was admitted into the strange community. This happened on August 30, 1872.

The three women now wore a kind of habit—a simple black gown but with no nun's veil—and they had taken vows. But they made no pretense of living like nuns. Sister Tondini used to say with cheerful cynicism that she kept her vows in her pocket. There was nothing specially scandalous about their conduct except that their mode of existence remained what it had always been—Sister Tondini and Sister Calza, those odd friends, quarreling shrilly, especially on the subject of Antonia's scape-grace nephew whom she kept well supplied with money. The six or seven orphan girls the place was supposed to look after were utterly neglected. Monsignor Serrati now chose Francesca to bring the House of Providence into some semblance of order.

"But Monsignor," she protested, "I can't do that. These women are nuns, and I—"

"You're as much of a nun as any of that crowd, Francesca. I want you to do this for me."

She shook her head. "No, Monsignor. You know very well that I want to be a missionary. To be stuck all my life in Codogno ..."

"Francesca, I'm not asking *that* of you. I merely ask you to go there for a while and reform the institution."

She laughed. "Monsignor, you can't be serious!"

"I'm perfectly serious, Francesca. What's going to become of those poor girls unless somebody like you goes to their rescue?"

She pondered this. "I'd like to do something to help them if I could, but—"

"No 'buts'; you'll go."

She still protested. "But Monsignor, I'm only twenty-four. Sister Antonia must be well over forty. You must know that she is not going to put up with my interfering."

"Then why not join them as a nun?"

"I've told you why not, Monsignor. I'm going to be a missionary."

"Don't you think you'll be a missionary by helping those girls? But if you raise that objection, I won't ask you to take the habit. Just go there for two weeks."

"Two weeks, Monsignor? What could I do in two weeks?"

"A lot. It's the summer vacation now. When it's over, you can go back to your school at Vidardo."

❦ ❦ ❦

Francesca never went back to Vidardo. From the beginning, she suspected that the situation at the House of Providence was not as simple as Monsignor Serrati imagined, but the very difficulties kept her there. The orphan girls clearly needed her, and she felt she could not desert them when her two weeks had come to an end. On the other hand, she was under the orders of Sister Antonia, and Sister Antonia resented her presence. There was a new cause for quarreling now, and when the storms raged, the girls would gather in Francesca's room for protection, while the so-called nuns banged at the door and threatened them.

If Francesca tried to calm Sister Antonia down, all she would get was insults. "Who do you think you are?" Antonia would scream at her. "An interloper! An interfering busybody!"

"But Sister, all that I'm trying to do—"

"I don't care what you're trying to do. You've got to understand, Francesca, that I'm boss here. It's on my money that we operate. What have you contributed? Nothing, except to make trouble. You have no standing in this house. You don't even wear the habit."

For an hour afterward they could hear the strident voice of Sister Antonia coming up from the kitchen where she was expatiating to Sister Teresa and Sister Giuseppa. Sister Giuseppa, a gentle, quiet soul, took no part in all this, but she had to listen. Those above, though they could not always catch the words, knew from their tone what it was Sister Antonia was saying.

The monsignor was a very patient man; still more so was the bishop. They had only themselves to thank that they had not dealt with the Tondini woman drastically long ago. Now it was in hope that they would make things better for Francesca that suggested that she consent to wear the habit. Then she could no longer be considered an outsider. Though this seemed to involve the abandonment of all her plans, she agreed. She was under no obligation to obey them in this matter; nevertheless, she obeyed as a mortification. It was something much harder than sleeping on bare boards.

❦ ❦ ❦

She had gone to Vidardo for two weeks—and had stayed two years. Now she had gone to Codogno for another two weeks—and this time had six years ahead of her, the six most dark and complicated years of her whole life. She was to emerge at the end completely formed and at last ready for her great career.

That Monsignor Serrati gave his young friend such a commission was a most striking proof of his confidence in her. As events were to show, he was mistaken in believing that Francesca—that anybody—could bring order out of chaos at the House of Providence. But his confidence in her being able to survive the shock of the spectacle of the religious life as lived there shows that he counted upon her piety as being capable of enduring anything. Had Francesca been less solidly constituted, she would in all probability have left, not only in disgust with this particular group of nuns, but with all nuns. It would not have been surprising if she had forgotten what she had seen among the Daughters of the Sacred Heart who had educated her and remembered only the fantastic Antonia Tondini and Teresa Calza in their daily bickerings.

Yet after she lived in this strange ménage for a couple of months, she and two of her pupils were invested in the habit on October 15, 1874, to be followed a little later by five other girls.

Francesca's courage and equanimity were never to be put to a harsher test. She had the simple black habit, it is true, but she had no authority—in fact, less authority now than ever. For three years she remained without vows, technically still a novice and subject to the idiosyncratic Tondini. Yet at the same time she was acting as a kind of novice mistress, gathering the girls in her room for spiritual conferences and assuring them that the day would come when they would all be missionaries. It was with this, her own ideal, that she inflamed them. Never did her dream seem more impossible than then; never did she hold to it more firmly.

Meanwhile, she and her little band worked hard at their sewing and embroidery so as to support a new group of orphans they had taken in, which eventually came to number about thirty. Though the House of Providence had not noticeably improved as a convent, it had at least begun to function more like the orphanage it was supposed to be.

The gathering by Francesca of an inner group of disciples was anomalous in the extreme. What was happening was the creation within the novitiate of a second secret novitiate. It had no formal constitution, nor was it officially recognized as existing, though the bishop knew that it did. Over it Francesca had no canonical authority, yet she ruled it by moral ascendency. It was the true life of the House of Providence, the force that was in the end to destroy it and change it into something else; but also the force that kept it going as long as it did. For Francesca, the strange experience was a necessary part of her spiritual development. For her, it was a real novitiate—one that formed a saint, one that only a saint could have borne.

Monsignor Serrati's object is patent. He was working for no more than the reform of an insignificant little orphanage that happened to be in his parish. He believed he could bring this about by grafting upon the House of Providence some new and better members. In this he was shown to be completely in error. The House of Providence was beyond repair. But one stands astonished at his attempt to fasten down Francesca Cabrini, of whose missionary ambitions he was well aware, to what was only a parochial enterprise. Even more is one astonished that Francesca should have consented to forego her own plans in order to further his.

Yet had she not done so—had she been insistent upon her own ideas—nothing would have come of the new religious institute she was to found. Quite unaware of what was to flow from her action, she may in a very real sense be said to have unconsciously founded her own Institute of the Missionary Sisters the day she accepted the habit of the House of Providence. It could not have come into being otherwise. Though this convent had a most inappropriate name, if only the character of la Tondini be considered, it was in truth a house where Providence signally showed its wisdom, its power, and its love.

Though the monsignor was not aware of all that went on—for Francesca never brought any complaints against Sister Antonia—he was keeping his eyes open. In his solicitude for his protégé, he was careful not to let her take her vows before he—acting as the bishop's delegate—was ready to act. He let her go on from 1874 to 1877 unbound by any religious profession. Then on September 13th he sent for her.

"Tomorrow, Francesca," he said, "you are going to take your vows. You know that woman is insane. Yet you are about to promise her obedience. What will you do if she orders you to throw yourself down the well?"

He got a surprising answer, but perhaps the answer he expected: "She is my superior, and I will obey her."

The monsignor had never had the slightest intention of letting things come to that pass. As soon as Francesca had made her profession, he told her to sit in the sanctuary as superior and receive the profession of the other Sisters. With tears in her eyes she obeyed. This meant that Antonia Tondini was not so much formally deposed as completely ignored.

Tondini's rage knew no bounds. Hitherto she had confined herself to insults; now she attempted physical violence upon Mother Cabrini, as she had at last become. The diminutive, delicate woman was saved only because the new Sisters gathered around her to protect her. That night—many nights—when alone in her room she gave way to tears, though at morning she lifted a face as serenely smiling as ever. For this weeping she was afterward to reproach herself, saying, "I wept a great deal, and a missionary must never weep. Not to complain when I had to suffer and to bear it all with patience and fortitude would have been a virtue ... but at that time I did not understand the value of the Cross and of suffering." These tears are not to be wondered at; more to be wondered at is her compunction.

🐾 🐾 🐾

This new difficulty marked a new stage in her development. She had always shown a special devotion to the Sacred Heart. From now on, that devotion deepened and became the center of her spirituality. In this she found so intense a consolation that her heart seemed to be wounded and on fire. There was but one way for her to meet the situation—that of casting herself completely upon God, confident that only by loving Him and by loving all His creatures would she be able to overcome a trial that consisted of a struggle every minute of the day. She knew of the jealousy by which she was surrounded and of the gossip that Tondini passed out to the town. In all kinds of small ways that insane woman found means of exercising her spite. At no time was Francesca given to making written records of the state of her soul, but in a notebook she was keeping at this time she wrote that henceforth she must stay with Jesus in the Garden of Olives, "in place of the disciples who sleep". The reference to Tondini and her partisans is obvious. Another entry is: "Thy mercy, O Lord, urges me to desire to suffer something for love of Thee, and to imitate Thy life, O my Jesus, which was one continuous martyrdom of pure suffering. Thou dost also make me feel the longing to humble myself for love of Thee. Enlighten me regarding the manner of accomplishing it in so many circumstances when I scarcely have the courage to put into effect Thy holy inspirations." But there is hardly any more direct reference to her difficulties than that. Francesca was the reverse of an introspective soul.

Another three years followed, even more difficult than the last three. As Francesca was now the superior of the House of Providence, it was her duty to exercise control. This meant—among other things—that she was obliged to stop the Tondini woman from giving the convent's money to her scamp of a nephew. But though Francesca managed to do this, she could not prevent Antonia from signing promissory notes when she did not have the actual cash to dispose of. This being the situation, she had to report it to the bishop.

Bishop Gelmini was anything but harsh toward this refractory nun. After he had appealed in vain to her to remember her vows, he offered to let her retire from the convent on a pension or to give her fifteen thousand lire in a lump sum. But though Antonia promised to behave, she was soon back at her old bad ways. She put in a claim for thirty-three thousand lire, the sum she said she had originally contributed, though much of this had been wasted without any accounting. When this claim was not admitted, she instituted an action in the civil courts against the bishop—and was at once excommunicated.

He had borne with her patiently, though he knew that she had ceased all practice of her religion, even to the extent of disregarding her Easter duty. His hope had been that she might be brought to a better frame of mind by the example of Francesca and the new nuns in the community. Now in face of the open scandal precipitated by Tondini's taking legal proceedings against him, he was compelled to act. At the end of 1880, he pronounced the House of Providence dissolved. Tondini was left in possession of the building, for the bishop did not want to contest the issue. He was immensely relieved that he had the opportunity of getting rid of the woman at any price.

Now the question was, what was to be done for Mother Cabrini and the seven Sisters she had trained? Bishop Gelmini sent for her and told her: "I know that you want to become a missionary. I know of no missionary order of women. Why not found one yourself?"

Taken utterly by surprise by this new turn of events, Francesca was for a moment silent. Then with a heart overflowing with gratitude to God that at last her opportunity had come, she looked the Bishop of Lodi in the face and said simply: "I will look for a house."

Chapter Three

THE IDYLL

There was an aura about those first days that was to glow in the nostalgic memory of the foundation. The dream that had seemed so impossible had come true. The little group of nuns were suddenly released from the murky shadows of the House of Providence to enter upon the idyllic peace of their own convent. That they had to suffer poverty at the outset only added something more rich to the golden skies. A poverty that extreme was an experience they were sometimes to have again; and even when the institute achieved splendor and success, its members as individuals remained poor. But there could hardly if ever again be anything like the sweet privations of Codogno when, as yet without a formal Rule, they were bound by nothing except a spontaneous and freely given love.

In part this may have been the charm of youth; if so, it was a charm that did not fade. Francesca, though she lived to be sixty-seven, never seemed to grow old in spirit; nor did her daughters. Yet they always looked back fondly to their beginnings. It was springtime for them, a lovely poem, a strain of music. As such, it lingered in their minds in tender radiance.

The names of the first group should be recorded. They were Sisters Salesia, Pesserini, Agostina, Colomba, Veronica, Franceschina, and a lay sister, Gaetanina, who worked

68

in the kitchen. For them and for the thousands who were to come after them, anonymity was to be their reward on earth. But as these were the seven who had gathered round Francesca in the House of Providence, and who went out with her to whatever the future held, and especially as they will not appear again in this story, let them shine for a moment now.

Before acting as he did at long last against Antonia Tondini, the bishop of Lodi made sure that some preparation had been made for the needs of Francesca and these seven young nuns, her disciples. Bishop Gelmini had had the idea of sending Mother Cabrini to some of the other convents in his diocese to invigorate them. Though probably none needed anything like the drastic reform that was vainly attempted at the House of Providence, there were few that would not have benefitted by being brought into contact with Francesca's charity and zeal. But she had objected to such an assignment, and now he saw that this plan would have to be dropped altogether. Francesca would have as much as she could do in attending to the founding of her own institute.

That loyal friend Monsignor Serrati did not fail her. As Francesca had gone to the House of Providence because of his pleading insistence, he had a responsibility in the matter. So he gave ten thousand lire toward the purchase of a house. On his own initiative, he made a deposit on one, in order that the Sisters might move into it at once. But immediately Francesca's independence of judgment appeared. Docile as she had been in going to Codogno and remaining there for six dark years, now that she was a foundress, she had to assume responsibilities that, so far, had not been hers. She continued to be, indeed, always grateful to the monsignor and as submissive toward him as was possible in the new situation. But she saw from the outset that his conception of her work was, like the bishop's, a good deal narrower than her own. That she refused the house selected for her was the first indication she gave that she meant to be free. She told the monsignor that she would look for a convent in the neighborhood of the Franciscan church.

The legend is that she did not know that behind that church there was a seventeenth-century friary that had lain abandoned and empty since the time of Napoleon. But on the face of it, this seems highly unlikely. Francesca had long been accustomed to pray before the statue of Our Lady of Grace in the Franciscan church. Moreover, as Codogno was a town of only eight thousand inhabitants, and as Francesca had lived there for six years, she must at least have heard of this friary, even if she had never seen it. She would have known that it would be far more suitable for her purpose than a house that would have to be remodeled before it could be used as a convent. Monsignor Serrati, by being ready without further argument to lose the deposit he had made, shows that he recognized that Francesca was right in her judgment. He may well have seen in her, too, a new spirit that he did not venture to oppose.

The friary, on what was then the Via Unione but is now the Via Cabrini, was at this time deserted except for a few mechanics' shops on the ground floor. It was somewhat in need of repairs but solidly built and just what Francesca wanted. A young architect from Milan employed by Bishop Gelmini was commissioned to inspect the place and make an offer to the proprietors. He conducted his enquiries with great discretion and gave out that the building was to be used as a storage for quicklime. He knew that if he said that it was to be a convent, again the price would go up. As the friary was of little value to the owners, they were glad to accept the price he offered. When Francesca heard of the quicklime story, she laughed. "Yes," she said, "he is speaking the truth. With our lime we are going to put up strong spiritual buildings all over the world." Yet it is worth noting that she herself was so ill that she was afraid to have the property held in her own name, as in the event of her death there would be inheritance taxes to pay. To save this expense, she got Monsignor Serrati and two other priests to become the legal owners.

On the very day that the deed was signed—November 10—the community moved into their motherhouse what few articles of furniture they possessed. How few these were is shown by the fact that they ate their first meal on a bench and went to bed in the dark, as they had no lamp. As to this, a second legend arose. Francesca, according to the story, guided each Sister to her room, finding her way along the pitch black corridors as though they were brightly lighted. That she did take each Sister to her room was later alluded to in one of her letters written from Buenos Aires, but she says nothing that supports the embellishments. As for her not having seen the place before she bought it, she was not that kind of person. We may reasonably suppose that in any event she and all the nuns went through the house on arrival before sitting down to their first meal. After all, those who carried the furniture in had to be told where it was to be put. The imaginative adornments must be dismissed. What the story does contain of truth is that the community had absolute confidence in their superior; from the first day they were wholly in her hands.

For their first supper, they did not have enough knives and forks and spoons to go round. But poor as the fare was, no meal had ever seemed more sumptuous. They

were at last in their own home. God had led them there.
Their work was about to begin.

The next days were spent in cleaning the place with a
vigorous scrubbing on hands and knees. One of the larger
rooms on the ground floor was prepared as a chapel. Over
the arch leading to it, the Sisters could faintly make out a
faded picture of Saint Francis of Assisi in ecstasy. This, like
the lunettes in the portico, had been saved from mutilation.

A few weeks later—on the Feast of Saint Francis Xavier,
December 3—Bishop Gelmini gave Francesca six thousand lire, though with some "strings" attached to the gift
that after his death were the cause of trouble. Part of that
money was used to renovate the chapel.

Monsignor Serrati had a gift for the chapel, too. He
brought the Sisters a statue of Our Lady to put in a niche
over the altar. This was rather disappointing to Francesca,
as she had planned to place a statue of the Sacred Heart
there as soon as she was able to get one. But she could not
well refuse the monsignor's present; to have done so might
have seemed discourteous to him and even to the Blessed
Mother. The question was settled when it was discovered
that his statue was a couple of inches too high to fit into
the niche. At this point Francesca brought out a framed
picture of the Sacred Heart. "This is not very grand," she
said, "but if ..."

"Very well, let's have it", said the monsignor; and up
it went.

In all the houses Francesca founded, or that have been
founded since her death, a statue of the Sacred Heart has
the position of honor in the chapel. Four days after their
arrival—on November 14, 1880—the monsignor said Mass
for them there for the first time, at an altar bare except for
two candles. That day is regarded as the birthday of the

institute. A month later the bishop of Lodi gave them his formal approval. The title of Missionary Salesians of the Sacred Heart was adopted.

The name "Salesian" was taken partly by way of compliment to Monsignor Serrati, who had a great devotion to Saint Francis de Sales, but was also a mark of Francesca's own devotion to that saint. It was, however, used only tentatively and was sometimes varied with others. In America, the group was first legally incorporated as the Salesian Sisters of the Holy Angels, and not until October 10, 1899, was the incorporation changed to the Missionary Sisters of the Sacred Heart. As such they are now canonically known. The word "Salesian" was eventually dropped to avoid confusion with Don Bosco's Salesian Sisters.

But the name of the Sacred Heart had already been used by several orders of women, including that founded in France by Saint Madeleine Sophie Barat and that of the nuns who had educated Francesca Cabrini. The fact would seem to be that, though Saint Francis de Sales continued to be regarded as one of their patrons, there was not much point in using his name. He was only one of several patrons. Saint Margaret Mary, because of her devotion to the Sacred Heart, was another; and Saint Joseph was taken as the spiritual director of the Sisters. Francesca used to say: "Our Foundress is the Mother of Grace; our Master, the Heart of Jesus; Saint Francis de Sales is our Manager; and Saint Francis Xavier, our Provider." She certainly put herself under very effective and comprehensive patronage. The title finally decided upon did exactly indicate what Francesca had always had in mind. As Missionary Sisters of the Sacred Heart, they at once proclaimed their purpose and the center of their devotion. The apostolic life was Francesca's concept of complete dedication.

As she was a missionary, Francesca now assumed "Saverio"—the Italianized form of Xavier—as her name in religion. But though she always signed herself in that style, she was referred to simply as Mother Cabrini, except when she was addressed as Mother General. She would never allow herself to be called "Mother Foundress", though she had been very punctilious in saying that the eccentric Antonia Tondini was the foundress of the House of Providence. In the case of her own congregation, as she was never tired of explaining, its founder was the Sacred Heart, and its foundress the Blessed Virgin. If any other founders had to be indicated—then these were Monsignor Serrati and Bishop Gelmini.

In this Francesca had justification, for it was patent that she had never tried to carry out designs of her own contriving but had been at most a passive instrument used by Providence. Though from her childhood she had dreamed of just such an order as this, it had come into being almost in spite of herself; actually because she had been willing to wait patiently for God to effect His own work.

❦ ❦ ❦

No mention is made of any election of a superior having taken place. Nobody seems to have thought of this. Francesca had been the superior appointed by Monsignor Serrati while they were still at the House of Providence. And though that institution had been dissolved, they carried on from that point, no other superior being even thinkable. But Francesca, though she took her position as much for granted as did everybody else, never regarded it as one of honor; it was merely that she was the natural head of this new family.

In drawing up Rules for her institute, Mother Cabrini had very few books to guide her. She studied Saint Alphonsus Liguori and the Jesuit writer Alphonsus Rodriguez, along with the works of Father Pinamonti. These and the *Imitation of Christ* and the Exercises of Saint Ignatius about completed the little library she had. But perhaps most useful of all for her purpose was her own experience in the House of Providence. If there was one thing she had learned from la Tondini, it was what not to do—a lesson of incalculable value. She understood now why those whom she recognized as being the real founders of her institute had kept her waiting so long. She dictated the Rules to one of the nuns, often on her knees or in tears; and her secretary was equally moved.

What Francesca presented by way of first draft to Monsignor Serrati in the summer of 1881 was considered to be hardly more than a general statement of principles, though as such it was greatly admired. But a couple of years later, after a careful examination on the part of Bishop Gelmini's coadjutor, Monsignor Angelo Bersani, and some revision that gave them a more definitely juridical form, the Rules were approved by episcopal decree and have never needed any material modification. Their acceptance by the Holy See, which was what Mother Cabrini had aimed at from the beginning, was to come a little later.

For the moment, she was satisfied with what had been accomplished; she saw that her institute was not yet quite ready to seek papal sanction. Further experience would have to be gained to justify that. The congregation would have to grow first. It was still a very small and apparently insignificant diocesan undertaking. She was confident that it was destined to a great expansion; she also knew that she would quietly have to set about the consolidation of what had been begun before proceeding to the next step.

❦ ❦ ❦

During those early years, the nuns who were qualified only to do domestic work were differentiated from the others as lay sisters. That distinction was afterward abolished, though many who joined the institute were competent only for kitchen and similar duties. But as all the Sisters, from Mother Cabrini down, did their share of this work, it was felt that any dividing of them into two groups was invidious. Therefore they were all set on an equal footing.

The habits the Sisters wore were those they had worn in the House of Providence. They were not rich enough to throw these away and to design something completely new. On the other hand, the fact of a new departure had somehow to be indicated. A few little adjustments and alterations sufficed. At the House of Providence, all the orphans who now constituted the community had been taught sewing and embroidery, and it was upon this work that they now mainly supported themselves. It was an easy matter for clever fingers to change their old habits—which were hardly more than simple dresses of black serge—almost beyond recognition. The chief distinguishing mark of the new habits was a heart cut out of black cloth and edged in red. It was afterward discarded as the need for that distinguishing mark disappeared.

Not until 1889, when Mother Cabrini and her first group of nuns came to the United States, was any veil worn, but only a white bonnet. When the veil was adopted, it consisted merely of a light piece of material. The eminently practical garb did not have a particle of the linen which, when lavish or elaborate, must be one of the greatest penances of conventual life. For women who visualized themselves as doing hard physical work in all kinds of climates and under all sorts of difficulties, glossy linen was a luxury they could not afford. Further to be unencumbered in their movements, they ceased to have rosaries dangling from their waists; they were just as handy when carried in the pocket.

❧ ❧ ❧

To start a religious order in those times called for an enormous amount of courage. Some people, her friends among them, said that Francesca must be mad to attempt a new foundation. Since 1870, Italy had been governed by men who were not at all favorable to the Church and who were quick to find a pretext for suppressing a religious community. For this reason, the ecclesiastical authorities were themselves not very enthusiastic about new foundations, thinking with some justice that they had enough to do to keep alive those already in existence. Their policy was broadly for grouping old orders together, or for severely restricting expansion, rather than for introducing untried experiments in the religious life. Even apart from the opposition that might be encountered from the State, the Church felt that there was already a sufficiency of such things for all necessary purposes.

It was characteristic of Francesca Cabrini that she did not make any use of extraneous aid, though she was in a position to do so. Her father's cousin, Agostino Depretis—he had the honor of being denounced by Carducci as "the shaggy, spectral wine-merchant from Stradella"—had become prime minister for the second time in 1881 and was to remain such until his death six years later. She even had no need to apply to him for protection, for he offered this of his own accord. But though he could have been very useful to her, she would not use him, preferring to trust herself entirely to Providence. The letters that passed between them about once a year were merely of a cousinly sort. Never would Francesca approach him in his character as prime minister.

The difficulties Francesca might encounter in Rome were better understood by Bishop Gelmini and Monsignor Serrati than herself. Knowing the situation as they did, they considered themselves very sensible in discouraging her from seeking to branch out. So long as an institute was content to remain a diocesan affair under the direct control of the bishop, it would have his protection. To extend the

work too far might excite opposition and would almost certainly give it a prominence that might make it subject to
attack. Their idea was that Francesca would be well advised
to go on as she had begun—that is, doing much the same
work that had been attempted by the House of Providence,
but of course doing it better than had been possible there.

These arguments may have been sound but were somewhat lacking in vision. From the outset, Francesca thought
of her organization as worldwide. All that her advisers
could do was to prevail upon her to put some curb upon
her impetuosity. When she spoke of her vast designs, the
monsignor would tell her, "But Mother, you *are* missionaries already!" Upon which Francesca would give him one
of her smiles and say, "I know that; but I am not *enough* of
a missionary as yet. This life will never satisfy me." Only
for the time being was she willing to accept the situation.

She had opened an academy and had also received a few
orphans. Indeed, to the end, the establishment of orphanages remained the principal feature of her work, the founding of hospitals being something she undertook reluctantly
and only because hospitals were so badly needed. Yet
an orphanage was never regarded merely as a means for
providing for the physical well-being of the needy; an
orphanage was primarily a school in which girls could be
educated according to what their subsequent life was likely
to require—above all in the Christian virtues. If other
types of schools—academies and colleges and hostels for
young women who were training to become teachers—
were afterward added to this original plan, these were no
more than a normal development from the original idea.

As the convent was large and the community small
as yet, some boarders were taken in addition to the girls

in the day school and the young women who were in a school of needlework. These were encouraged to go daily to Communion, though this was long before the days when Pius X was to promote the practice. There was even an extension of this work, for during Lent the Sisters went to the Franciscan church nearby to conduct classes for girls and women that would help them to make better Confessions and Communions. Already Francesca was showing her readiness to perform any task that needed to be done. Her idea of education was a very broad one. She never thought of her activities as specialized. Any kind of work, so long as it was for the salvation of souls, was her work.

These early years at Codogno had the sweetness of an idyll but were looked upon as the preparation for the program of carrying the Gospel to all lands. For this Francesca first had to train her nuns; and while she was training them, she could also quietly occupy herself with such small tasks as teaching embroidery and catechism. "But", as she often told Bishop Gelmini, "don't think that my institute can be confined to one city or one diocese. The whole world is not wide enough for me."

At this the bishop gently smiled. Her enthusiasm, flashing from those bright blue eyes, pleased him; but he feared that she might make the mistake of attempting too much. He knew that she was frequently ill—so ill that she had to give up and go to bed, and that even at best her health was never very good. How was it going to be possible for one so frail to shoulder the gigantic tasks she was already planning? What he wondered was whether she would live long enough to establish this one community firmly enough to ensure its lasting after she was gone. In his prudence he believed she would accomplish more by restraining her ardor. He smiled again, then sighed a little; oh well, perhaps she would learn all this before it was too late. It was not only for his own sake that he wished to hold her in Codogno, but for hers. Neither he nor the monsignor had any conception of her destiny.

❦ ❦ ❦

Francesca was now just turned thirty, but she still looked very much of a child. So ethereal was her appearance that she seemed almost to be a disembodied spirit as she flitted through the house, apparently not even touching the floor with her feet, so lightly, so swiftly did she pass. But she was in spite of all this a very matured and determined woman. She was also a very wise one. She recognized that for the present she would have to confine herself to the formation of the young women—almost all of them of the sturdy Lombard peasant stock—who were now joining her in ever increasing numbers. She had a wonderful fascination, and there was no dearth of vocations. She attracted souls and showed her power of inflaming them with her own spirit and ideals.

Even so, she was not satisfied with the progress she was making. There were already more than enough nuns for the tasks immediately to hand, but she was always looking ahead to the time when her wider activities would begin, and therefore she always kept an eye open for suitable candidates for her community. Rapidly as they came, they did not come rapidly enough to suit her. Accordingly she did a thing that is unique among founders of religious orders. It was a thing so extraordinary that some people have been rather shocked at it. Indeed, when the process for her beatification was being conducted, the Devil's Advocate, hard pressed to find a fault in her, seized upon this. She casually asked Mother Giovanna Francesca Grassi, the superior of the Daughters of the Sacred Heart at Arluno, who had educated her and had afterward refused her when she had wanted to join them, to let her have any postulants or novices that the community did not feel up to their standards. She may have been thinking, in part, of delicate girls who, like herself, were in danger of being sent away on account of their health; but she had something else in mind as well.

About this Monsignor Seratti spoke to Bishop Gelmini when next he saw him. He made a special trip to Lodi on this account, though he made it appear that he had merely dropped in for a friendly call. As they sat over a glass of wine, he let the bishop bring the subject of Mother Cabrini up.

"How are our good Sisters at Codogno, Monsignor?"

The monsignor did not look up but played with his glass, pushing it slowly backward and forward and gazing at it with his strong, serious eyes. "A beautiful spirit, Your Excellency. But I sometimes think Mother Cabrini is rushing ahead too fast."

The gentle old bishop smiled. "I often think so, too." He paused; then he asked, "Well, what has she been doing now?"

Monsignor Serrati told him about her request to the nuns at Arluno. "She's so anxious to build up her institute that she seems ready to take almost anybody. By now she ought to have learned that unsuitable people can spoil a community."

The bishop sipped at his wine. "Don't worry on that score, Monsignor. If she does get unsuitable people, she'll soon get rid of them. And another time I shall not be so lenient as I was with Tondini. That's something I reproach myself with."

"Not at all, Your Excellency. Look what came of it!"

"I know. God overrules even the mistakes of bishops. But I don't think that Mother Cabrini is making any mistake. Properly understood, that request is very much to her credit. If there is anybody who can make something out of unpromising material, she's the person. If these girls have the necessary good will, there is no need to ask for exceptional talents. The molding she can impart to the character—that and the grace of God—will make up for everything." He paused before asking a question: "What would you say was her supreme natural gift?"

Monsignor Seratti did not hesitate. "She's a born teacher. We know that."

"Exactly. And she knows it, too. That will provide for everything."

He finished his wine and smiled at the monsignor. They both felt that there was no need to say anything more.

🐾 🐾 🐾

On the other hand, when a community of nuns wished to join Francesca in a body, she refused them. There were too many of them for her to absorb, and as most of them were women who were already formed, set in their opinions and habits, she did not think she could do anything with them. It was a different story when she could get hold of a teachable young girl. In that case, always assuming that the grace of a vocation was conferred, she could be reforged.

When next the bishop dropped in on Monsignor Serrati, he said: "Of course she's quite right there. A vocation is something that, in the majority of instances, has to be developed."

The monsignor grunted assent. "I know. It doesn't drop full-fledged out of the skies."

The bishop went on: "Theoretically speaking, the supernatural should have all the freer road in a gifted personality. And it does, when natural gifts are willing to give grace its opportunity. But it is all too common knowledge that natural gifts tend to make their possessors vain, though one would suppose that the obvious reflection that no credit is due to the recipient ought to be sufficient to prevent any absurd self-esteem. That's why the simple and the humble, who are without any special talents, often make more progress in the spiritual life than do the brilliant."

The monsignor interposed. "Mother Cabrini is herself a woman of exceptional natural gifts, Your Excellency."

"She certainly is. But she understands that her daughters are for the most part girls of only average or less than average parts. She knows how to raise them to God, vastly heightening their ability by making them depend not on themselves but on an energy outside of themselves. Never have I seen anyone who has more skill in drawing out the best in people. I have an idea that our little Francesca is going to astonish us one of these days."

"She's astonishing *me* already."

Her main work during those years was the formation of the young women who entered her institute—that and the long hours she spent in contemplation by way of further forming herself. It was noticed that when she came out of chapel, it was with a face that positively glowed. She seemed to be transfigured after prayer. The bishop and the monsignor had agreed that her chief natural talent was pedagogical, and it was being employed all the time through those busy days, but largely to supernatural ends. She did little formal teaching, her external duties being already of an administrative rather than of an educational sort; but by spiritual conferences and private interviews, she so put her imprint upon the Missionary Sisters that not a nun ever joined her but showed for the rest of her life that the hand of Mother Cabrini had been upon her.

She was always very kind but also always very firm. To rule she had first to conquer the vivacity of her own temperament. Like Saint Francis de Sales, she was by nature quick-tempered; like him, she managed to keep that fact hidden, so that most people supposed that she was born with her sweetness of disposition. It was something that was not achieved at a stroke, and to the end of her life she had to keep a guard on herself. But by the time she had founded her Sisterhood she had become a calm, smiling woman, whose wit alone suggested the possibility of fire under her exterior.

Because of the sort of material she was gathering, and the nature of the work the Sisters were to do, she kept her institute to such devotional practices as were easy and within their comprehension. She had, for that matter, no theory of spirituality; she belonged to no school. Sublime mystical considerations were not laid before her daughters, as these might have proved bewildering. A great many prayers in common, including the Little Office of the Blessed Virgin, some private meditation, and always the cultivation of simplicity, humility and (above all) of obedience sufficed. That was the spirit of her Foundation. She went so far as to introduce a prayer to the Sacred Heart to be said daily in which she asked, "May the institute perish rather than that Thy spirit decline in it."

❧ ❧ ❧

From the start, the question of what was and what was not possible was ruled out. This was not out of overweening self-confidence, for Francesca was unassertive, retiring, and even timid by nature. It was because of her confidence in God. Almost every day one heard on her lips the words of Saint Paul, "I can do all things in Him who strengtheneth me." They became her private motto and afterward the motto of the institute. She wished all the Sisters to have the same trust. Early in her career, she had decided that she must not be asked to do only what was possible. Now she told her nuns that they must be prepared for the performance of impossibilities. "Nothing", she said, "is ever to daunt you. You are to press on, not of yourselves, but under obedience. I have already learned that whenever I failed in any undertaking, it was because I trusted too much in my own powers. None of us will fail if we leave everything in the hands of God. Under Him the question of possible and impossible ceases to have any meaning."

🍂 🍂 🍂

It soon became apparent to the nuns at Codogno that they might expect anything to happen. A number of incidents occurred that, though some of them may be accounted for on natural grounds, pointed to the marvelous, perhaps the miraculous. Francesca herself would not allow them to be called miracles; she could not prevent the Sisters from considering them precisely that. They occurred in those early years; they were to occur all through her life.

One day Francesca told a Sister to go to their wine-merchant to buy some wine for the community. Being Italians, they took the drinking of a little wine with their meals as a matter of course. The trouble on this occasion was that Mother Cabrini had no money to pay for the wine, and she already owed a bill.

The Sister thought she could arrange the thing: the wine-merchant came from her hometown, and she knew him. He would give them credit. Off she went for the wine.

The man looked a bit glum when he heard that he would have to wait for his money. "I'd better ask my partner about this", he said.

She caught scraps of their conversation from the next room. The partner said, "Oh no; those Sisters are so poor. God knows when we'll get paid!"

When the nun told Francesca that she had been refused, she seemed disappointed at first. But suddenly she asked, "Haven't you got any money?"

"No", was the reply. "Last night after shopping I found a penny in my pocket, but before I went to bed I handed that over to the treasurer."

"How much money does the man want?"

"Forty lire, Mother."

At this Francesca raised her eyes to heaven and her lips moved in prayer. Then bowing her head before a statue of the Sacred Heart as though in thanksgiving, she asked again, "Are you *sure* you have no money in your pocket?"

"Quite sure, Mother."

"Sister, I don't think you can have looked very well."

Upon this, the Sister turned her pocket out to prove that there was no money there. All that it contained were her beads, a notebook, and a handkerchief.

"What are we going to do about it, Daughter?"

"I don't know what to say except that the Lord will take care of it."

"Daughter, look in your pocket again."

This seemed quite useless, as she had just turned it out. But she obeyed, and to her astonishment she found two twenty-lire notes.

She got frightened this time, thinking that Mother Cabrini would suppose that she had attempted deception. She might get sent away for this apparent infraction of the rule of poverty. Hiding money—that was a serious offence. But being a simple soul, she told Mother Cabrini just what was in her mind.

In return she got a smile and the assurance, "Don't be afraid. I shall not send you away for this. I wish I had a hundred daughters as candid as you are."

When she went back to the wine-merchant with the notes, he was a bit sarcastic. "I see you found the money, after all! I rather thought you would."

The young nun told him exactly what had happened, and he was so touched that he said, "Well, if that is the case, I'll give you all the wine in my cellar." And he did in fact send in a couple of barrels of wine for nothing.

🌿 🌿 🌿

A somewhat similar story was told by a Sister who was sent to the kitchen to help the cook. She found her in great distress because the milk container was empty. So she went to Mother Cabrini's room and told her about it. "We do not have a drop of milk and the cook needs some at once. What are we to do?"

"Are you sure you looked well?"

"Yes, Mother; Sister Frances and I both looked. There is not a drop."

Again the eyes went up to the statue of the Sacred Heart. Then Francesca smiled and said, "Go down and look again—thoroughly this time."

The can was full to the brim. When the Sister carried it up to Mother Cabrini to show her, the answer was merely another smile. But when Sister Frances saw the milk she cried out, "Our Mother is a saint! She performs miracles!"

A little later Francesca sent for the nun who had found the milk and ordered her to say nothing about the incident.

"But, Mother, Sister Frances knows about it already."

Francesca laughed. "In that case, don't tell anybody else."

🌿 🌿 🌿

To be poor in that convent did not matter. Thus when Francesca heard that the bread-bin was empty except for a few stale crusts, she said, "You couldn't have looked properly. Go look again."

The Sister knew positively that there was no bread there, but out of obedience she did look—and found the bin full of fresh loaves. Wonderingly she asked the cook and the portress whether anybody could have brought bread in. "No," they both said, "Nobody did. How could anybody have bought bread when there isn't a penny in the house?"

This time they did not have the courage to speak about the matter. It was Mother Cabrini who said, "So you did find the bread!"

"Yes, Mother. I found a lot of fresh loaves."

There was a moment's silence. Then came the off-hand comment, "That shows you could not have looked in the first place."

❧ ❧ ❧

Francesca was not content, however, with always supplying their wants in this way. Poor as her health was, and though she suffered from frequent fevers, she was indefatigable in doing her share of the household duties, from which of course she could have been excused as superior. She helped also in the embroidery school—especially when it was necessary to work late into the night to put through some rush order; and she was constantly in the wardrobe and even the chicken-run. No detail was too small for her vigilance. And however hurried and worried she might be, the whole community noticed that she, above all others, gave them an example of the kind of serene sweetness taught by their patron Saint Francis de Sales.

If there was any talk of miracles, she passed it off lightly by saying that, had any miracle occurred, it was due to obedience. For in her eyes obedience was the all-important thing. No other form of asceticism was needed than the life of the community well lived and the Rule faithfully observed. "To become perfect," she said, "all you have to do is to obey perfectly. When you renounce your personal inclinations, you accept a mortification countersigned with the Cross of Christ."

Only in this way, she assured them, could they gain the secret of interior joy. That joy would not fail them in trials, if they remembered that these were sent by God; they would have it even when they were ill, so long as they accepted everything with gratitude. The words came with special force from the one among them who was suffering most. In the Rules she wrote: "When they are not able, on account of illness, to attend to all the common practices, the religious should frequently raise their hearts to God, keeping united with Him and offering Him their sufferings without complaint." Were they not at such times the little poor of Christ? Any kind of grumbling she detested, even if it was only about the weather. Still more she disliked to hear her nuns speak of the crosses they had to bear. Warm and constant as was her sympathy, she could be somewhat sharp when she heard a whine of self-pity, however piously it might be expressed. Why should they talk of crosses? "The true daughter of the institute", she used to say, "has no cross to carry, because the Mother takes care to carry the burdens of all." What she wanted was that they should keep their thoughts fixed on God and not on themselves.

Work and prayer, the old monastic ideals—these she made thoroughly her own. And seldom can they have been more closely combined, the active and the contemplative life, the modes of Martha and Mary. Hers was an order dedicated to so much hard physical work that it would seem that little time could be left for prayer. But that was not Francesca's concept at all. Six hours a day were given to prayer and contemplation, not counting the Friday adorations and the weekly saying of the Office of the Dead. The guiding principle was that no external duties should be allowed to interfere with the aspirations of the soul. For anybody to say that she was too busy to pray was no excuse. Rather it should be: the more the work, the greater the need for prayer. Apostolic though their purpose was, they were not to forget for a moment that they were Brides of Christ.

❦ ❦ ❦

Saints soon appeared among them. In May 1884, they buried the first of the Sisters to die, Giuseppina Cremaschi. In her last hour she said, "I'm going to found a house of the institute in heaven."

A few months later, Sister Ancilla Maria followed her. As she lay dying, she said to Francesca, "When I am in heaven I shall obtain all the graces you wish for the Order. Tell me what you want." When Francesca told her, she answered, "I shall obtain all this for you from the Sacred Heart of Jesus."

A few hours after her death, while the Sisters were at recreation, a bright light crossed the courtyard. Several of the nuns exclaimed, "There's Sister Ancilla going to Paradise!" When the people in the town heard that she had gone, they exclaimed, "A saint is dead!" Crowding into the convent, they begged for relics of her. A young woman who was dying of consumption asked, in the hope of being cured, that she might help to carry Sister Ancilla's coffin to the grave. At every step she felt herself growing stronger, though the burden was heavy. She came back completely cured.

But it was Francesca herself who was their great saint. During those first days she had had Sister Franceschina

Cairo as her roommate. One night this nun awoke and saw that the room was flooded with light.

"Mother, Mother!" she cried. "Did you see that?"

The calm reply came, "Yes, I saw it; it's nothing. Go to sleep."

The following evening, Sister Franceschina found that her bed had been moved into another cell. Never again, if it could possibly be avoided, was any nun allowed to sleep in the same room with Mother Cabrini.

PART II

THE DREAM AT NOONDAY

Chapter Four

THE ASSAULT ON ROME

The assault was not precipitate. Francesca Cabrini crept toward the Holy City before coming to the frontal attack and allowed her work to expand locally first. It was indispensable that she have a sufficient number of Sisters for her purpose before trying to carry it out, and those Sisters had to be completely formed for the work ahead of them. All this took time—however eagerly Francesca pressed on.

Yet as early as the spring of 1884, she found that she already had too many nuns to be able to house them all in the convent at Codogno; so she decided to enlarge the building. Monsignor Serrati—who had always been cautious by nature and was growing more cautious with increasing age—was against this. "Why build?" he asked. "Would it not be better to keep your numbers small?"

"But there are postulants applying to me all the time, Monsignor."

"Then turn them away."

The advice startled and even hurt Francesca. It seemed to be setting limits to God's designs. She told the monsignor so.

"But the expense, Mother!" he said. "You know you haven't much money."

That objection did appear to be unanswerable. The builder's estimate was for twenty-four thousand lire—more than twice what she had paid for the old friary. But nothing was impossible to Francesca. Instead of leaving everything in the hands of the contractors, she got the idea of setting the Sisters to work on the building. Under the supervision of one of them who was the daughter of a bricklayer, the nuns climbed the scaffolding after the workmen had left for the day and carried up baskets of bricks and buckets of cement. To the last glimmer of twilight, and again before the bricklayers arrived very early in the morning, these strong country girls toiled, finding the work hard but thinking it fun. How clever it was of their Mother to have thought of this! The Sister in charge of them was later, in the United States, to do a good deal of just such building, as Francesca on several occasions acted as her own contractor there. But this was after some experience had been gained. At Codogno, the experiment did not turn out very successfully.

One day a man presented himself at the convent. When Francesca went to the parlor to see him, he said, "I have come from the municipal authorities."

"Yes?"

"I am sorry, Mother Cabrini, but—well, perhaps you had better read this order."

She took the paper and read. "This means ..." She said looking from the paper to his face. She knew what it meant.

"It means that wall will have to be reinforced by props. If not, it is likely to fall down, and somebody will get hurt, perhaps killed."

She answered at once. "Of course that must not happen. I'll attend to it. You can tell the Building Commission so."

Her swift mind had already reached its decision. The bricklayer-Sisters would repair their bad work. It was more difficult than putting up the wall in the first instance, but undismayed the Sisters put out buttresses, crude but secure. A great saving of money was effected. With very little outlay, the convent doubled its size; better still, it had potentially doubled its spiritual power.

With that the time had come to make a further branching out.

❧ ❧ ❧

The second foundation had already been effected, two years after Mother Cabrini and her seven young followers left the House of Providence. It was not, however, of the kind that gave any indication—unless perhaps to the very discerning—of the direction in which she was moving. In November 1882, four Sisters, headed by a superior who was only twenty-five years old, left for Grumello, a small town near Cremona. Francesca went with them, in order to open the house, something she always did, with only one exception, whenever a new foundation was made, though these foundations of hers came to extend through three continents before her death.

The little group left Codogno in sedate excitement. Francesca, while outwardly more calm than they were, had a breast on fire, a gaze fixed on far horizons. When the farewells had been made, she turned to her traveling companions and said in an even tone, "Well, we leave now. Now we begin."

Out of Codogno the five nuns rode in the kind of simple carriage used in country districts, and behind them came a farm wagon laden with their furniture and kitchen utensils. Nobody who saw them rolling down the road would have supposed that this was the beginning of missionary journeys that were to exceed even those made by Saint Francis Xavier. Not even the monsignor or the bishop fully realized its significance, though they knew of

Francesca's ambitions. At the back of their minds was a
hope that a few little enterprises of this sort would help
to use up her energy and so keep her where they wanted
her to remain. But the Sisters understood; from now on
they might expect a summons to go anywhere; they were
already on the march. The idyllic family life of Codogno,
where they were all safely together, was nearing its end.
There were some tears at parting, but smiling faces and
shining eyes as well. Some of them would probably soon
be in China. Francesca had fired every one of them with
her own missionary enthusiasm.

Yet at Grumello they did on a small scale no more than
they had been doing at Codogno; they were even obliged,
because of the fewness of their numbers, to do less.
There was no orphanage, only a free day school for girls,
in which very sensibly the practical needs of those who
attended were considered. There was therefore a great deal
of emphasis laid upon cooking and needlework, for most
of these girls would become the wives of workingmen and
farmers. But as in Codogno, there were also classes for the
religious instruction of the women of the place. In the eyes
of the world, nothing had happened except that another
small convent had been opened. In the eyes of Francesca
and her nuns, it was incalculably more than that. The institute had begun to spread; it would go on spreading until it
reached the ends of the world.

❧ ❧ ❧

Yet after that no further move was made for two years.
Then in 1884, a house was opened in Milan, the arch-
diocese to which the bishop of Lodi was associated as a
suffragan. By going there, the Missionary Sisters, though
their intention was to expand—and to expand farther than
anybody imagined possible—put themselves in a position,

so it seemed, of being tethered more securely than ever in Lombardy. It did not prove to be a tethering at all.

The establishment of the Milan convent had the appearance of being very casually made. As Mother Cabrini was sending a nun there to buy a religious statue, she told her to make enquiries at the same time as to a house that might be available for them. Knowing a priest in Milan, this Sister looked him up and talked to him about the matter. Perhaps he could advise her. It so happened that he was the very man who could help them. He had a boarding school in his parish, and it was just then in need of somebody who could take charge of it. There and then he offered it to the Missionary Sisters.

This time Francesca took eight of her nuns to take possession of it. But she changed the character of the school by converting it into a residence for those intending to become teachers. She was to found several institutions of this kind, for she realized how badly they were needed by young women who came, many of them for the first time in their lives, from their country homes into a large city. The whole weight of the secular normal schools was, as she knew, being thrown subtly—and sometimes with naked heaviness—in favor of what was called liberalism, a complete secularity of outlook. Francesca saw that teachers, more than any other class of people, needed to be taught. By keeping them good Christians, she would make sure of their exercising the right kind of influence upon their students. These hostels of hers were a missionary activity; through them, at one remove, she meant to lay her hand upon the religious life of the nation.

Writing in 1906 from Chicago to the normal students in her hostel in Rome, she told them: "You, my good daughters, in your great mission of education, are the first cooperators in the missionary works of the Sacred Heart, and for this reason you are specially dear to my heart in the great family that Jesus has given me." It was her concept of this specialized activity.

Up to this time, Francesca had done her work in villages and small towns. From this time on, it was a settled policy with her to locate her establishments, whenever feasible, in large cities. Milan suited her well, not only for that reason but because it was one of the most important of the ecclesiastical focal-points of Italy. Not a few religious congregations had been founded there and were content with it as a center of operations. It could never be this in Francesca's eyes. To her, Milan was primarily a stage on the road to Rome.

What she immediately found by going to Milan was a field of opportunities for the local extension of her work. Had she wished it, she could have confined herself to that and still have found plenty to do for the rest of her life. The next year saw her established at Borghetto, and there were calls from Casalpusterlengo and Livagra. But all the time her blue vivacious eyes were fastened upon Rome. Rome! Rome! There was where she had to be. She always had said that she needed to base her institute on the Rock of Peter. Though all her work so far had been within the Lombard low country—with seven schools of one sort or another, instituted within seven years after she had founded the Missionary Sisters—she regarded this as no more than the preliminary to something far more important. It was to be Rome—and after Rome the whole earth.

The autumn of 1887 burned gold and bronze. Francesca's order had so far been only a diocesan concern, directly under the control of the two local bishops. For her even to think of obtaining papal approval so soon appeared to many of her advisers foolish and almost presumptuous.

There was one of her close friends who had shown more understanding of her ambitions than had anybody else. This was Monsignor Bersani, the coadjutor bishop of Lodi. When he died in the June of that year, his passing was not only a great sorrow to Francesca but seemed to be the removal of one of the main supports upon which she had counted. Then the next morning, as she was about to go to the altar rail to receive Communion, she heard, she thought, his voice saying, "Mother, receive it for me." For a whole month, she offered all her Communions for the repose of his soul. After that she seemed to see him smiling at her and heard him saying, "It is enough now. I thank you for this. You have helped me. From now on I shall help you." She knew that the time was near when she would need the aid of a friend in heaven.

But though there were also friends still on earth who believed she was right in going to Rome—among them a Jesuit who preached a retreat at Codogno and the Canon of Crema—Monsignor Serrati again strongly advised against her going farther afield. As Bishop Gelmini of Lodi could not be consulted, because he was ill just then and died early the following year, and as Bishop Bersani was now dead, Monsignor Serrati's opinions fell with a weight all the harder to resist.

The monsignor was now the only one left of those who could be regarded as co-founders of the institute. He had to be listened to for that reason, and because he had always shown himself so firm a friend. He was full of misgivings, and he looked upon himself as doing her a service by warning her that the time was not ripe for what she proposed.

"You will never succeed", he told her. "You don't know Rome as I do. There you will only get scoffed at, and when you come back to Codogno you will be the laughingstock of the town."

As Francesca was not greatly shaken by that argument, he tried to turn her aside by saying in his blunt way, "These are things that should be left to the saints to do." He thought that ought to stop her. He knew that the thing that most dismays a saint is to seem to be claiming to be one. Upon Francesca that delicate form of intimidation did not work.

As she could not reach Bishop Gelmini owing to his illness, she tried to see Archbishop Luigi Calabiana of Milan. Twice she called, only to be told that he was out. But she persisted and went a third time.

He came down to her and showed himself distinctly annoyed. "What makes you want to go to Rome? Isn't Milan good enough for you?"

"Your Excellency", she returned mildly—but he could not fail to notice the flash in her eyes—"Your Excellency, I have *always* intended to go to Rome. Milan is a beautiful city, but it can never be enough for me."

"Mother," he answered, "you have received diocesan approval. Be satisfied with that. Give up these absurd notions of yours."

He gave this opinion so emphatically that Francesca wondered whether she had not been put under obedience. He seemed to have forbidden this journey to Rome. In face of that, Francesca hesitated. She could not resist authority, and yet she was sure that God was calling her.

In her perplexity, she laid the question before her friend Monsignor Mantegazza. What, she asked him, had been the archbishop's intention?

He had no doubt at all. The archbishop, so he assured her, would not have meant to give a positive prohibition but only a personal expression of his views.

"Are you certain of that, Monsignor?" she asked.

"Perfectly, Mother. No bishop would put you under obedience in such a matter. You may go to Rome with a clear conscience. You won't be disobedient. Look, I'll take the responsibility. Don't annoy him further by trying to see him again. Go, and I'll explain everything to him afterward."

Just then Francesca had a dream in which the Infant Jesus appeared to her. From the Child's mouth she heard the words, "Go to Rome."

She woke quivering with delight. All the same a dream would have counted for nothing with her in the face of a definite episcopal order; but as Monsignor Mantegazza had been positive on this point, it was possible for her to believe that she had received a form of divine inspiration. She was to have many such dreams all through her life, and while she was careful not to attach too much importance to them—even when what she modestly described as dreams may really have been visions—she was, in actual fact, often guided by them, hardheaded and practical woman though she was. They may of course have been merely a vivid corroboration of her intuitions, but as she felt that these intuitions came from God, she acted upon them as such.

She acted now. We have her own laconic note on what she did. It reads: "F. Cabrini, always burning with the desire to go on foreign missions, but on the other hand not wishing to go or send Sisters without the approval or blessing of the Sovereign Pontiff, the representative of Christ on earth, came to Rome in September 1887."

She left Milan on the 24th of the month. It was characteristic of her that she took as companion, not one of the more vigorous and capable Sisters—these were needed for work elsewhere—but Serafina, who was selected because her health did not make her good for much. That this threw an additional burden on her own shoulders was something she did not mind. The two nuns, with all their belongings packed in a single shabby suitcase, struck down direct to Genoa.

From there the railway runs most of the way to Pisa, and even beyond, within sight of the sea. It was the first time that Francesca, from the inland plains of Lombardy, had seen it, except in imagination in the days when she used to launch her paper boats filled with violets. Now it stretched out wide and calm and glittering under the moonlight. From that time on, it was to be almost her native element. The phobia she had had since the day she had nearly been drowned at Livagra disappeared, never to trouble her again. Instead the sea, in whichever of its varying moods she was to behold it, became for her a symbol of the immensity of God. Why fear again what was to be the road to the missions?

Only a woman of the greatest intrepidity would have attempted what she was about to do. Those who had advised her against going to Rome had not been merely trying to keep her for themselves, though that motive may have been mixed with a sincere desire to spare her a wound. They realized better than she could what rebuffs she was likely to encounter. And even she knew quite well that she would be looked upon only as a provincial nun who had happened to found one of those diocesan orders that were everywhere. As such she had no claim to special consideration. But she was also convinced that she was being called by God. It was with boundless faith in Him and her vocation that she set out on what so many people told her was a fool's errand.

When Bishop Gelmini had said in 1880, "I do not know of any order of missionary nuns; so why not found one yourself?" he had spoken with prophetic insight but also with imperfect information. Yet he may be pardoned for not having heard of that Breton lady, Hélène de Chappotin de Neuville, who as Mother Mary of the Passion had founded the Franciscan Missionaries of Mary in 1877. Francesca had been in correspondence with her as a kindred spirit, and it was at her convent that she stayed for her first six weeks in Rome. In Mother Mary and in the General of the reorganized Friars Minor, Bernardino da Portogruaro, she found enthusiastic supporters and wise counsellors.

As always with Francesca, she made friends, carrying them off their feet by her enthusiasm. And, what is more, she realized the value of friends. No instrument that might be useful to her was ever neglected. At the same time, she did not depend on them too much. The Friend of friends was the one she finally counted upon.

On the very day of her arrival, Francesca made a pilgrimage to the altar of Saint Francis Xavier in the Chiesa del Gesù. His body—buried first in quicklime on Sancian Island off Canton—was still incorrupt at Goa in India. But his right hand that had baptized so many thousands of pagans was preserved at the Gesù. He was her patron. She had taken his name. It was fitting that she go at once to put her cause under his protection. Friends on earth were good; friends in heaven were still better.

❧ ❧ ❧

She had two objects in going to Rome. One was to obtain papal approval of her institute, the other was permission to open a house there from which all the subsequent operations of the institute might be directed. This would free her from complete dependence on local bishops and give her a center for the work that she conceived as worldwide. Though little enough of her subsequent life was to be spent in Italy, it was officially from Italy, or more specifically from Rome, that everything was directed.

Perhaps it was as well that Francesca had no experience of the Curia's ordinary mode of procedure. Had she had this, she might have despaired, for sometimes it almost seems that papal departments dispose of business by leaving it indefinitely undealt with. At best any dealings with cautious ecclesiastical officials call for plenty of time and an even greater amount of diplomatic finesse. As it was, Francesca cut through red tape at a stroke, refusing to be put off and carrying everything before her by her impetuosity. Her very ignorance of customary procedure was probably an advantage, for she managed to impress everybody by her ardor and zeal. Now for the first time in her life, she was brought into contact with extremely exalted personages, and, with everything at stake, she seemed suddenly to acquire an extraordinary ability in the management of affairs. Her personal charm counted for a good deal. More important than that was the fact that the officials were not so official in outlook as not to suspect that they were encountering a saint.

Francesca had never been in Rome before. Its splendors and antiquities stirred her imagination. On every side there were things that stormed her heart. But the sights themselves were not permitted to overwhelm her. Her mind was fastened on its objective, her eyes fixed all day in prayer on the tabernacle. Rome surged around her, and she prayed. In the gorgeous churches rich with marble and gold, she heard nothing and saw nothing. She was alone with God.

As for the business on which she had come, she was told that she would have to see the cardinal-vicar, Lucido

Maria Parocchi, a Lombard like herself, as he was the person to whom application had to be made for permission to establish a house in Rome. She lost no time in going to him; Francesca always acted with the greatest promptitude. Her first interview with the cardinal was on the 28th, only three days after her arrival.

At the outset she received decided discouragement. The cardinal began, as is customary, by asking her if she had brought any letters of recommendation. If she had thought of securing them, she had not been able to do so. Bishop Gelmini had been ill, and the archbishop of Milan had been too much opposed to her plans for her to venture to ask him for recommendations. Yet this was something that she could hardly explain to the cardinal-vicar without damaging herself. She had simply to say that she had no letters, and the cardinalitial eyebrows arched. Could this nun from the provinces be so simple as all this? Surely she should know that, though the possession of such letters is often of little help, their absence is a detriment! He looked at her again. Candid, yes; but he saw she was very wide-awake.

"But why", he asked her, "should you wish to come here? It's much too short a time since the founding of your institute. In Codogno you can do an immense amount of good, but you are not needed in Rome. Here religious houses are like the flowers of spring; there are too many of them already. You had better go back to Codogno."

He was not unkindly. As he talked to the Francesca of the smiling face and the flashing eyes, he became interested in the person he saw before him. He thought her project hopeless, but he found himself asking for an account of her institute. "Now what", he said blandly, "would you say was its distinctive spirit?"

At this Sister Serafina cut in with voluble explanations. Francesca had to stop her. Then she answered Cardinal

Parocchi, "Your Eminence, I am not quite sure whether it *has* developed a distinctive spirit as yet."

Delighted by her honesty, the cardinal smiled again. But the answer confirmed him in his belief that she ought to make sure that the Order had developed before coming to Rome. He thought he knew how to deal with a situation of this sort. "Well," he said, "I will give you permission to found a house in Rome when you can show me that you have enough capital for the purpose."

The promise was also a blow. What capital did Francesca possess? All the same she asked him what he would consider sufficient.

"Oh, half a million lire." That he imagined to be a very clever way of getting rid of her. He had laid down a condition which he was sure she would never be able to fulfill.

He rose to dismiss the two nuns, who at this rose too and then knelt to kiss his ring It seemed to be the collapse of all their hopes. Where could they get such a sum of money? But though Francesca was deathly white, she managed to murmur *"Deo gratias!"* and when they emerged from the cardinal's apartment she tried to cheer her *socia* by saying, "Courage, daughter! You will see that the Lord will change his heart."

❦ ❦ ❦

For the moment there was nothing to do except pray. She had been praying hard already; now she prayed harder than ever. She did not return to Codogno; she waited in Rome.

At about the same time that she had seen the cardinal-vicar, she had presented her Rules to the body commissioned to sit in judgment upon such matters, the Congregation of Bishops and Regulars. As this was a committee, it was still less to be hurried than was an individual cardinal. It did not hand down its decision until March 12 of the following year—and even that was exceptionally swift work—when a decree of praise was issued for the institute, although the definitive approval of the constitutions did not come for nearly twenty years. Again it was the Roman method of proceeding with caution.

The approval of the Rules, however, was not the most urgent matter. Francesca's immediate concern was getting permission to open a house in Rome. And despite the discouraging attitude of Cardinal Parocchi, she wrote to ask whether he would see her again. That he consented to do so shows that he must have been impressed.

"But I don't know what more I can say than I said before", he told her.

Francesca had come prepared with a bold suggestion. "Your Eminence, could you not consult the Holy Father about this?"

The cardinal was not a man given to gasping. But he might well have gasped at the idea that he should directly approach the pope about such a thing. Looking at the determined and intrepid woman before him, he felt a new interest in her. He was beginning to discover what many others discovered in their time that it was not easy to say "No" to Francesca Cabrini, even though he was a cardinal and she a nun from the provinces. He leaned forward on the table and looked at her a long while. At last he spoke: "Very well, I *will* speak to the pope about you."

"That is very kind of Your Eminence."

"But don't pin any hope on this. The Holy Father is away at present at his summer residence. When he comes back ... Only I don't see how anything can be done for you."

That the cardinal had said as much as he had was a good deal, though it gave no assurance as to the outcome.

Francesca went away radiant with joy. When she heard a few days later that the cardinal had confided to a friend that the Lord was changing his heart with regard to these nuns—using the very words that she had used—she exclaimed, "This is too much! This is too much!" She had always been confident of success; she now perceived the finger of God moving.

Meanwhile letters of recommendation had arrived from Lombardy. And Monsignor Mantegazza wrote that he had seen the archbishop of Milan and was authorized to say that the archbishop had only meant to give advice, not to issue an order. He added, "You are free to do what you think best." The ground was being cleared very rapidly.

Two weeks of almost intolerable strain for Francesca followed. Then at her third interview with the cardinal-vicar, he seemed a different man. As soon as the nuns entered his room, he beamed upon them. He had his graceful but slightly grim joke all prepared.

"Well, Mother Cabrini," he asked at once, "are you ready to obey?"

"Of course, Your Eminence."

"In that case I shall not allow you to establish a house in Rome." He paused to see how she would take it, and she did not flinch. "Instead, I order you to found *two* houses."

Relishing his wit and the surprised delight of the nuns, he went on, "You must found two houses—a free school for the poor at Porta Pia and a kindergarten at Aspra in the Sabina."

But with the permission came a heavy obligation. Francesca had got much more than she had bargained for. To obtain nuns to staff two houses created a problem. Another problem was that of financial resources.

The cardinal proposed to do no more for the school at Porta Pia than equip it; the Sisters would have to pay the rent and maintain themselves. And at Aspra, they were to receive only four hundred lire a year. Yet this was a gift-horse that could not be looked in the mouth. In confident obedience, Francesca without hesitation addressed herself to her task.

The news when it reached Lombardy thrilled the Sisters and their friends. The most sanguine among them had not expected so much success. That it had come brought forth donations even from those who had been gloomy in their warnings. Monsignor Serrati was specially generous, giving five-hundred lire to cover the expenses of five Sisters who were to go to Rome and another thousand to help generally in the foundation. Though none of the sums given were large, they sufficed; Francesca would make them suffice.

❦ ❦ ❦

Francesca Cabrini was accustomed to act with the utmost dispatch and decision, though only after prayer. There were to be occasions in the years to come when she was to enter a strange foreign city and have a house functioning there in a couple of weeks. Once the road was open, nothing was ever able to hold her back. On October 31, she rented an apartment near the Porta Pia in the Palazzo Majocchi, and then she set out for the Sabina.

The journey was not a long one, but it was made difficult on account of the weather and the poor means of transportation. She and the nuns assigned to Aspra left at six in the morning, undeterred by the fact that the rain was falling in torrents and a strong wind blowing.

"Mother," asked one of them, "do you think we should go today? Why not wait till tomorrow?" one of them asked.

"Today" was the only answer. Opening her umbrella, Francesca trotted ahead, pushing against the wind until her umbrella was blown inside out. After that she ran on with the wrecked steel and silk tucked under her arm. "Hurry! Hurry!" she turned back to call to them as they ran behind. "We must catch this train."

By the time they got to the station, they were already wet to the skin and splashed with mud. Nor did the train help them much. The window of their compartment would not shut, and the rain and wind blew in. And at Poggio Mirteto, the nearest station to Aspra, there was no cabriolet at hand. For nearly an hour they waited, shivering in their wet clothes until a station porter had pity on them and invited them into a little room where they were able to thaw out a bit near a fire.

The cab came at last—an open one. That meant another two hours in the vile weather, as they crawled slowly over the hills and down the steep valleys. An early snow had fallen there, and the air was cold. Francesca tried to console the Sisters by reminding them of Saint Teresa's experiences on the rough roads of Spain. At least they did not have that upset which made Saint Teresa humorously complain to Christ, "If that's the way you treat your friends, little wonder that you have so few!"

It is hardly to be wondered at that Francesca returned to Rome ill and with a fever. But this deterred her no more than the weather could. She used to say that for her the way to get well was to do some work. So she set about preparing the apartment in the Via Nomentana for the reception of the nuns who were to teach in the Porta Pia school.

The funds at her disposal did not permit the buying of new furniture, even of the cheapest sort. She decided to pick up what she needed at auctions, and though this would take time, she sent word to the Sisters at Codogno who were to staff the Roman school to come on at once. On the Feast of All Saints, November 1, five of them arrived. Like the two nuns already there, they had to sleep for the time being on straw and had to wash in the scullery. But a start was made.

Meanwhile Francesca went every day to public auctions. Fever or no fever, she was out early in the morning, not even waiting for breakfast after Mass, so as to get to work without delay. There she stood on her feet in the salesrooms until late in the afternoon the auctioneer laid his hammer down. Sometimes she took a little bread and cheese along, but that was all she got to eat until supper.

Piece by piece she picked up such articles of furniture as were indispensable. She had a shrewd eye and a small sum of money was made to stretch a long way. Yet often after she had bid in competition with others there, and was all worn out, she had to let what she wanted go, because somebody else, just before the "Going! Going! Gone!" offered a few lire more than she decided she could afford. She would never throw away a penny out of weariness; if she did not get what she was looking for that day, she would wait until the next, ill as she was. Bit by bit she furnished the apartment in the Palazzo Majocchi in this way. Until then straw had to suffice for beds and a couple of boards stretched between washstands as a refectory table. It recalled the first night at their convent at Codogno. They were all very happy.

The finishing touch came when Cardinal Parocchi himself called to see them at the Via Nomentana. By now this great dignitary who had stipulated for resources of half a million lire was almost making pets of his new protégés. In the parlor where Francesca received him, he observed a statue of Our Lady. As the crown was not on the Blessed

Virgin's head but lying on the pedestal, he asked, "When are you going to crown her?"

It was now Francesca's opportunity to get even with a little joke. Demurely she answered, "Our Lady has been waiting to be crowned by him whose heart she has changed."

Chapter Five

THE PLIGHT OF THE DISPERSED

The immediate objective had been gained with Cardinal Parocchi's permission to establish a house in Rome. Consolidation of that position came when on March 12, 1888, the Rules as drawn up at Codogno were approved. It was the day when the annual novena to Saint Francis Xavier ended; Francesca took this as very characteristic of the courtesy of that great Basque gentleman. She learned afterward that when a preliminary report on the Rules had been shown to the pope, Leo had exclaimed enthusiastically, "Approve them, approve them!" That was why a piece of business of a kind that sometimes dragged on for years was disposed of in a few months. The period of waiting had seemed long to Francesca; to those accustomed to these things it seemed wonderfully short. Francesca had every reason to congratulate herself. But that was something she never thought of doing: she had placed the issue in the hands of God, and she had never had the slightest doubt as to the outcome. Her heart went up in gratitude.

It may be that some of the friends she had made helped more than she knew. In Cardinal Parocchi she had a powerful protector. But in the General of the Franciscans, Father Bernardino, and in Father Salna, the prior of the

Dominicans at the Minerva—who happened also to be a member of the congregation that passed on religious Rules—she also had men who were able to do a good deal for her. Father Salna would put his hand on her head and call her his child, and the Franciscan used to say that whenever he saw her his heart filled with joy. She had begun to show the power of getting things done that was to be so characteristic of her.

Her charm she had always had, but in the retirement of the convents, it had not been drawn out in just this way. In the seclusion from the world in which she had lived for fifteen years, she was always preparing for the time of her activity. But until then her influence had been exercised only very quietly upon the group of young nuns she had gathered around her. Among them her naturally shy temperament had kept her willingly inconspicuous. Now the day had at last arrived when other qualities appeared—intrepidity and an ability in management hardly suspected before. They were all the more effective because of being exercised by one who had lost nothing of the grace humility gives. She was from now on, not a different woman, but a greater woman. Rome gave her a new outlook and a new confidence. She was at the heart of Christendom and part of a new world. That drew out the latent force in her—that and the assurance that God was now leading her to the destiny of which she had dreamed for thirty years.

This destiny was to prove to be somewhat different from what she had expected. Rather, while remaining essentially the same, it took a different form.

The fact that Leo XIII had taken a direct part in the approval of her Rules showed his special interest, though she and the pope had so far not met. When that did happen, she was to receive from him not that kind of sanction usually given and that follows a stereotyped official pattern. His was to be a personal and explicit commission.

❧ ❧ ❧

It came about in what seemed a very roundabout manner.

A few months before Francesca made her journey to Rome, some Benedictine nuns at Castelsangiovanni had requested to be affiliated with Francesca's order, offering a school and orphanage. Nothing was done about the matter at the time, but in Rome Francesca met the bishop of the diocese, Giovanni Battista Scalabrini of Piacenza. It was because of this ripening friendship that she was induced to go to the United States.

The bishop had about this time published his pamphlet *Italian Emigration to America*. It created something of a sensation, for it dealt with a problem everybody in Italy knew to exist but that nobody had stated so clearly. From the warmth of his heart he had written: "I see those poor Italian immigrants in a foreign land, among people who do not speak their language, easily falling a prey to cruel exploitation ... fatigued, sick, sighing in vain for their quaint and humble little towns in Italy, and finally dying without the consolation of their dearest ones, without the enlivening words of faith which hold out to them the reward the Lord has promised to the good and the unfortunate. Yet those who do succeed in making a decent living—they are the very ones who, feeling aloof from their native country, forget every idea of the supernatural, every precept of Christian teaching, and each day they lose more of their former religious feelings, since those sentiments are not nourished with a good Christian life, and thus evil inclinations overcome the loftiest ideals." The same idea was put more succinctly in a letter from an Italian in America that was read before the Chamber of Deputies in the days when Francesca's cousin, Agostino Depretis, was prime minister. One terrible sentence ran: "Here we live like animals; one lives and dies without a priest, without teachers and without doctors."

Bishop Scalabrini did more than write a book. Since 1876, when he was sent to Piacenza, he had had a burning concern in the plight of the dispersed. In his own diocese, he found that twenty-eight thousand of its people were living in foreign countries, because they were unable to exist in their own land. He was deeply distressed by the situation and did all in his power to bring it to the attention of the country, going up and down lecturing upon it. For the material aid of the immigrants he founded the Saint Raphael's Society and, in 1888, the Congregation of Saint Charles Borromeo to minister to their spiritual needs.

Even so, what had by now been accomplished was pitifully inadequate. Two Fathers and a lay brother had taken over a former Protestant church in New York, dedicating it to Saint Joachim. Five other priests and two lay brothers had gone to South America. But at least the bishop was doing what he could. "There in America," he wrote, "the Italians, feeling isolated from their native country, completely disregard every precept of Christian life and day by day lose more of their former religious piety.... At this point, I confess, I feel humiliated both in my capacity as a priest and as an Italian."

He had visited the United States to gain information at first hand, and his conclusions were supported by the bishops who met in the Third Plenary Council of Baltimore. There could be no doubt at all that the Italians in America were in a desperate condition.

❧ ❧ ❧

Other national groups of immigrants in America had previously presented a problem—similar in some respects but in others vastly different. The Irish for a long while did not have enough priests, and some of those who arrived among them were men their bishops at home were not particularly sorry to unload on the United States with high recommendations. But such men were, after all, only a small minority among the clergy. Compared with the Italians, the Irish had always possessed an abundance of priests and good ones.

The Germans, too, from the beginning had pastors who knew their own language. Though they were neglected in this or that section of the country, yet as they tended to gather in compact little German pockets, they could be easily reached. They were taking over whole rural sections of the Middle West, and in some cities—such as Cincinnati and Milwaukee—one could at times almost imagine one was in Germany itself.

Moreover, the Germans were served by powerful religious orders. Boniface Wimmer had established the first Benedictine abbey near Pittsburgh, and from that abbey one foundation after another was to come. The Fathers of the Precious Blood were in Ohio. Though perhaps everything was not quite satisfactory even among the Germans, it is at least true that they were relatively well off both materially and spiritually.

As for the Irish, though they had suffered hard things at the hands of the Know Nothings, who hated them for both social and religious reasons, they had ways of protecting themselves. Both in Boston and Philadelphia Nativists discovered that it was not very safe to tread on an Irishman's coattails. In New York, when the truculent John Hughes was archbishop, nobody dared to try it at all. The Irishman's fighting spirit, his aptitude for politics, his articulateness, and his ability to rise in the world soon made him respected, even by those who did not like him.

With the Italians it was very different. They were a gentle people and were utterly helpless before those who exploited them, many of whom were their fellow-countrymen—agents who went about Italy inducing them to emigrate and the *padroni* into whose clutches they fell upon arrival. The early Irish had indeed done hard work with pick and shovel on canals and roads and railways and had had a monopoly of the longshoremen's work; but they had graduated from these occupations. Anything poorly paid and thankless, anything dangerous—that was now left to the Italians, and it was almost the only thing left to them.

For this state of things it is not very easy, nor perhaps would it be very fair, to fix any blame on individuals or even on particular groups. The vast majority of those arriving in the United States were from the south of Italy and Sicily; and nearly all of them were unskilled farm laborers. Most of the Italian artisans went for seasonal employment to nearby European countries and then returned home. Not many such came to the United States: most of those who did were waiters and barbers and the like.

The Italian *contadini*, primitive though their methods were, could in many instances have obtained employment as farm-laborers. They generally would not accept such work, as they found they could save even less while doing it than they could as navvies. And their consuming idea being to save as much as possible, usually with the dream of going back to Italy as rich *signori*, they were willing to live in such squalor that this alone made them universally despised.

Many, however, in fact did return to Italy. During the years immediately following Mother Cabrini's arrival, for every five immigrants who arrived, two went back, while South America regurgitated an even higher proportion. Not all of these stayed in Italy. A large number intended only to make a visit; others were disappointed in their old life. But the dream of repatriation filled thousands who never were able to make it come true. It was for this that they desperately saved.

Yet they had little of what one thinks of as patriotism. They left Italy because, as they used to put it, if they had stayed there they would have had to eat one another. With equal frankness they used to say that Italy for them was any country that would give them a living. But they did have very strong local attachments. Rather than patriotism, they had *campanilismo*, parochial loyalty.

This, however, was greatly to their disadvantage in America, where such a sentiment could not be so much as comprehended. It prevented their unity. It made for a factionalism that was perhaps rarely bitter but that made the various provincial or city groups gather in little enclaves within the Little Italies themselves. It was very difficult to get any community of these immigrants to work together for common betterment. This factionalism was one of the things that Francesca Cabrini was to find most hampering to her work; it was also the thing that she, perhaps more than anybody else, helped to break down.

🍀 🍀 🍀

Another factor that created a serious problem was that two-thirds of the immigrants coming to the United States were men. Uprooted from their native soil and separated from their families, the effect of immigration upon them may be readily imagined. Not only that, but there were many criminal elements among them; if brigandage disappeared in Sicily, it was less because of the efforts of the police than because the brigands left their country for their country's good. The presence of these people in America got all Italians, most of whom were peaceable and orderly and sober and industrious, a bad name. As now and then knives were drawn by hot-blooded men in a quarrel, many people imagined that all Italians carried stilettos, as some people still seem to imagine that every Negro carries a razor for use as a weapon.

Yet the general judgment must be that the Italians were a very useful group to have. Even when they were being most ruthlessly exploited, they were useful. The clothing manufacturers who employed Italian women (at sweated wages) and unkindly said that they were as cheap as children and little better, were nevertheless glad to have them. And though in the railroad-building gangs the Italians had less muscular strength than the Irish who had preceded them, they made up for this by their steadiness and persistence and tractability. They were, if it comes to that, often too tractable. They made themselves unpopular with American organized labor by their unwillingness to strike and their willingness even to be used as strike-breakers. Yet the sum of their qualities gave them a decent balance in the social ledger.

For a long time they were regarded with universal contempt. The combative Irish despised people who would not—who could not—fight for their rights. But how was it possible for them to do much for themselves? Huddled into the insanitary slums of the Little Italies, the men might learn a few words of English—just enough for their daily tasks. The women seldom learned even that much. As for the children, they ran wild, except for such boys as could pick up a few nickels selling papers or shining shoes.

❦ ❦ ❦

Probably no race, not even excepting the Blacks, has been so poorly thought of in the United States as that which has produced Dante and Saint Thomas Aquinas and Michelangelo and Leonardo da Vinci. Indeed, those who wanted a still more insulting term than "wop" or "dago" found it when they called the Italians "white niggers". A good many of the poorer immigrants were illiterate, but surely none could have been quite so ignorant as their coarse-grained detractors.

The social side of the problem was, however, only one, and not the worst, side. The Italians found little opportunity to practice their religion in America. Those who, in spite of all discouragement, went to church, found themselves herded into basement chapels, something they bitterly resented. In disgust, some would thereupon call themselves free-thinkers; others went over to Protestantism, especially as this was made to their economic advantage. And the anticlericalism that was imported from Italy took in America extreme forms.

Those who did hear Mass regularly could seldom find a priest able to hear their confession. Chicago, which was the best off of the larger American cities in this respect, had as late as 1899 only one priest for every seven thousand five hundred Italians. In New Orleans, the proportion was one priest to every thirty thousand, and in New York, a quarter of a million Italian Catholics had five churches to which nineteen priests were attached. This for a people who had come from a land where there was one priest for every three hundred and seventy souls!

The consequence was that for the vast majority all contact with spiritual things was completely severed. Not even when dying could they find a priest to attend them. While living, the conduct of these hitherto inoffensive people was often of a kind that shocked the staidly respectable. Despair drove them to the devil that waits for unfortunates.

The nature of the rough and dangerous work they were forced to do—since no other work was open to them—resulted in many deaths and still more permanent mutilations. Then they had nowhere to turn. Their children were taken from them and brought up in public or private institutions where they inevitably lost the remnants of their faith. Those who were obliged to go to the free ward of the hospitals—and where else could they go?—often were unable to tell the doctors what was the matter with them. If they got well, it was only to return to a life of squalor; if they died, it was in loneliness and desperation. We can hardly wonder that this most amiable and gentle of peoples tended to grow bitter and, in their bitterness, antagonistic to religion. The surprising thing is that their Catholic traditions survived among them at all.

Leo XIII, when issuing his famous encyclical *Rerum Novarum*, did not have in mind only the oppressed and dispersed Italians; he was giving the world principles of universal application. But he knew when writing of "a yoke little better than that of slavery itself" that to no people did it apply more than to his fellow-countrymen in America. He understood perfectly, too, that the oppression they suffered was not merely that of economic injustice, but that this injustice made it virtually impossible for large numbers among them to live a decent Christian life. That he had spoken as he did was something that the vast majority of the poor and illiterate never heard; those who did know, the exploiters of the poor, disregarded his words. The way so many of these exploiters made a parade of their church connections, though few of them were Catholics, created a widespread association of ideas that linked Christianity with capitalism. Even in Italy, a land little industrialized, an unjust system of land tenure had often created a similar impression. In capitalistic America, the moral could be drawn with devastating effect. A vague antagonism to religion was the all too common consequence.

In 1889, when Francesca Cabrini arrived for the first time in New York, immigration to the United States was far from being at its peak. Then the yearly average of Italians to arrive was only about 50,000. More went to Brazil and even to the Argentine. Later the emigration to Brazil dropped sharply, and that to the Argentine rose only slowly. But emigration to the United States rose steadily until after 1902 it was over 200,000 every year. During the period of Mother Cabrini's work in this country, the total of immigrants must have been close to four million, though it must be remembered that at least a million and a half of these went back and that many among the four million are included several times in the statistics because of their several entries.

For Italy the problem was very acute, and the government made several attempts to check the outward flow of the population. In many places an entire countryside was stripped bare. Whole villages were left empty, whole districts had to change their mode of life because there were not enough people left to maintain the former economy. It was a state of affairs that weighed heavily on the heart of the pope, both as an Italian patriot and the Father of Christendom. Yet except for the heroic but inadequate efforts of Bishop Scalabrini and the men he had recruited, hardly anything was being done for the souls of those now scattered abroad. In such a situation, it was natural that Leo XIII thought of sending aid by getting an order of Italian nuns to go to America.

The first attempts at persuasion brought to bear upon Francesca Cabrini came from Bishop Scalabrini. He thought, however, of the Missionary Sisters as auxiliaries to his Congregation of Saint Charles Borromeo. That alone was sufficient to make Francesca disinclined to accept the charge he proposed. To do her work effectively, she knew that she would have to maintain her independence and have a free hand. As events were to show, she was completely right. The bishop had started with what was with her the worst possible argument.

All the same, she could not but recognize his zeal. Her heart went out to his American schemes, even when she told him, as she had previously told Monsignor Serrati, that the world was too small for her. Though New York and its environs already had a population greater than that of some European countries, she believed she would be too restricted there. If she went at all, she saw that she would have to take in the whole of the United States; and to begin her missionary activities in a country so opposed to Catholics—and especially to Italians—she feared would be to draw more territory into her scope than, for the moment, she would be able to handle. To accept might bring her up against difficulties that would prove insurmountable.

The bishop was not easily to be put off. He probably spoke to the pope about his idea of getting an order of Italian nuns for America, and he certainly got into contact with Archbishop Corrigan of New York about his project. He realized that he was dealing not only with an enthusiast in Francesca but with a very practical woman. The only means of persuading her was that of having something definite to present. When the assurance of welcome came, he might be able to use it as a means of forcing Mother Cabrini's hesitant hand.

Chapter Six

UNDER OBEDIENCE TO LEO

Two organizations had it in their power to do something for the Italians in America. These were the Italian State and the Catholic Church. Unfortunately they were often not in very close harmony. Since 1870, the government had been under the control of the so-called Liberals and so was jealous of anything that the Church might attempt. The *Riforma*, the semi-official paper, put the issue in these words: "The government cannot be indifferent to this situation, but while the present conflict exists between the Vatican and Italy, we may reasonably doubt whether the pope's emissaries will work in accordance with our national interests. Moreover, it is not desirable that the Italians present themselves in foreign countries as a religious and clerical element." To put it in another way: official Italy did not want priests and nuns to have anything to do with the dispersed people of the nation.

Yet it was only priests and nuns who could work effectively among them, even for social alleviation. The Italian government could (and in fact did) make its protest when some outrage occurred too grievous to be borne. But the occasion for that offered itself only rarely. There were no means of making representations merely on the ground that Italians suffered unfair discrimination, or were taken advantage of, or were despised. The American government was not responsible for the actions of individual Americans, nor were those actions themselves as a rule of so demonstrably unjust a character that any protest on their account would have been entertained. Not only that, but one of the greatest evils was the exploitation of Italians by Italians, by the horde of commission agents who contrived to get these poor people into their clutches. Unable to do much itself for the immigrant, the Italian government nevertheless put obstacles in the way of the only organization that was in a position to do anything—always on the ground, of course, that it was not desirable that Italians should present themselves in foreign countries as a religious or clerical element.

Later, it is true, there was something of a change of heart in this respect. But it occurred only toward the end of Mother Cabrini's career in the United States, and only after she had proved the social value of her enterprises. Then there came small subsidies for her undertakings and decorations for herself and grand ambassadorial compliments. But she had to start under conditions unfavorable to her work, though she was working for Italy as well as for God. "My Italianity", she was to say, "is in the hearts of the poor who are the people and the soul of my faith." It was in this spirit that she went to America. She was not Italian in any exclusive sense; in fact, she accepted her American mission only because she saw its crying need and because the pope told her to go. Even so, she refused to limit her work to America, though she was to become naturalized as an American citizen. But her work was to be, among other things, one of the most notable pieces of social service ever performed for Italians, though it was not quite of her own choosing but was forced on her by circumstances.

She did not decide all at once. After she had been urged to go by Bishop Scalabrini and had received Archbishop

Corrigan's invitation, she still remained undecided. When she consulted Monsignor Serrati, asking, "What shall I say to the bishop?" he gave the characteristic answer, "Say nothing." It was in keeping with all the advice he gave her. He feared she was going too fast and that she might be undertaking something she was not able to carry through.

He had some reason for his misgivings. Francesca herself, when first approached by Bishop Scalabrini, described his schemes as dream castles. The monsignor could not but recall that when she had bought her first convent at Codogno eight years earlier, she believed herself near to death. And her health had not improved since then. What he did not realize was that, despite ill-health, she had drawn increasingly upon great reservoirs of spiritual strength. He was getting old, and he saw that Francesca had ideas very different from his own. He was inclined merely to shrug his shoulders when asked his opinion about anything.

For her he was by no means the last court of appeal. In December 1888, Francesca left Codogno again for Rome. This time she meant to consult the pope.

❧ ❧ ❧

By now Francesca had a number of influential friends in Rome; so to arrange for a private audience with Leo XIII was not very difficult. Such a favor is not usually given to an obscure nun, even when she is at the head of a small diocesan order. But it was somewhat different in her case; the pope could be reminded that he had been very pleased with the Rules she had drawn up for her institute when they had been shown to him the previous year. And Cardinal Parocchi and several other dignitaries who already knew Francesca were able to assure His Holiness that she was a woman well worth knowing.

She went into the pope's presence with a heart full of reverence for his high office. But hers was also a heart which so burned with desire to serve God in accordance with what Christ's representative on earth would say that love gave her an easy familiarity as she knelt before him. Shy and unobtrusive? She was all that. She also had the naturalness of manner that comes from forgetfulness of self. He looked down into the open countenance of the woman before him and saw a face that, without being beautiful in its features, was made beautiful by its spiritual light. There he saw candor and courage and compassion. At first glance he knew that here was somebody remarkable.

One could tell the same thing of him at the first glance. His was the highest office in the world, and yet—as rarely enough happens with holders of high office—one also saw a man to be venerated for his personal qualities. Poet, scholar, wit, statesman—anybody could have perceived at once that he was all these, a great man as well as an exalted personage. The keen deep eyes in the withered sensitive face showed his quality. Without any loss of dignity, he was able to be affable and even intimate, though there were some who also discovered that he had a quick temper and a sharp tongue. From the first moment of meeting, Leo and Francesca were to be lifelong friends.

Yet at that first meeting Francesca said nothing to the pope about America, though she had come to Rome to consult him about her going there. The reason for this was that she had been expecting further word from Archbishop Corrigan in New York, and, as it had not reached her, she thought it best not to bring up the subject of America during this interview. The conversation, therefore, was only about the institute she had founded and in which Leo was already interested. He learned from her that its members now numbered a hundred and forty-five, a good accomplishment in eight years but perhaps hardly enough to warrant the undertaking of which she was thinking. She answered the pope's questions; he blessed her; a friendship was formed. But for the moment that was all.

Bishop Scalabrini, however, was now pressing Francesca for a definite answer about going to the United States.

To obtain the guidance she sought, she prayed, and asked for prayers, and began a novena to the Venerable Antonia Belloni, a Clarissian Sister of Codogno whose cause for beatification had been presented to Rome. The fact that Antonia came from Codogno made her, Francesca thought, the most appropriate patroness to invoke.

Before the novena was finished, Francesca had another of her famous dreams. These she always seemed to have at times when she needed illumination in her perplexities. In this dream, she saw Antonia Belloni, who told her that on the following day she would get the letter from the archbishop of New York for which she was waiting. Behind the candidate for beatification there appeared a host of saints—and who should be among them but Francesca's own mother! From her came the reproach: "Why is it that after all your desire to go to the missions you now hesitate?" Last of all appeared a vision of Our Lady and the Sacred Heart. On Christ's white robe was the monogram IHS, to which he pointed, saying, "Why do you fear, my child? You must go to take my name to far-off countries. Take courage. I am with you."

The next morning, on her way to the Vatican, she met Bishop Scalabrini. He laughed when she told him about her dream, and so did she. She never took such things as seriously as some of her nuns did.

Leaving him, she went into Saint Peter's and prayed for an hour. When she got home, she found a carriage drawn up before the Palazzo Majocchi. Bishop Scalabrini was waiting for her, a letter in his hand. "You and your dreams!" he said by way of greeting. "But Archbishop Corrigan *has* written. Now get ready to go."

❧ ❧ ❧

Already she had consulted other friends in Rome. And most of them approved of the American mission, though one bishop felt as Monsignor Serrati did, that she was being very imprudent in setting out for a country like the United States in such poor health and with no knowledge of the English language or any material resources. But Cardinal Parocchi thought she was right, as did Cardinals Simeoni and Rampolla. She even aroused the admiration of the socialist deputy Maiocchi who, though officially anticlerical, would creep into the Sisters' chapel to lay a little offering at the feet of the Child Mary.

Nobody, however, doubted that what she proposed doing was admirable in itself. The only question was whether it was wise, whether it was even feasible. A little while before she had consulted her physician in Rome, Dr. Morini, and he had told her that she had about two years to live. Now in deference to the qualms of some of the Sisters, she consulted him again about her health.

"Do you really want my opinion?" he asked her.

"Of course, doctor."

"Then it's this: if you stay in Italy you will die of a broken heart. Your ailments can't be cured except by God. Go to America—then perhaps you'll get better."

A few days later she knelt before Leo. Until he had spoken she would do nothing. She left it to him to decide between China and the United States. He decided in favor of the United States. After that she felt no hesitation or doubt whatever. To those who were still worried about her health she said, "Obedience will take care of everything." The pope had given her his blessing. "With it," she said, "I would go with a feeling of security to the end of the world."

On February 16, 1889, she wrote to Archbishop Corrigan from Rome. Bishop Scalabrini, she told him, had advised her to go first with only one Sister, but she added that as this would involve too much delay, she intended to sail with a group in May, if not before. A month before this, Bishop Scalabrini had written to the archbishop saying that the Sisters had decided to come. On March 8, she obtained her credentials from the Congregation of Propaganda. After that it was only a question of packing for the journey.

Only a woman of boundless compassion and courage would have dared to accept the commission. But having accepted it, Francesca acted with extreme directness and speed. As soon as she had obtained her credentials from Cardinal Simeoni—this explicitly stated that she was going to the United States "by order of this Sacred Congregation of Propaganda"—she was off to Codogno to make final preparations. There on March 19, the Feast of Saint Joseph, Bishop Scalabrini presided over a ceremony. It was fitting that he should be there, for he more than any other man, except the pope himself, was responsible for the American enterprise. To Francesca Cabrini and each of the Sisters selected to go with her to New York he gave the missionary crucifix.

Monsignor Serrati also was present, and he went to put them on the train that was to take them to Paris, the first stage of the journey; for they were to sail from Le Havre. While saying farewell to him, Francesca spoke lightly of what she was doing. She was so overjoyed that all her physical ailments were forgotten and were as though they had never been. Nobody who saw her little quick darting figure would have supposed that she was looked upon as having one foot already in the grave. Here was a radiant child—who was also a woman in complete command of the situation.

"Monsignor," she said, "this trip of ours is nothing—nothing at all—compared to the long journey that has to be made by the missionaries who go to Asia and the islands of the Pacific. You need not worry about me and my health. God is being merciful to my weakness in sending me to a civilized country."

Monsignor Serrati had never quite approved of Francesca's missionary ambitions. He had done all he could to hold her safe in Lombardy. But this was no time to say that all over again. Seeing her eagerness, he wondered if perhaps she was not right after all. And he caught what he felt was a touch of regret that she was only going to the United States, that she was giving up China. She and all the nuns knelt down on the station platform to receive his blessing. With it went the affection and admiration of his rugged character.

One of the Sisters chosen for the mission was very young. For that reason she was allowed to sit next to Francesca on the train, and all night she slept with her head on Francesca's shoulder. When she awoke in the morning, the child-nun was greatly embarrassed at the discomfort she must have inflicted, but Francesca merely smiled at her apologies and said, "Where could you rest better than leaning on your Mother?" The answer charmed them all. They were all exultant. Their long-dreamed-of work was about to begin.

❦ ❦ ❦

There was a day in Paris—only one day, for Francesca never spent a longer time upon her journeys than was absolutely necessary. That day was spent with their friends, the Franciscan Missionaries of Mary. But Mother Cabrini did what she always did when passing through Paris—she made a visit to the basilica of the Sacred Heart on Montmartre. It was the shrine of her great devotion.

Then the journey to Le Havre. And as the *Bourgogne* eased out of its dock, the group of nuns gathered on the deck and sang, somewhat tremulously, the *Ave Maris Stella*. It was ever afterward the hymn of their voyages, sung every day that they were able to assemble on deck.

That, however, happened only rarely on this voyage. To these women from inland Lombardy the sea was a fearsome thing, as it was to most of the fifteen hundred immigrants on board. But lest we should be tempted to be too scornful of their terrors, we ought to remember that the ships of those days were not like our palatial trans-Atlantic liners and that only the oldest and slowest of the steamers were assigned to the transportation of steerage immigrants. By way of cheering up her nuns, she told them, "I'm very glad we have this rough weather. It's a sign that we have the blessing of God." At which the Sisters smiled wanly and moaned in their berths.

After the sea there came the shock of discovering that Archbishop Corrigan had not expected them and that he disapproved of the location on East Fifty-Ninth Street which had been selected by the Contessa Cesnola as their orphanage. All that Francesca could do for the moment was to stay at the orphanage of the Sisters of Charity on Madison Avenue and Fifty-First Street and hope that the archbishop would change his mind.

She gradually won him over. Probably there were several interviews, but the letters she wrote him show her tactful mode of approach. On April 6 she wrote to thank him for his "paternal care"—he had, after all, found them a place in which to live—and at the same time she sent him a picture that she said the pope had blessed for him. A week later, she wrote asking to be allowed to take possession of her "little house", explaining that though the Sisters of Charity with whom she was staying showed her "exquisite kindness", she felt that she and her nuns must be a bother to them. On April 18 there was another letter in which she thanked the archbishop for "the generous contribution" she had received from him. Probably it was on this day that he and the Contessa Cesnola had met and she had gone down on her knees so dramatically and he had at last consented to Francesca's taking possession of the house on Fifty-Ninth Street. At any rate, she entered it three days later with his blessing.

It must be admitted that the archbishop's objection to the location of the orphanage was not without point. The house on Fifty-Ninth Street proved too expensive to maintain, and a year later Francesca moved to 135 East Forty-Third Street. Yet it was not merely a question of expense; Archbishop Corrigan feared that there would be criticism when ragged and dirty children swarmed into a select neighborhood—all the more criticism perhaps because Francesca was going to call the place the Asylum of the Holy Angels. However, he yielded gracefully in the end before the accomplished fact, and on May 3 he formally opened the house by saying Mass there.

Five days later, the first of the orphans arrived. They were two grubby little girls wearing nothing but a few soiled rags. Yet Francesca welcomed them as angels, seeing the image of God in them. "Poor little things!" she exclaimed. "But now remember, I'm your mother; in every one of these Sisters you have a mother. This is your home now."

The first thing she had to do was to give them a bath and to comb their tangled hair. The second thing she had to do was to cut up her petticoat to make them dresses. What a change there was at once! Though dresses made out of a petticoat were hardly very *chic*, at least they had been made by a clever needlewoman, and to these children they seemed finery.

Francesca's generous heart asked for no reward. Nevertheless, she got it. One of these two little girls on growing up joined the Missionary Sisters.

🐾 🐾 🐾

Francesca knew as well as did the archbishop that the contessa's five thousand dollars would not last very long, so she lost no time in casting about for expedients for increasing it. The Italian consul in New York, Signor Riva, was applied to for a subsidy but returned the cold answer that he had other plans for the future of the colony. He did not say what these were, but it was clear that he had no intention of doing anything for any group connected with the Church. His attitude, as Francesca soon discovered, was rather general among the Italian officials. An attempt to get an appropriation from the municipal authorities also failed. And when the contessa wanted to raise money by means of a lottery, the archbishop would not allow it. Francesca saw that the only support she could obtain would be that given by personal well-wishers.

She at once went to work herself; at the same time she set others to work for her. However little they might raise, it would all be useful. On May 26, she wrote to the archbishop asking him to give an endorsement to a Miss Williams who wished to seek subscriptions for the orphanage. And the contessa's daughters, Gabriella and Luisa, also went out among their friends, adding most of their own pocket-money to what they obtained. Money did come in, money must have come in for the work to have been maintained; without it, Francesca could not have supported the four hundred destitute children she collected within four months. But most of the money was in small sums, and the existence of the orphanage remained very precarious.

There had to be a good deal of direct begging in New York's Little Italy. Every day a couple of the Sisters went on these excursions, and sometimes Francesca herself went with them. It is from her account of a typical day that we know the kind of thing that happened when the Sisters made their rounds in the Italian quarter. And Francesca said that she found it really rather a pleasant experience.

The best place to go was of course the long Mulberry Street in downtown Manhattan, for though one end of it was still settled by the Irish, the other had already been taken over by the Italians, together with most of the short streets branching off. From block to block the atmosphere changed, or changed enough to be noticeable by an Italian, though other people would see no difference. This was because the immigrants from the various provinces gathered together, keeping their local customs and their local dialects. To the rare American who wandered there, everything—whether it was of Venezia or the Abruzzi or Calabria or Sicily—was simply Italian. Francesca and her nuns caught at once all the shades and nuances; it was this knowledge that made them understand just how to handle the people they met.

Not always were they well received; being from the North, they were often objects of suspicion to those from the South. Italian sectionalism and anticlericalism caused some refusals when they went into the ramshackle bustling little stores to beg. But they also got many small contributions, and sometimes contributions that were large when the poverty of the givers was considered. Mostly pennies were dropped into their bag, but nickels and dimes and quarters, and even a few dollars, found their way there as well.

By way of identification, they carried a subscription booklet, and this they produced when they received dollar subscriptions, so that the name of the donor might be signed—when he was able to sign his name. But the Sisters went with large baskets on their arms, for food as well as money was very acceptable. One man gave them a little tin milk container, another a wooden bucket of apple preserves. Meat, cans of tomato sauce, vegetables—these came in small quantities but mounted until the nuns were staggering under their load. One grand haul, quite unexpected, was made when a fish-dealer put a salmon nearly a yard long into a basket.

The owner of the chief vegetable market turned out to be a very good Catholic.

"Have you a wagon?" he asked.

"No, only this bag."

"Well, what is it that you would like? Greens, garlic, pumpkins?"

"Whatever you like to give us."

They could hardly carry the stuff away.

Into another store they went. There they were asked again, "What would you like?"

Francesca smiled and produced the empty milk container they had been given. "Well, if you could give us a little sugar . . ." she suggested.

The container was large enough to hold five pounds and the storekeeper made his joke, "You don't mean to say that you expect me to fill it for you!"

Francesca returned the jest. "Oh no, that would be too much. Perhaps a cupful . . ."

He took the container and filled it to the brim.

There were places where they got a refusal, but then the man next door would run after them with a string of onions or a dime.

"Sisters, sisters!" he said, when he caught up with them. "You don't know your way around yet, I can see that. You go to the wrong places, where they will never give you anything. Always come to me." And with a magnificent gesture, he handed them ten cents as though he were giving ten dollars.

It was tiring work, but it did bring in supplies and money. Without this begging, the orphanage could not have kept going. Day after day, the Sisters combed the Little Italy, each day having new experiences and learning from them how to spend their time to the best advantage. They never knew what might not happen on Mulberry Street with its medley of stores and stalls, its small banks, which the immigrants often preferred to the much sounder official bank maintained for them. In these they got word of jobs or lodgings or had their letters written for them—all of course for a commission or a fee. And in the basements where stale beer was sold at a cent a glass, the padrone lay in wait for his victims. It was a seething hive of movement and color and strange scents, at once lively and sordid. But it was the main harvest field for the Sisters sent out begging.

On the day about which Francesca wrote her record, she noticed a young lady in the crowded streetcar on which they rode back looking very attentively at them. She could tell from the nuns' crammed baskets what they had been doing. Out from her handbag she drew a dollar bill, folded it in her palm, and then, just before she got out of the streetcar, slipped her little offering in Francesca's hand.

"This is for your poor", she said.

The tone of Francesca's account indicates that she considered this a rather good day. It was a decided help in feeding the four hundred children she had gathered. One of the nuns who was with her said of those times in New York, "We never lacked bread", but there must often have been lacking a number of things almost as necessary to life. It was always touch and go at the orphanage. However, by their begging and that of their friends who went out for them with subscription lists and the help that came from other communities—especially from the Foundling Hospital of the Sisters of Charity and from the Bon Secours nuns, from the Religious of the Sacred Heart at Manhattanville and from the Holy Cross Sisters—Francesca's orphanage somehow managed to survive.

The orphanage, supported in this hand-to-mouth fashion, was from the outset looked upon as the all-important work of the Missionary Sisters. Only by such means could homeless children, especially those of Italian parents, be preserved from the activities of the proselytizing agencies. Yet even before Francesca was able to open the orphanage, she set a couple of Sisters to work at Saint Joachim's Church on Roosevelt Street. Though the conducting of parochial schools was not thought of as the distinctive function of her institute, Francesca never refused it when it needed to be done and there was nobody else to do it. She was to show before long that she was prepared to adapt herself to any form of work, even to work to which she felt some natural repugnance. The establishment of schools for the Italian poor therefore was a prominent feature in her Order.

At this stage of the country's development, there was a valid argument that only by having churches and schools for the various national groups could they be kept Catholic. And this argument, in some sections, still has some validity. But at that time there were groups who were pressing the case too much. This was ultimately to result in a bitter controversy between those Catholic leaders who believed that the good of the Church in America called for the Americanization of the immigrants and those other leaders who wished to gather the people of their own race and tongue into islands that were largely separated from the general life of the country. This, however, did not apply to the Italians. In their case, the obvious immediate need was schools in which, by maintaining the Italian tradition, their religion could also be maintained. Among them there was no belligerent nationalism. It was simply a matter of practical necessity and was considered to be merely an interim program.

Without waiting for a school to be ready—it was later supplied at 26 Roosevelt Street—Francesca and her Sisters set to work at Saint Joachim's on the very first Sunday they were in New York, looking after the children during Mass and going there again in the afternoon to give classes in catechism.

This, however, was only the start. Before April was out, they had a day school in operation there. The church itself had to be used for this purpose. One class was conducted in the choir loft; another was held under it, a curtain dividing the rest of the church from view; a third met in a room opening off the sacristy. There were of course no desks, nor could the supply of books have been adequate. But this day-by-day improvisation served to bring the Sisters into contact with the Little Italy of the lower East Side.

There were great disadvantages in trying to run a school in this way. The lessons had frequently to be interrupted on account of a wedding or a funeral, and as the church was kept open all day for such as wished to make a visit to the Blessed Sacrament, it was hard to rivet the attention of the children upon their studies. Yet two hundred children were instructed daily, perhaps not very efficiently, if judged by modern educational standards, but wonderfully well if judged, as the matter should be, by the purpose in mind.

But Francesca did not end there. For those children who were attending public schools, catechism classes were held on Sunday, between the Masses. At the same time, in another part of the church, conferences on Christian doctrine were given in Italian to older girls and young women. Saint Joachim's was becoming a center of Italian life.

Nor did Francesca limit herself even to formal instruction. As many of the Italians had dropped all practice of religion, she sought them out in their own homes. Squalid enough many of these were, sometimes with several families crowded into one room. Into many a dive and den into which the police themselves were afraid to enter, Francesca and her nuns went with serene and smiling faces, making friends even among those antagonistic to religion.

Usually, however, it was not so much antagonism that they encountered as an indifference created by long-endured despair. As it was the Easter season, she would ask: "What was the last time you went to confession?"

She grew accustomed to the answer, "I don't remember. It may be twenty or thirty years—before I left my home in Italy."

"But now Easter is approaching. Aren't you going to fulfill your Easter duty?"

"Sister, when I return to Italy, I shall go to confession; in this country, one is not accustomed to attend Mass. We have no chance to think of anything except earning our daily bread."

It was clear that these people had not maliciously cut themselves off from the Church but that they felt themselves abandoned. Now some little ray of hope was being brought to them, one that broadened and brightened as Mother Cabrini became, in the years that were to follow, better known among them. Though the majority had acquired a habit of indifference that was not easy to break down, there were hundreds that year who were led to practice their religion because of the Missionary Sisters. And even those who remained indifferent were usually willing enough that their children should receive instruction in their faith.

To get more effectively at the Italian district, and also to spare the Sisters who were teaching at Saint Joachim's the journey from what was then uptown, Francesca took a house for them at White Street. The name was not very appropriate for a place so dark and dirty. But it had the advantages of being near the school and having a large yard that could be used as a playground for the children and for the exercises of the *festas*.

It was to be used only until the Roosevelt Street house was ready for occupancy. Because it was so temporary an abode, the Scalabriniani Fathers seemed to think that it was not necessary to furnish it. They supplied the Sisters with beds but no mattresses, and one table had to serve as a pantry and for nearly everything else. As for the stove, it was broken and therefore could not be used for cooking. However, as the weather was so torrid, the Sisters did not mind eating only cold food.

Privations never dismayed them. What did seem discouraging was the magnitude of their task and the meager means they had to perform it. New York at that time contained close to two hundred thousand Italians, and every boat that arrived from Europe brought several hundred more. That many of these went on to other sections of the country only meant that Mother Cabrini would eventually have to follow them there. Yet what could she expect to accomplish with a handful of nuns? She saw that if she were to do much she would have to open at least ten such centers in the New York area alone. As she wrote in a letter, "We are a small group that is swallowed up in such an infinite sea."

What was encouraging was the way the children responded to the affection shown them. Francesca visited the school every day, and whenever she was there the little girls—often very dirty and neglected—would cluster round her. She usually had a small gift for each of them, if it was only a piece of candy. They in turn brought the Sisters their gifts, a bunch of carrots, a head of lettuce, or a couple of lemons. One arrived knocking at the door late one night and solemnly presented the Sister who opened to her with a peacock feather and a tiny looking glass. Equally charming was a Protestant girl who arrived one day with a little statue of the Blessed Virgin.

Things like these always delighted Francesca. But as she pored over the map of the United States, trying to figure the all but incomprehensible distances and picking the strategic points for attack, she had borne forcibly upon her the difficulties she would have to face. Yet more than ever she was convinced that God had called her to this great work. How it was to be carried out she did not know, but her trust was absolute. That the pope who was the Vicar of Christ had sent her to America made her sure that she would not fail; obedient to him, she was being obedient to Christ. At this time she may have thought of herself as chosen to carry out the divine will. Later in life, looking back upon it all, she was to say that she was not even God's instrument; she was nothing but a witness of His infinite power.

🦋 🦋 🦋

Archbishop Corrigan and she were now great friends. He had not changed his opinion about the unsuitability of East

Fifty-Ninth Street for an orphanage, but he had come to see the value of the work that Francesca and her nuns were doing. In order to make her better acquainted with American conditions, he would sometimes invite her to accompany him when he had to make a visitation in the country. One day when they were at Peekskill, the archbishop took her outside and, pointing across the Hudson, said, "Now *there*, Mother, is where you should establish yourself." It may be that he had nothing more definite in mind than that the open country would be a suitable place for the housing of children. More probably he already was thinking about something he was not prepared to talk about yet.

Francesca gave a swift sidelong look to his face and murmured tactfully, "May it please God that Your Excellency prove to be a prophet."

She had arrived in New York on the last day of March; on July 20, she sailed for Italy, taking with her two Irish girls as postulants from the parish of Saint Lawrence O'Toole, which has since been replaced by the Jesuit church on Park Avenue. Now things in New York had been started, and she knew that it would not do for her to be absent from Codogno too long. Her vitalizing presence was needed, and she wished to select other nuns for the American mission. Then she would come back with them.

From Italy the two little postulants, Loretto Garvey and Elizabeth Desmond, wrote the archbishop a letter in which they told him: "It is the desire of our Reverend Mother that we, her two first Americans, shall become saints."

Chapter Seven

SECOND AMERICAN JOURNEY

Francesca Cabrini was now forty. The Institute of Missionary Sisters she had founded was not yet ten years old. A few of the older nuns had reached the age of thirty, but most of the Sisters were much younger than that, many of them being still in their teens. The spirit of the institute was one of youth and vigor and adventure, and the youngest and most daring heart among them was that of their Mother.

What their General had to relate on her return to Italy was electrifying. Her account of the poverty and hardships and difficulties encountered in New York was to the brave souls trained by her an inducement to greater effort and devotion. What Francesca had to tell at firsthand about the state of the Italian immigrants in the United States, so far from depressing them, made them see all the more clearly how great an honor it was to have such a charge committed to them. The need, the need—that was what mattered. To give up the idea of evangelizing pagan lands—insofar as they can be said ever to have given it up—had been a sacrifice, but it brought no repining. If they did not go to the field to which the pope had assigned them, their own dispersed fellow-countrymen would become pagans. All recognized where their immediate duty lay.

At Codogno, Francesca spent a month stirring up the ardor of her nuns and then passed on to each of her

convents in Lombardy in turn. It was not merely by formal
spiritual conferences that she did this, or even by little talks
to the community about the work waiting in America; a
story in private conversation, a word, even a smile, had its
effect. The mere presence of Francesa called out love and
a desire to serve. Everywhere she went there was rejoicing
that their Mother was with them again; everywhere there
was an eager hope of being selected for the missions. It all
added to Francesca's own ardor; she saw that there could
be no doubt that in these generous and compassionate
hearts burned the disposition God required in His apostles.

There was a sorrow, too, for Francesca at Codogno.
At the time when Antonia Tondini and Teresa Calza had
been excommunicated by Bishop Gelmini—who thus put
an end to the strange religious community of the House of
Providence—the cook of the institution, Giuseppa Alberici,
escaped ecclesiastical censure. She was an inoffensive and
pious soul and had never been implicated in the doings of
the other women of which, in her humble position, she
had even been unaware. Before long she was admitted into
Francesca's new institute. Now she died while reciting the
Gloria. It was another link broken with the past.

After Lombardy came Rome. There Francesca saw the
friends who had encouraged her in what had seemed so
hopeless a task. While there were still some misgivings as
to whether she had not undertaken more than she would
be able to carry out, these were much less now, since people saw that she had at least been able to overcome her first
difficulties. In the radiance of her joy, she seemed to them
a new woman, yet some of them had never expected to
see her again, so ill was she when she left.

Again Francesca had a private audience with the pope.
She told him of what had been done and of what was

crying to be done. It was not necessary to go into the kind of reception she had had on arrival in New York, for all that had been happily rectified. But she could speak of the orphanage that she had in operation, of the school she had established at Saint Joachim's. From that foothold, which was now sufficiently secure, she knew that she would be able to advance all over the huge country. Her difficulties were things she made light of; what she enlarged upon were the opportunities for work among the Italian immigrants.

Listening to the little enthusiast kneeling before him, the pope's gaunt visage bent over her head, and he blessed her again. It was his insight that had sent her to the United States; it was at his command that she had gone. His long reign was giving the papacy a prestige such as it had not enjoyed since the Middle Ages, and not the least of his strokes of genius was the commission he laid upon Francesca Cabrini. More than ever now he was her firm friend and supporter.

Before long there arrived an explanation of Archbishop Corrigan's enigmatic words at Peekskill, when he had pointed to the other side of the Hudson and said that she should establish an orphanage there. Francesca was now told that the Jesuits were going to give up their novitiate in the Catskills and migrate to the Eastern bank of the river. Their property was offered her at an extremely low price. She was informed that the grounds were beautiful and extensive; that there were two large houses and a smaller one that had been used by the employees on the farm; but she was not informed that the water supply was inadequate. This was the reason the Jesuits were prepared to dispose of Manresa at an absurdly small figure.

There was, however, no doubt that Francesca was being offered a bargain. There is also no question that bargains often have to be refused for lack of money. But the terms were made as easy as possible, and some backing was obtained from friends in Italy. Even so, for Francesca even to think of buying Manresa showed the utmost daring, a daring that struck many as highly imprudent. It turned out to be one of the best bits of business this notable business-woman ever carried through.

Francesca had had another of her wonderful dreams. In it she saw a large house in a wooded estate. She saw farm-lands and orchards and a wide river. All this just before she had even so much as heard of Manresa. When word about it reached her, she was startled. Could Manresa be the place of which she had dreamed? On April 18, 1890, she sailed again for New York—this time accompanied by seven Sisters—to find out.

At Milan she assembled the group chosen to go with her. It was the morning of the day on which they were to take the train for Paris. Francesca went forward at the begin-ning instead of the end of Mass to receive Communion. She was tired, and she did not wish to remain in the chapel and so to defer her thanksgiving. There was still so much to do before she left. It was just then that the superior of the house, not recognizing her in the dim light, stopped her and told her that Communion would be distributed later. Without a word, Francesca went back to her place. She did not often have the opportunity of being obedient within the communities of which she was the General. She was glad to take the opportunity when it occurred.

With this second voyage to New York began that series of diary-letters which constitute so important a source for all her biographers. Ordinarily she had no time to write anything except brief notes, mostly on business, and though these are plentiful, they tell us little about herself. Now for the entertainment and instruction of those left behind she wrote, sitting in a chair on deck, just jotting down whatever things occurred to her. She used a faintly lined paper and a pencil, never making any erasures, but composed, as she put it, between one wave and another.

These letters are probably unique of their kind in the history of the saints. For though others have written far more voluminously than Francesca ever did, the great voyagers among them have usually said little about what they saw of interesting people and places and have usually confined themselves rather strictly to an account of their work. It was so, at least, with Francesca Saverio's famous patron, Saint Francis Xavier. His letters are full of an impassioned ardor, and they reveal him, as her letters reveal herself— though in neither case could that have been the intention. But only occasionally, and then incidentally, does Xavier speak as a traveler, his sole purpose being to inflame readers with a desire to serve God as missionaries to the heathen. While Francesca was not without that desire, and may well have had his letters in mind as a model, she was also able to be chatty and amusing. She never imagined that these letters would be published after her death, still less that they would ever be used as a textbook for the study of Italian literature in schools. She intended nothing but keeping in touch with her daughters; all these letters were written to be read "in the family".

Those who received them already knew her well; those who never knew her may find much of her here. Among other things that they may discover—though all this was quite unconscious on her part—is how it happened that people were so anxious to do things for her. She had no idea that she was giving herself away as an extremely fascinating person. But that she must have been a fascinating person is evident, for everywhere we find people fascinated by her. What she thought she was relating were the many acts of kindness done her; what she actually shows us, without knowing it, was that she was the sort of person to whom everybody wanted to be kind. She seems to have made no voyage on which she was not the pet—one might almost say the mascot—of the ship's company. With this went a good deal of shrewdness on her part, which also comes out in these letters; for she made a practice of always approaching the head man in the steamship agency, and when she got on board she always went at once to introduce herself to the captain. These people she charmed, and these were the ones able to do much for her. Then it would be, "Oh Mother, I would not dream of making you and your Sisters pay the full fare! Now these are good accommodations, and you can have them at half-price." Or the captain would come to her cabins and say, "Mother, these are not good enough for you. If you will come with me ... The stewards will take care of your baggage." Then, after having paid for small cabins deep down in the ship, Francesca would find herself in a grand suite opening right on the deck, the best quarters on board.

This serves as a clue to the way that she, with very little financial resources at her command, should have been able to accomplish so much. What she asked for she almost invariably got; often she did not have to ask at all, for people pressed gifts and favors upon her. That she charmed them shows that she must have been charming. Whatever her supernatural endowments, she also possessed natural qualities that were irresistible. No doubt they were heightened by grace, and those drawn to her were attracted (even though unconsciously) by the divine love so visible in her. But the foundation of everything was a simple, unaffected naturalness. Always at ease, never at a loss in any situation, she carried everything before her.

It may be that we could safely reconstruct the incidents of her first voyage to New York from what she tells us about her second. On the other hand, this may not be so at all. In March 1889, the weather had been foul, and Francesca herself possibly did not quite escape seasickness. But April of the following year was mild, and in the interval Francesca had crossed the Atlantic twice, and she was now able to regard herself as a seasoned salt. This made her rather amused at the terrors and the mainly psychological seasickness of her companions. Her voyages gave her the only chance she ever got for a rest, and she came to enjoy them mightily. The ocean she thought of as her element, and she never felt in better health than when breathing its keen clean air. One is left with a conviction that she lived as long as she did because of the benefit she derived from her long sea voyages.

She began her diary-letter the day she got on board—again on a ship carrying nine hundred immigrants, mostly Italians, to America. But as her arrival at Le Havre was at five in the afternoon, and the boat was not to sail until the next morning, there was not much to relate. She merely gave an account of the journey to Paris. It had been uneventful except for the railway carriage in which the nuns were riding having broken down. At two in the morning, they had sleepily to get out and find another. There may not have been much danger, but they all thanked God for their preservation, made a fervent spiritual communion—and went placidly to sleep again. At Paris the next morning, there was Mass at the Church of Our Lady of Victories, the reception of actual Communion this time, and then the journey to Le Havre. The amount of news is slight; but the keynote of all the letters is struck at once: that the true missionary must have courage and that for her there are no distances in separation, as she remains united to all her Sisters in the Sacred Heart. The natural sorrow Francesca confesses to have experienced at parting is swallowed up in the joy she finds, and knows that they all find, in labors and crosses.

The next day they went in the morning to pay their respects to the captain, who was at once captivated. Then on deck they recited the *Ave Maris Stella*, not singing it, for the simple reason that they were afraid they might disturb the other passengers. But they were sure that the Blessed Virgin listened to the melody in their hearts. The sea appeared to them, as to Francesca, a symbol of the grandeur of God.

As soon as the ship left the dock the seasickness began. Sister Battistina had hardly felt the ship move when instantly she grew dizzy and half an hour later sought refuge in her berth. Not so with Francesca. Now that they were out to sea a charming idea occurred to her: she wished she could have a special boat built for the Missionaries to carry them all over the world. She would name it the *Christopher*, the Christ-bearer. But she added sensibly: "These are futile thoughts, and I do not permit them to occupy my mind." They merely served for a little diversion; she was still something of a child playing with paper boats full of violets.

Playful fancies unfortunately were not of much use to the others just then. One nun—Sister Ignatius—went to breakfast at half-past ten with Mother Cabrini and tried to eat; but halfway through the meal she had to make a quick departure. As for Francesca: "I alone remained and stayed until breakfast was over. I don't remember an occasion when I enjoyed my breakfast so much." If she had any little innocent vanity, it was about the way she found and kept her sea legs.

The next day—Sunday—the sea was so calm that it seemed like a lake. But though Mother Cabrini had managed to get them all to go on deck the previous evening for a little air, it was hard to persuade them to leave their cabins now. One who did venture up was in so dazed a condition that she was wearing her habit inside out and so had to be hurried below again.

None of them could be induced to eat any breakfast. The slightest movement of the boat seemed a storm to them. Sister Eletta would have liked to have had the boat stopped, at any rate during meals. Francesca told this to their steward to make him laugh. He was a man with a big brown beard and looked so kind that she decided that he resembled Saint Francis de Sales. That they were under the direct care of their patron was another harmless fancy she found very pleasing.

She entered into a little conspiracy with him. Bananas had been served, and one of the Sisters had a curious repugnance to the fruit. So Francesca got her Saint Francis de Sales to bring this Sister some bananas fried and to offer them as veal-brain. She explained to him elaborately, before them all, that this veal brain should be very well done, as the Sister had a delicate stomach. Thus disguised, the obnoxious bananas were devoured with gusto. Not till then did Francesca tell the banana-hating Sister what it was she had eaten.

Whatever the mood of the sea, Francesca found in it an image of the divine. Now that it was so calm, she saw in it the tranquility of a soul that lives in the tranquility of the grace of God. "God commands," she wrote; "the sea obeys. If also in religion every Sister would obey her superior—with perfect submission, that is, without relying on her own judgment—what peace, what paradisal sweetness would be hers."

There were other reflections that possibly did not greatly appeal at that moment to poor Sisters Assunta and Eletta, groaning in their berths. But no doubt they edified those safe on dry land at Codogno. "I want all of you", their General told them, "to take on wings and fly swiftly to repose in that blessed peace possessed by a soul that is all for God." Wings! Wings were always Francesca's private emblem of the spiritual life.

The next two days were somewhat rough, and Sister Eletta was praying hard that God would calm the sea. She, like all the others, kept to her cabin, only Francesca remaining on deck and going to meals. Now and then she would visit her daughters and try to cheer them up with small jokes and funny stories. When these did not work, she sometimes found, she said, that a little scolding was efficacious. But Sister Giovanna could laugh deep in her misery, and even Sister Agostina was able to muster a smile. They were amused when Sister Eletta in her simplicity asked how it was that the great circle of the horizon always remained the same distance away. But poor Bernardina and Battistina lay there like the dead, never saying a word all day, and the sight at last made Francesca feel seasick herself. Yet the next morning she got up early to look at the magnificent spectacle of the towering waves. Into her letter went the reflection: "How beautiful is the sea in its great motion! How the waves swell and foam! Enchanting!"

That night something went wrong with one of the engines and the ship had to stop while it was being repaired. The blowing of the foghorns woke Mother Cabrini, and she got up and dressed to find out what was wrong. But when Sister Eletta ran to her in terror, she only laughed heartily so as to chase away her fears. When after a sleepless night Francesca saw sea gulls in the morning, she again toyed with the fancy that they were their guardian angels—or perhaps represented "the many dear young virgins who come to our institute to be missionaries."

The morning of the next day she was able to dwell upon something a good deal more solid than pretty images: the ship was surrounded by icebergs. Had the engine not broken down, it would have encountered them at night and there would probably have been a collision.

Thankfulness for their escape served to banish all seasickness, for though the sea was still rough, the Sisters came up on deck where they said the Little Office together and sang the *Ave Maris Stella*. The other passengers appeared to think it fortunate to have praying nuns among them. One gentleman after another came up to join the group of Sisters. The sense of relief made everybody sparkle now.

There was a new opportunity for pious considerations. As Francesca had been so much in the salt air, the skin began to peel from her nose and forehead. This she took to be a sign that God wanted her to change her life and be converted. "Pray, pray!" she commented. "I am in need of your intercession. When I am converted and begin to lead a good life, it is certain that this will obtain many beautiful graces for the institute."

A Protestant gentleman—one living in New York where he was married to a Catholic wife—invited them to attend a concert that evening. Though Francesca told him that they could not do that, he presented her with six tickets for the lottery that was to be held. From others they eventually got fifteen tickets, but after seeing the prizes, Francesca decided that there was nothing that would be of any use to them. The Englishman told them that they had undertaken a very difficult mission and that he did not think they had much chance of success. In reply, Francesca told him that it was precisely because of the difficulties that they had undertaken it.

As for the luck in the lottery, Francesca was hoping for something better than winning one of the prizes: she was praying for the conversion of her English friend. Because she found it hard to make herself understood when she tried to explain Catholic beliefs to him, Sister Bernardina started to make a novena that their Mother would obtain the grace to speak English. Francesca said that she feared the day of judgment would arrive before that happened.

On the last day of the month they docked in New York. They had been nearly two weeks at sea and were glad to land. It was a somewhat battered and bedraggled little company that slept that night in the orphanage of the Holy Angels.

❧ ❧ ❧

Mother Cabrini had come to America to look at the house and estate the Jesuits had offered to sell. She lost no time in going there. As soon as she saw it, she exclaimed, "Why, this is the very place I saw in my dreams!" No wonder that the Sisters used to say that her dreams were really visions. They were not so pleased when she added, "This is where I shall be buried." The thought of her ever dying dismayed them.

In spite of her dreams, Francesca was a very practical person, and practical considerations decided her now: the beautiful location within easy reach of New York, the furniture that went with the house, old and shabby but serviceable—and the low price. She noted the shortage of water but did not let that deter her. Here was a place where it would be possible to house three hundred girls.

Coming to it out of the city slums, they would look upon it as a paradise.

The drawback about the water eventually proved to be no drawback at all. From the outset, Francesca felt sure that there must be a good well, if only she could find it. But for the moment there was no water on the property except a small supply that came from an inadequate well—just enough for drinking. For all other purposes the nuns—helped by the orphans—would have to carry water up the steep banks of the Hudson, a toiling climb of twenty minutes, and wash their linen there, too. In spite of this, Francesca did not hesitate to close with such a bargain.

She kept watching the ground to see if anywhere there was persistent dampness. Meanwhile she prayed to Our Lady of Graces. When her keen eye did locate what she thought a likely spot on the hillside, she ordered a well dug there; after that they had all the water they needed. A statue of the Blessed Virgin—put in position by Francesca's own hands—was erected beside it. And people still go there to pray and to drink from what they call Our Lady's miraculous spring. The Jesuits, looking across from their new establishment at Poughkeepsie, came to be sorry that they had ever given up Manresa, now known as West Park.

Francesca loved this place and was always talking of going to live there when she retired from her Generalship. This was something she was never able to do. But after her death, her nuns saw to it that her prophecy about her burial-place should be fulfilled; for they carried her body there from Chicago, and there it remained until it was transferred to the chapel of the Mother Cabrini High School in New York. It was at West Park, too, that she had the American novices under her eye, under her hand, during frequent visits. She wished whenever possible to give their characters a direct personal molding. And at West Park she had the happy children of the orphanage around her. She saw to it that this should be a home for them, nothing that corresponds to the somewhat grim idea that comes to the mind when an orphanage is mentioned. The children, being in large numbers, had of course to be under school discipline, but it was under a discipline no more severe than that of a school. Francesca was not, as with the principal of a school, *in loco parentis;* she was their Mother, all the nuns were the mothers of these children, showering love upon them. Whenever she could snatch a little time from her duties, she would go among them, drawing them around her in the garden, coming out with small gifts of fruit or candy. "Here comes Mother Cabrini!" one would cry as soon as she appeared, and at once a crowd of merry little girls would crowd around her. Not only for them but for Francesca West Park was very near paradise.

Again there was a stay in America of only three and a half months—just long enough to get West Park in operation and to move the reception-center in the city from Fifty-Ninth Street to 135 East Forty-Third Street. Then on August 16, Francesca sailed with two girls—Elizabeth and Ann—who were to enter the novitiate at Codogno. For not until 1891 did she make West Park the novitiate for the United States.

That the weather was delightful, and that the crossing took less than a week, Francesca credited to the presence on board of seven Religious of the Sacred Heart who were on their way to their motherhouse at Paris to prepare for their profession. But the calm did not prevent Elizabeth and Ann from getting sick. While they shut themselves up, woe-begone, in their cabin, Francesca sat on deck, meditating and talking to the other passengers and scribbling.

She did not scribble much on this journey, however; there was nothing in particular to write about. The main incident recorded was her making friends with a Protestant lady on board by playing with her dog. To be able to make converts of such people was always one of Francesca's ambitions, though she never got in touch with Protestants except in passing and so was able to do little. This time her regret was that she was not better instructed— presumably she meant in the tenets of the Protestant sects—but she gave the lady the address of the convent in Rome, in which city she intended to pass the winter. There the Sisters might be able to do what she could not do herself.

There are several touches in this brief letter that are very characteristic of Francesca, who was always intensely interested in everything she saw and ingenious in discovering in the beauty of nature a divine significance. In mid-ocean she was always on deck until eleven at night, fascinated by the sea. By day she would stand by the stern for hours looking at the milky furrow of the ship, and at night she gazed delighted at the sparkling phosphorescence of the sea. "It looked", she wrote, "like so many lanterns of a thousand colors on the waves round the ship." Though she made no mystical application of this, she enjoyed it nonetheless.

By six in the morning, she was on deck again, making her meditation. The cool, clean, sharp air not only invigorated her; it also seemed to help her thoughts. They ran on the fortunate and happy life of those to whom God gave a religious vocation. "Love is not loved, my daughters!" she wrote. "Love is not loved! And how can we remain cold, indifferent, and almost without heart at this thought? ... If we do not burn with love, we do not deserve the title that ennobles us, elevates us, makes us great, and even a portent to the angels in heaven."

Chapter Eight

CENTRAL AMERICA

What was by far the most important incident of that journey back to Europe remained unmentioned in Francesca's
letter. This was probably because she thought it as well to
say nothing until there was more to say, since by speaking
too soon she might raise hopes that would afterward be
disappointed. But it is also possible that she kept silence
so as not to dismay those left behind in New York. For
nothing less was involved—hardly two years after she had
made a start in the United States, and while the work there
needed all the support it could get—than establishing herself in Central America. A wealthy lady from Nicaragua
named Elena Arellano had offered Francesca a house in
Granada and was begging for a school to be opened there.

That Francesca should even have entertained such a
proposal might seem very strange. It would appear to have
been more than enough that she had accepted the dispersed and poverty-stricken Italians in the United States as
her special charge. Almost immediately to scatter her meager forces upon a project that had little to do with the Italians, and still less to do with the poor and oppressed, strikes
the casual observer as being strategically a bad move. The
explanation is that Francesca had not thought of limiting
her missionary activities to one country or to one social
class. Though she never was able to go to China, she used

to say, "The world is only a small ball for the Missionary Sisters. See how the Infant Savior holds it in His hands!" Her sole concern was to save souls, and she knew that the well-to-do needed spiritual help just as badly as the poor. From what Doña Elena had told her, they needed it even more badly. This was the beginning of a series of foundations in Central and South America of what would be called select academies for the education of Spanish-speaking girls.

It is astonishing that such an enterprise should have been undertaken by a community that, so far, was wholly Italian. It is even more astonishing that this enterprise succeeded and did not interfere with what Francesca was to do for her fellow-countrymen on the northern continent. That she accepted it proves her zeal and her courage; but in the end it also showed her good judgment. She counted upon God; at the same time, she counted upon the vigor and enthusiasm of her congregation. Small as it still was, she could feel its pulsing life and, so, confidently went forward.

Francesca's decision was made only after she had consulted Cardinal Rampolla, the Vatican secretary of state. In reaching it, she committed herself—as she clearly understood from the start—to a good deal more than the establishment of a single house in Granada. It meant going on to South America; it meant giving her institute an international character; it meant proceeding to the founding of houses in Paris and Madrid and London, if only to supply her South American schools with teachers. Nicaragua was therefore a new turning point in Francesca's career.

❧ ❧ ❧

In Italy, while she was preparing for this, she busied herself with opening at Rome a residence house for normal-school students such as she already had at Milan. Donations

were secured for this purpose from the Princesses Francesca
Massimo and Carlotta Antici Mattei, and a committee was
formed that was presided over by the Contessa Guenda-
lina della Somaglia and included some of the most aristocratic members of Roman society. Francesca had become
a great personage among them by now. For a moment
then, and several times afterward, there was what might
have proved a danger—that hers would turn into an order
working among the rich and fashionable. To Francesca it
was no real danger at all; it was merely that she drew from
such people whatever help they could give. Her institute
lost nothing of its original spirit; it remained one whose
chief distinction was its devotion to the poor.

On arriving at New York in mid-September 1891, she
at once took to West Park the twenty-nine nuns she had
brought with her. But she went back to New York herself
the same evening so as to book the passages for the fourteen
Sisters who were destined for Nicaragua. It was less than
two and a half years since she had first set foot in America,
and already she had fifty nuns gathered there, if we count
the seven girls to whom the habit was now given. It was
a wonderful achievement in so short a space of time. We
begin to see how it was that she felt she was able to accept
a new burden without diminishing her strength. Her conviction always was that, the more she undertook, the more
recruits she would get. To promise difficulties and dangers
is an inducement to generous hearts. Francesca's courage
was already starting to pay dividends.

Yet at the last minute, it seemed as though the Nicaraguan plan would fall through. The money Francesca had
counted upon to pay for the tickets failed to arrive, and the
boat was to sail in two days. That night she had a dream

in which she saw Our Lady with open arms praying to her
Son for them. The next morning she went to Archbishop
Corrigan and told him in what situation she found herself. Though the archbishop did not have the money just
then, he was able to borrow it from one of his priests. His
getting it for her seemed to Francesca miraculous, and as
a reminder of this incident she prescribed that three times a
day the *Memorare* should be said by the Sisters in the same
attitude in which she had seen the Blessed Virgin—with
open arms.

On October 10 they were able to sail as planned.

On their previous voyages, the Sisters do not appear to
have encountered more than rolling seas; this time, they
ran into a hurricane raging up from the Caribbean, encountering it as soon as they got beyond Sandy Hook. As Francesca wrote in her diary: "We do not expect this voyage
to be as smooth and beautiful as the last, seeing that we are
concerned with a new mission, and this needs great graces
and therefore new graces to make us more worthy of it."
The fact that they had set out in the teeth of a hurricane
was, from this point of view, an excellent sign. However,
for a while there was a real likelihood that they would all
be drowned. Like the nuns celebrated in Gerard Manley
Hopkins's poem "The Wreck of the Deutschland", they
experienced "wind's burly and beat of endragoned seas".
All that night, under a black sky suddenly shattered by
lightning, under the thunder and the hail, with waves that
swept the ship from end to end and that threatened at
each assault to capsize her, the Sisters prayed and prepared
themselves for death. Francesca was pierced to the heart
at the thought of these young nuns dying while on their
way to their first mission, but she urged them to accept

the will of God. So as to meet any emergency, she dressed, while the fourteen Sisters all remained in their berths, ready to die but huddling comfortably under the bed-clothes. She left them there, keeping her own watch in the state-room, from which she could come at once to summon them should there be a wreck. Until then, she decided, they might as well stay where they were.

As it was October, the month of the rosary, Francesca kept praying to the Blessed Virgin, and to her she lighted the candle of Our Lady of Loreto that she had brought with her. This was considered specially efficacious against storms at sea. Her prayers also went up to Saint Aloysius, the patron of Catholic youth. Now was the time for him to come to the rescue of these young nuns.

The prayers were heard. Other ships were wrecked off the New Jersey coast that night, but the *New York*, on which the Sisters were traveling, managed to strike for the open sea and so got out of the path of the hurricane. A dawn of slate-grey and ashes showed the seas still heavily swelling, but the worst of the storm was over by then. Their thanks went up to Mary, "Like a mother full of compassion for each one of us who, in our danger, invoked her with faith. Oh, what a joy to be children of such a mother!"

Francesca was writing on October 15, the first time she was able to write at all on that voyage. It was the feast of Saint Teresa, and that reminded Francesca of the discomforts of her voyages over the rugged country of Spain. She felt sure that it must be Teresa who had sent them such a blue, glittering day after all that they had gone through. When two days later they anchored off Fortune Island in the Bahamas, she strained her eyes to try to make out the steeple of a church. She wished to salute, even though from far off, the Blessed Sacrament. It was now a Friday, and she knew that on that day all the Missionary Sisters would be at adoration. It was also the feast day of their patroness, Saint Margaret Mary, who had done so much to promote devotion to the Sacred Heart. The time sequence struck Francesca as significant.

The day ended with a concert. A deputation headed by a Guatemalan colonel came over to the Sisters as they were taking their places at dinner and asked them if they would not consent to go on the program.

"I'm afraid not, Colonel", Francesca said, "Singing at concerts is a bit out of the line of nuns."

"But Mother Cabrini," he persisted, "this is something a little different. It's only in the family."

She shook her head, and he had to try again. "This concert", he told her, "is in honor of the captain, and you know that we all owe our lives to his skill and courage."

Francesca pondered this a moment. As it was put to her like that, she could hardly refuse. "All right, Colonel", she said. "But I must make one condition."

"Any condition you like, Mother Cabrini."

"A very simple one. Could you not put down our names at the opening of the program? Then after we have given our little performance you will not mind if we retire."

What she did was to prepare a short address to the captain, which she read. Then all the nuns went on deck, leaving the other passengers to finish the entertainment. But they had hardly settled themselves in their chairs when the colonel, accompanied this time by the ship's doctor, came out and begged for an encore.

"You hear how they're still clapping", the colonel said.

"But what can we do for an encore?" Francesca wanted to know.

The doctor was ready with his suggestion. "Mother, what about some of those hymns we've heard you singing?"

They went back and sang in unison *Gesù, mio ver conforto* and *Maria, che dolci affetti*. Everybody was charmed; they did not suspect that these hymns were being sung as a prayer for their conversion.

On October 19, the *New York* came to anchor in the port of Colón on the Panamanian coast, just where the Eastern entrance to the canal was being dug. Here the purser had their luggage carried ashore and put on the train free of charge, and the captain and all the ship's officers came to see them before the train pulled out of the station. Even the stewards and some of the sailors came to say goodbye. "One would think", Francesca wrote, "that we were leaving our own families!"

The journey across the isthmus seemed to Francesca like a page out of the *Annals of the Propagation of the Faith*, from which she had learned her geography as a child. Everywhere there were coconut palms and banana trees and tamarinds with their beautiful little glossy leaves. Gazing out of the window of the train, she excitedly saw brilliantly enameled colors under a turquoise sky and glimpses of gorgeous birds and exotic flowers and butterflies of gold, crimson, green, and black. Now at last she really felt like a foreign missionary—especially when they passed villages of thatched or wooden houses, mainly occupied by Blacks or Chinese. She was deeply shocked, however, to notice how little attention the Black women paid to decency in dress and compared them unfavorably with the well-trousered Chinese. As the nuns could do nothing else for these people, they said the rosary for them. "Let the Blessed Virgin", Francesca exclaimed, "be honored in this country of palms and flowers, which are an image of her!" She meant to try to bring that about.

Upon arriving at Panama, they went immediately on board the waiting ship, supposing that it was going to sail that night. When they found that there was going to be a wait of two days, they managed to hire a rowboat next morning and go on shore. It was the first time they had been in so frail a craft, and they were all frightened. But as they had been without Mass for ten days, they felt a great desire for Holy Communion, and this served to overcome their terrors.

On their way back to the ship—rather less frightened by now at their trip—they were singing hymns, and hundreds of birds flew after them, singing too. This delighted Francesca, who had a special fondness for birds and in whose mind the image of flight constantly occurred. "Put on wings!" she used to tell her nuns. "The road to heaven is so narrow, rocky, thorny, that only by flying can one travel over it." Some of the Sisters began to speculate what was signified by these birds. Francesca offered the interpretation that the birds represented those who would join the institute. One of the Sisters had a different opinion: no, they were the souls they were destined to convert. The naïve little argument was still going on when several thousand more birds flew toward them, almost darkening the brilliant sky. Upon this Francesca gave in: no doubt they *were* the souls the Sisters were going to save; there were too many of them for even her sanguine mind to suppose they represented future Sisters.

With such pleasant fancies they amused themselves until they got on board. But Francesca, who was sitting in the stern with her hand dangling in the water, was bitten by something she first thought must be a shark and then decided was only a crab. Apparently nobody had any mystical explanations to offer about that.

The next tedious day, while they were still detained in the harbor of Panama, some of the Sisters wanted to take a boat again and visit some islands nearby. As it was a question of only a ten minutes' trip, Mother Cabrini was willing enough to let them go. But she herself remained on board. To brave the choppy sea in a rowboat in order to go to Holy Communion was one thing; pleasure excursions were something else again. "You go, if you like", she told them. "No islands for me!" She confessed in her diary-letter that she still dreaded the sea, "And if there is no holy motive in view, I have no courage to go where I fear danger, unless I am sent by obedience." There were some remaining traces in her of her childish phobia against deep water. Except when it was obliterated by the exhilaration that uplifted her, it could reappear. There were still occasions when she permitted herself to be timid. But the Sisters who went on their little picnic enjoyed it as though they were children. On their return, they exhibited the delicately tinted shells they had gathered on the beach.

Striking northward along the Pacific coast, the boat stopped for a while at Punta Arenas in Costa Rica. There they were visited by the bishop, who whispered audibly to his secretary, "We must get them here, too." He then told them—having a better idea than they had of what they might encounter—that if they ever needed a shelter, they would find one in his diocese. Francesca decided that this intelligent and energetic German was just the right sort of man for Central America.

On October 25, they at last entered the lovely Gulf of Nicaragua and anchored off Corinto at seven in the morning. Before them was a beautiful panorama of nearby hills and palm-fringed shores with white houses beyond, gleaming in the sun, and a volcano in the distance. No sooner had they anchored when two boats adorned with flags and full of soldiers gaudy with gold lace put off toward them, with brass bands playing. The president of the republic and the bishop had sent representatives to meet the nuns. It was all very Latin-American in its flamboyance. A good breakfast was waiting for them in the town, and the president had sent them complimentary tickets to León. This sort of official welcome was very agreeable. As time was to show, however, it did not mean much more than that nuns were something of a curiosity in those parts.

It was mainly out of curiosity, too, that a large crowd assembled when they arrived at León that evening. The nuns tried to get off the train without being observed and to slip by a side door out of the station. It was useless: the vicar-general of the diocese had come to greet them and insisted on reading an address in the bishop's name. Then in the carriages drawn up for them they were escorted between files of soldiers to an apartment provided by the bishop in a hotel. In the evening, the leaders of local society made a formally solemn call and begged Francesca to leave seven of the Sisters there. She found it hard to convince them that she was unable to divide her forces but promised to do what she could later.

At Granada, their destination, there was similar enthusiasm. This time the crowds would not allow the carriages to come up, as they wanted to inspect the nuns at close quarters. Francesca was almost afraid that the people's devotion—or curiosity—would make martyrs of them. But between lines of soldiers a procession was formed, and they went on foot to the cathedral where the priests sang a *Te Deum* before escorting them to the house that was to be their academy. It was all so hectic that Francesca had to warn her band that the same crowds that shouted "Hosannah!" were a few days later howling, "Crucify him!" More than the soil of that country was volcanic. Had it not been for what they had suffered on their journey from New York, she would have been made very uneasy by the vociferous reception.

❦ ❦ ❦

As it was, things soon proved sufficiently disturbing. On the evening of their arrival, they found that Doña Elena Arellano was to give them a fine dinner. They also found that the half-native women who were to wait on them were naked to the waist.

Francesca instantly gave a little cry of consternation.

Her hostess turned to her. "What is it, Mother?" she asked anxiously.

"Those women! It's indecent."

Doña Elena explained, "This is the custom of the country."

"And you don't mind?"

"I never think of it. We're all used to it."

Francesca made herself clear, "Well, Doña Elena, *we're* not used to it. We can't allow this."

The half-naked native waitresses had to drape sheets and towels over their shoulders before the nuns would start their dinner.

Worse was to follow. Only 5 percent of the population was of pure Spanish blood. Another 5 percent was purely Indian. The rest of the people were of mixed white, Black, and Indian strains. This and the hot enervating climate had resulted in a great laxity of moral standards. Even the women who attended Mass and went to Communion were often scantily clad, and it was all taken for granted until the nuns contrived to persuade them to be a bit more seemly in their dress.

But the worst thing of all was that a high proportion of the children to be registered at the Sisters' school were illegitimate; and that, too, was taken for granted. While there may have been something to be said in favor of the fathers who openly acknowledged all their offspring, Francesca made up her mind that for her to admit such children would be a kind of condonation of immorality. She put her foot down and announced that she would not accept those who were of illegitimate birth. She did this as tactfully as possible, by forming a committee of parents and then inducing them to pass the regulation she wished; but everybody in the town of course knew that she was responsible for the ban.

This raised a fiercer storm than the one Francesca had run into off the New Jersey coast. One of those whose children was refused—a very wealthy and influential man—was deeply incensed. In face of what he might do, Francesca was advised to come to some sort of a compromise. She was not to be moved.

The offended people proceeded from threats to acts of violence. Night after night, men were around the convent firing guns and battering on the door. Francesca admitted that she was really frightened, and for a whole week every time she went to bed she quite expected an assassin to break into her room. The slightest noise made her jump nervously; yet she looked forward with a visionary joy to possible martyrdom. But probably there was no actual intention of murder; it may have been that it was expected that these demonstrations would be sufficient to intimidate Mother Cabrini. In Nicaragua, one way of getting rid of an unwanted tenant is still that of hiring a mob to make a noise around the house. But Francesca held her ground, and after a while she was left in peace. So far from having injured herself by excluding illegitimate children from her school, she had won further respect by her resoluteness. Children who could be accepted arrived in such numbers that the academy had to be moved within a few months to a larger building.

There were other inconveniences, though of a minor sort. The heat was intense. Earthquakes were so frequent that the Sisters, afraid that the house might topple down on their heads, put all their beds in the central porch that ran along all sides of the building. An active volcano was not very far away. This open-air sleeping helped to enable them to endure the sultry nights, but it also brought them into too close a proximity with strange insects and reptiles. Francesca, under her mosquito-netting spread over a folding-cot, pictured to herself beetles and snakes crawling up to her. She got so little sleep on this account that one young nun appointed herself Mother Cabrini's *matasapos*, toad-killer. Yet toads and snakes were preferable to the cowardly mob that had tried to terrify them by howling around the convent at night. As for the reptiles, and even the frequent earthquakes, the Sisters soon got used to them.

Still other difficulties were encountered, however. Three of the nuns—including the local superior—contracted typhoid, one of them nearly dying. They were brought safely through by the devoted nursing given them by Mother Cabrini herself. But though the climate and the water were unhealthy, the Sisters had to be most careful not so much as to hint that Nicaragua was not the earthly paradise its inhabitants believed it to be. Still greater tact had to be exercised in keeping as much aloof from the life of Granada as possible. There were many local jealousies, and the only way of avoiding getting involved in these was for the Sisters to refuse all presents that were pressed upon them. The gifts were no doubt usually offered without ulterior motive, for whatever their faults may have been, the Nicaraguans were generous. On the other hand, one could never be quite sure that what seemed to be generosity was not a subtle form of politics—an attempt to win them over to this side or that by putting them under an obligation. Extreme caution was necessary in dealing with such people.

Such were the difficulties. Those that could not be overcome—the climate and the reptiles and the earthquakes—were accepted by the Sisters as part of their lot. Mother Cabrini reminded them of the words of their patron, Saint Francis Xavier: "He who goes holy to the missions will find many opportunities to sanctify himself still more; but he who goes poorly provided with holiness runs the risk of losing what virtue he possesses." She clearly perceived that nothing could be accomplished there except by force of personal sanctity.

After having formally opened the school on December 3, her patron's feast day—Francesca gracing the occasion by making a little speech in the best Spanish she could muster, trilling it out in her high little voice—she stayed on until she saw that the foundation was going to be a success. As soon as that moment arrived, she left for the United States. It was the beginning of March 1892.

Chapter Nine

NEW ORLEANS

Francesca Cabrini returned to the United States by a different route from the one by which she had come. It was nothing to her that it was a far more difficult route; for by taking it she would see parts of Nicaragua through which she had not passed. Also she would be able to visit New Orleans.

Her object in this was not mere sightseeing. She always wished to acquaint herself with conditions in the countries she visited. All she knew of Nicaragua was what she knew of Granada, except for glimpses of other towns on her way there. But she was aware that an aristocratic and wealthy city, settled so largely by descendants of the *Conquistadores*, was hardly typical of the sparsely settled interior. As the only way of obtaining first-hand information was by going there herself, she decided to make the journey this time across Lake Nicaragua and the San Juan River. Like Saint Francis Xavier, whose name she had taken, her plan was to go ahead to select the places where a mission was most likely to be fruitful. She had never thought of limiting herself to Granada.

The journey Francesca made was not very long in actual miles, but it took a month, partly because it could be made only very slowly but also in part because of her side excursions. Across the lake it was all easy enough, but after that

the turbulent San Juan ran in a southeasterly direction between Nicaragua and Costa Rica. Since Francesca's time, it
has been made navigable to fairly large ships by a series of
canals, but fifty years ago it was in some places passable only
by canoes, so sharply does it descend from the mountains
of the east. Where, on the other hand, the country was flat,
it was often swampy and half choked with roots of trees.
Clearings there were, but most of it was a dark, sinister
tangle of jungle vines and thickets. Francesca learned a lot
more geography on this occasion.

Twelve times she had to change steamers—if the small
riverboats and lighters by which she usually traveled are
to be so described, and these could never move at night
for fear of running aground. Sometimes the passage could
only be made in a canoe, and at least once Francesca and
Sister Mercedes Cepeda, the nun with her, were caught
in a tropical downpour of rain. In an instant, they were
gasping and blinded by the solid sheet of water.

Mice, along with other vermin, were often found in
the cabins of the boats they had to take. Then poor Sister
Mercedes eyed Francesca with dismay.

"At least they are rather amusing to watch", Francesca
told her consolingly.

"I'd find it more amusing to be able to go to bed", Sister Mercedes said.

"So would I, Sister. No more than you do I want to
have them running over me in the middle of the night."

"Ugh!" Sister Mercedes shuddered at the thought.

Francesca laughed. But she had her full share of small
feminine fears. There was only one thing they could do.
They sought refuge in the tiny state-room, and there,
while Sister Mercedes made herself as comfortable as she
could on a sofa, Francesca stood all night on guard—on
guard and praying.

One of her main purposes on this trip was to see the Mosquitia Reserve, which stretches up as a strip from San Juan del Norte (the former Greytown) most of the way to Honduras. Francesca had planned this a long time in advance, as Cardinal Rampolla had asked her to go there. The Indians of the reservation were not of pure blood, for the Blacks, and to some slight extent the whites, had mingled with them. But their culture (such as it was) remained basically Indian. From 1630, when an English chartered company had established itself there, the British had claimed a protectorate until 1850, always with an eye to making the San Juan into a canal. War between England and the United States nearly came of this, but in the end the dispute was compromised by the cession of the coast to Nicaragua, which gave a kind of autonomy to the Indians. That autonomy, too, was eventually surrendered to Nicaragua, but at the time of Francesca's visit it still existed.

Her heart at once went out to these squat, dark-skinned but not unintelligent people who were, especially from the religious point of view, so utterly deserted. On the steamer that was taking her to Bluefields, she met two of their chiefs, and they greatly impressed her. And while waiting for the boat at the port at the mouth of the river, she visited the Indians in their huts to speak a few kind words to them. This is her account of what she saw: "Overcoming their shyness and yielding to their respect for the 'Black Gowns', as they call the Sisters and the priests, they begged us to send them Sisters and priests to instruct them and save them. The poor things! How I felt for them! I would have opened a house at once had I the means to do so."

This was never to prove possible. Two years later, the Sisters at Granada were themselves summarily ejected by a new revolutionary government. And by that time the Mosquitia Reserve had been turned into the political

department of Zelaya. One more of Francesca's many
missionary dreams had to remain untranslated into actual-
ity. Though she did start a subscription in Europe for the
founding of a mission among the Indians, circumstances
brought the design to nothing. The chief factor was the
seizing of power in 1893 by that José Santos Zelaya who
modestly gave his name to the Mosquitia Reserve, but
whose regime was officially described by the United States
as "a blot on the history of Nicaragua".

❦ ❦ ❦

In making this arduous trip through Nicaragua, Francesca
had more in mind than even a visit to the Indians. From
Bluefields—which still kept its English name as a relic
of the British protectorate—she could have taken a ship
direct to New York, which would have been the easiest
and most comfortable route. Instead, she decided to visit
New Orleans.

There were several reasons for her wishing to do so. A
great many Italians had gone to the southern states in the
hope of being able to do there something resembling the
work to which they were accustomed. Though the raising
of cotton was new to them, it was at least work in the
fields, a kind of farming. Moreover, Louisiana had a warm
climate, and the state had a high proportion of Catholics—
higher than any other part of the heavily Protestant South.

On all these scores, the immigrants were disappointed.
The weather, though warm, was very different from that
of Italy. And though employment was offered them on
the plantations, the wages were extremely low, because
of inevitable competition with the Blacks. Everything
possible was done to prevent the Italians from obtaining
independence as cotton-raisers. And the creole aristocracy
looked down upon the newcomers. Even Catholics were
afraid that the local prestige they enjoyed would be lost

if they were swamped by the influx of a race as much despised there as anywhere else.

In Louisiana, in fact, the worst of all the outrages against the Italians occurred. For whereas in the North the immigrants merely suffered from exploitation, in the South the terrible weapon of lynching was drawn against them.

It has often been observed that lynching has little to do with a popular indignation that, impatient of the slow process of the law, exacts an immediate penalty. It rather springs from a generalized hatred or a generalized fear, and this is always ready to fasten itself upon any available victim, without much consideration of his guilt. It is sometimes even a way of enlivening a dull existence with the sharpest of excitements. Though it is by no means invariably directed against Blacks, or invariably occurs in the South—for several of the worst cases of lynching in the past twenty-five years [i.e., between 1920 and 1945—EDITOR] have occurred in California, where those hanged by the mob were white Americans—the South has been chiefly notorious for this form of sport.

Here was the immediate reason why Mother Cabrini went to New Orleans.

A year before her arrival there, in the spring of 1892, a band of young Italians had been arrested on a charge of murdering the chief of police. Three were found guilty and condemned for the crime; eleven had been acquitted; and some others were awaiting trial. Just then the mob, inflamed by the press, got out of hand, and they pushed upon the prison, where the acquitted men were still awaiting their release, howling the cry of "Kill the Italians!" As so often happens in such cases, the prison officials, secretly sympathizing with the lynchers, put up only a perfunctory resistance. That the arrested men were Sicilians was enough; this meant that they must all be armed with stilettos and all members of the Mafia. All of them were dragged out and hanged on trees and lampposts. For days their bodies were allowed to dangle there—not so much as a warning to murderers as a gentle hint that the Italians were to consider themselves classed with Blacks.

A thrill of horror ran through the hundreds of thousands of their compatriots scattered throughout the United States. The Italian government made strong representations to President Harrison, and when he replied that the matter was one beyond his jurisdiction, diplomatic relations between the two countries were broken off. This made the lynchers see that they might act with impunity, and as a crime of this sort is often an incitation to another, in the years that followed several such outbursts stained the American name, though none was on quite the same scale. Henry Cabot Lodge, writing in the *North American Review* for May 1891, though of course deploring the outrage, found the principal lesson to be drawn was that immigration should be restricted.

Francesca had been deeply shocked by the New Orleans lynching, and this unquestionably was one of her chief reasons for visiting the city. Her way was always that of trying to obtain information on the spot, of analyzing the problem and of finding out how best to solve it before proceeding to action. Believing as she did that the Italians would themselves have to remove the prejudice against them, she saw that this could be most effectually brought about by providing them with the religious and moral aid they needed.

The archbishop, Francis Janssens, a vigorous Dutchman who was still under fifty, received her cordially and begged her to establish a mission, as did Father Gambera of the Scalabriniani. The archbishop recognized the needs of the Italian members of his flock, but like most of the American bishops, he could do little for them. What he saw at once was that Francesca was just the woman the situation required. He was to show most signally the kind of man he was by the way five years later he met death. It occurred when he was at sea on his way to Europe. Suddenly stricken, he had just sufficient time to kneel down in his cabin and say, "My Lord, I thank Thee. I am ready." Francesca promised him that she would send some Sisters to New Orleans as soon as possible.

❧ ❧ ❧

Two months later she fulfilled her promise.

She fulfilled it despite the fact that she had no material means at her disposal. Undeterred by this and moved only by her compassion and confidence in God, she set about giving relief in a way that nobody but herself would have ventured upon.

She assigned three Sisters to the task—one of them a girl of seventeen. Though here, as elsewhere, this nun's recollections have been drawn upon, her extreme modesty will not allow her name to appear. As Francesca at that moment happened to be even more than usually short of money, she could not buy their tickets all the way to New Orleans, but only to an intermediary city not yet visited by her daughters. From there they would have to work their way by begging.

It was by these methods that they slowly moved toward their destination. As far as their money would carry them, that far they went. Then they got out, found a local convent willing to give them shelter for a night or two, and spent the days asking for contributions in the local Little Italy.

These contributions had to be drawn from a people nearly all of whom were bitterly poor. The Sisters mostly received only nickels and dimes, though now and then a man squeezed out a quarter or even a dollar.

"So you are on your way to New Orleans. We Italians need some help there, Sister."

"That's why we are going. Those poor men that they
hanged last year!"

"But what can *you* do, Sister?"

"We will do anything we can—anything."

If that was the right way to appeal to some people, on
others it had a bad effect.

"Sisters can do nothing in New Orleans. How are you
going to stop Italians being lynched? Priests and nuns are
no good for this sort of thing; they only keep our people ignorant."

"Are you an anticlerical?"

"Certainly I am anticlerical. You go somewhere else. I
do not give my money to the Church."

Another man, though not an anticlerical, would refuse
to give.

"No, Sister. There is nothing that can be done. Not in
New Orleans. In New York, maybe; you go back to New
York. I am a poor man and cannot waste money."

But in spite of rebuffs—and to these they were accustomed by now—a few dollars would be scraped together.
As soon as they had enough to buy tickets to the next city,
they went there and repeated their performance. Slowly,
stage by difficult stage, they made their way south. But
they got to New Orleans in the end.

The three nuns arrived there at eleven at night, a very
dark night. With their bundles tucked under their arms,
they started to walk into the blackness—they did not
know where.

Just then the youngest of the Sisters had an idea. Clapping her hands with joy at its brilliance, she said, "Do you
remember what Saint Francis of Assisi made Brother Leo
do once? Well, I am going to do the same thing." Handing
her package to one of the other Sisters, she started to twirl
round and round. She kept on, as a child does, until she
was dizzy and about to fall. When she stopped, she said,

"We'll be like Brother Leo. My face is pointing down that street. Let's go there. The Lord will guide us."

They went forward, still having no idea as to where they were going. Suddenly a carriage, driven rapidly, came out of the darkness behind and passed them. A few minutes later it returned, the horse now coming at a walk, and stopped.

"You are not the Italian Sisters we heard were coming?" the driver asked.

They said they were.

"Well, Father Gambera told me about you. I will take you to his house."

The Sister who had done the twirling ventured to ask, "Is Father Gambera's house down the road we were going?"

"Yes, Sister."

She clapped her hands again. "You see!" she cried delighted, "I told you that was the way to find it."

This priest and his brother took them to get lodgings. What they found was a room containing nothing but three beds covered with mosquito-netting. As they thought this too luxurious for them, they removed it, and of course rose in the morning covered with bites. The next night they decided that a mosquito-net was not contrary to their vow of poverty.

🐾 🐾 🐾

Francesca had told them that, as soon as they saw any promise of success, they were to wire her and that she would come on at once. One day they collected the magnificent sum of seventeen dollars and thirty cents, so they sent her the telegram, "Success! Please come." On August 6 she arrived, accompanied by four other nuns. She always wished to open any new convent herself.

There was, however, nothing that could be called a convent. All that they had was three rented rooms in

a tenement house on Saint Philip's Street. It was occupied mostly by Blacks, a couple of families often being
in the same room, and yet being sometimes able to take in
lodgers. The large courtyard was a kind of general living room for everybody. There the noisy people congre-
gated, usually very hilarious in spite of their misery and not
infrequently drunk. Naked pickaninnies played, and semi-
naked women quarreled in the same place. At night there
was singing and the strumming of banjoes. Sleep was
always impossible before the small hours.

The only cooking the nuns could do was on a crude
brick barbecue, which was also in the public yard. There
they ate their meals, such as they were, with a bench for
a refectory table, mangy dogs and pot-bellied children
hanging around for scraps. Water was scarce and, as it was
drawn straight out of the Mississippi, almost undrinkable.
Fearful of typhoid, the Sisters had to go from door to door
begging for a jug of water that had been filtered. When at
last they obtained a convent of their own, Mother Cabrini
ordered that there should always be at the door a jar of
good water for any thirsty caller.

It was this same sprawling tenement house that Francesca
bought a week after arrival. She found that it was going
cheap—a great advantage. That it was at the center of the
Italian settlement—if the Italians could be said to have had
one in a city where only the Black quarter was open to
them—was also an advantage. From this place the Sisters
were within call of anybody who needed them. That part of
the street became almost a strip of Italian territory.

By August, Francesca had her convent there and a
chapel housing the Blessed Sacrament. And when the
crowds that gathered for Mass on Sundays grew too large
for their little chapel, the courtyard was covered with an
awning and a portable altar was erected on a platform.
The same courtyard served very well for social or patriotic

gatherings. It was used also to give religious instruction to those who could be induced to attend. Orphans began to be collected; a school was started. The New Orleans mission had been established almost overnight.

Because of the lack of Italian-speaking priests, much that might be called pastoral work devolved on the Sisters. They often had to help the dying to make acts of contrition and of faith, hope, and charity. At any hour of the day or night, mothers would come to them with sick babies in their arms. These the Sisters had to baptize. Archbishop Janssens so highly approved of them that, instead of ringing the bell like everybody else, he had his special signal: when they heard his cane knocking on the door, they knew who it was.

The mission prospered, though not notably at first from the financial point of view. Francesca herself went out begging, even when the Sisters asked her not to do this lest she be overcome by the heat. "No," she said, "I'm coming, too. This sort of thing is a bit distasteful to me, and I don't want my daughters to undertake any duty that I refuse." All of them looked upon poverty as a blessing sent by God. What was evident from the start was that neglected souls were being reached and that some ray of hope was being cast on the lives of the unhappy Italians. The Saint Philip's Street convent was for them a social settlement as well as a mission. Except for the sullen groups holding apart, the Sisters had provided New Orleans with an Italian meeting-ground. It was achieved only by enthusiastic self-sacrifice. The fashionable academy of Granada had by no means led Mother Cabrini to depart from her main objective.

Nor did the Sisters confine themselves to the city. There, indeed, they had enough and more than enough to do. But they also went out in twos and threes to the rice fields and cotton plantations of Louisiana and Mississippi in search of isolated groups. Everywhere they had the same end in view—the salvation of souls, the alleviation of misery. Merely to hear a sympathetic word in his native tongue brought tears to the eyes of many a despairing and embittered man. Memories of Italy, memories of the religion he had so long ceased to practice came back. Perhaps in many cases not much more than that was accomplished, though even in such cases only God could know what good had been done. But there was also plenty of evidence of rich fruit. A priest who could understand Italian went from this place to that to hear confessions, to say Mass, and to administer Holy Communion. These people were not really lost to Catholicism, but until now they had had little opportunity to practice it. The opportunities were still inadequate; that they were being provided at all was due to the abnegation of the Missionary Sisters. Archbishop Janssens would sometimes go with them to the plantations and, with the open sky as his cathedral roof and a kitchen chair as his episcopal throne, administer the Sacrament of Confirmation.

If Francesca always wished to open a new mission herself, she always would leave it as soon as she saw that the Sisters were able to continue the work without her help. She set them on their feet and then expected them to march. Her words at parting were: "You can go ahead now; everyone to her own mission." They all looked back with a kind of nostalgia to this period of privation as to a golden age, an idyll upon which the memory might linger forever in love.

Chapter Ten

THE FIRST HOSPITAL

One of the things that stands out most strikingly in Francesca Cabrini's character is her flexibility, her willingness to adapt herself to circumstances. She never said, "This is the work I want to do"; what she said was, "This is the work that needs to be done." It was so even from the outset of her career when, contrary to all her inclinations, she not only entered the House of Providence but consented to remain there under vows. That seemed to be the end of everything she had ever hoped for, but was really its beginning. It could not have been so—whatever her adaptability—had she not been rooted in humility and obedience. Her flexibility was part of her sanctity and is not to be accounted for on any other ground.

The same thing may be seen in her readiness to lay aside her life-long dream of going as a missionary to China the moment that Pope Leo XIII asked her to go to the United States instead. And she had hardly got to the United States and begun her work among the poor Italians before she saw an opportunity of doing some good in Nicaragua—and so established a house there.

This, however, did not mean that she ever completely renounced the idea of China. Though she herself was never able to take the Orient into her sphere of operations, she did not forget the Chinese, and her institute now works among them, with Chinese women as members. Similarly, she no sooner had got her academy started in Granada than she was making plans for taking the Gospel to the Nicaraguan Indians, as later she talked about the Eskimos and the Pueblos and even North Africa. She bounded herself only by the limits of the world, and any kind of work, so long as it could be thought of as having a missionary significance, was work she was ready to undertake.

All the same, every religious society has to specialize to some extent, and this was particularly true of one like hers, still young and meager in numbers. Otherwise, there is so much diffusion of energy that ineffectiveness results. Mother Cabrini's specialization was that of teaching poor Italians, and she did not really diverge from this when establishing her academies and colleges and normal schools. Institutions of this type had in fact already begun to be staffed by her nuns. But if within education itself there was one department she made distinctively her own, it was the founding of orphanages in which destitute girls could be trained to become virtuous Christian women. She had come to New York to take over the institution offered to her on East Fifty-Ninth Street by the Contessa Cesnola, and she had only put it on a firmer basis by transferring it to West Park. Francesca was still thinking of orphanages as her main activity.

It was a distinct shock to her when she was asked in 1891 to take charge of a hospital. This seemed to her quite outside of the limits she had set herself—wide as these were.

Yet she recognized the need of hospitals for Italian immigrants in the United States. She well knew that most of these men were engaged in occupations of a rough and dangerous sort in which accidents frequently occurred. She also understood—nobody better—that the slums into which they were crowded made them extremely susceptible to disease. And she was aware of what happened to those who were obliged to go into the wards of the public hospitals, for she had often visited the one on Randall's Island. In such places, the poor were frequently treated almost as though they were criminals. And even in the most efficient general hospitals, the attention given to non-paying patients is—even today—often less solicitous than that received by the well-to-do in their private rooms. It is not altogether without reason that the poor in all countries still regard a hospital with what the comfortable consider a superstitious horror.

All this fell with special weight upon a people like the Italians, who were so very isolated in a strange land. Sensitive as they were, they cannot be blamed for also being suspicious. Nor can it be said that they did not have good grounds for feeling as they did. Their sufferings in America were perhaps all the sharper because their resentment was inarticulate. In free clinics and dispensaries, people were not always treated with the most delicate consideration by busy doctors and nurses; nor did they get more than the bare minimum in the hospital wards. In such a situation they were helpless and silent and bitter.

Nor was this all. Ignorant as these Italians commonly were of the English language, it was hard, even for those who wished to be kind to them, to get into contact with them. What had to be done was done efficiently, but with an appearance of coldness, however much those who were looking after the patients wished they could show a keener personal interest than was possible under the circumstances. This was brought home to Francesca one day when, visiting one of the public hospitals, a man asked her to read him a letter he had received from Italy three months before. He had waited all that time for even this little service. He was now so delighted that he had found somebody who could read him his letter—and then so stricken with grief when Francesca had to read out the news it contained of the death of his mother. Tears came to her eyes as well as his own while she read.

For such people a stay in a hospital was an experience of devastating loneliness. Their sick bodies received some attention; the fact that they had still sicker souls was rarely thought of at all. When it *was* thought of, it was not easy to find Italian-speaking priests who could hear their confessions and bring them the consolations of religion in their last hours.

One side of the problem—the need of a hospital for Italians—had been recognized by the Italian community. But that community was poor and could do little. Moreover, it was so split into factions that a united effort was virtually impossible. Funds had been collected for a Garibaldi Hospital—whose very name suggested that it was to be purely secular if not actually anticlerical in atmosphere. But the funds had not been enough to build a hospital on the projected scale, and they had slipped through the hands of the promoters because of the long delay, so that nothing had come of the scheme.

Then Bishop Scalabrini had taken it upon himself to establish a small Italian hospital on East 109th Street, putting it under the management of his Fathers of Saint Charles Borromeo. There they could indeed look after the spiritual needs of the patients, but their lack of knowledge of hospital work soon got them into difficulties. Under Father Morelli—a good but not a very capable man—the hospital was so obviously a failure that the bishop had to recall to Italy the Sisters he had sent to look after it. In his desperation, Bishop Scalabrini had begged Francesca when she was last in Italy to assume the management.

The choice was clear. She would either have to do what was asked of her, or the hospital would have to close. Yet for a number of reasons she was disinclined to accept this responsibility. She feared that the day and night demands that the conducting of a hospital would make upon her nuns might be detrimental to their religious spirit—the particular kind of religious spirit she sought. Moreover, compassionate as she was, she had a fastidiousness that made her turn from anything like physical putrefaction with inextinguishable disgust. When it was absolutely necessary—as in the case of the sufferers from smallpox whom she had nursed when a girl in Sant' Angelo, or in that of the old woman dying of cancer whom she and her sister Rose had nursed, or in that of her own nuns when they were sick—she had been able to conquer this repugnance. But she had not as yet conquered it so completely as to be willing to take charge of a hospital to which all kinds of people—men, women, and children alike—would have to be admitted.

What she did in this state of uncertainty was what she always did at such times: she prayed hard, and she sought advice. As she had gone to the United States to do missionary work, she laid her difficulties before Cardinal Simeoni, the prefect of the Propaganda Fide, as the proper authority to consult. His opinion was that she should undertake this task, one that while primarily a corporal work of mercy had also great spiritual value. Though there were Catholic hospitals functioning in New York, there was none among them that was at once Italian and Catholic. Francesca could take charge of it and still regard herself as a missionary; by means of a hospital she could save souls. This view was confirmed by the letter of recommendation dated July 16, 1891, sent her by the cardinal-vicar, which had direct reference to hospital work.

What also contributed to her decision was another of her dreams. This time she saw Our Lady with her sleeves rolled up and her skirt pinned back, going from one bed to another in a hospital ward as a nurse. As soon as Francesca recognized the Mother of the Afflicted, she sprang forward offering her help. Upon this Our Lady said, "I am doing what you refuse to do." After that there was no more hesitation. If Francesca brought so large a number of Sisters with her from Italy in September 1891, it was because ten of them had to be assigned to the Scalabriniani hospital. She put them to work before she left for Nicaragua.

Even under the direction of the Missionary Sisters, the hospital failed, though through no fault of theirs. Francesca had to hurry back from New Orleans in the spring of 1892 to deal with the situation. Bishop Scalabrini's view had always been that the Sisters were to be auxiliaries to his Fathers, and it was this that had made Francesca reluctant to go to America in the first place. Now this auxiliary relationship was having an interpretation put upon it by Father Morelli at the hospital that she could not accept. She had always meant to be independent, which was why she had pressed so early in her career for the papal recognition that would make her dependent directly on the pope. In taking over the hospital, she had expected to be allowed a free hand.

It came out at once that she was not to be given her freedom there. The point of view of Father Morelli was that the Sisters would be very useful to him, but were to remain under his control. At the same time, after having undertaken to pay each of the ten Sisters working at the hospital a monthly salary of twenty-five dollars, he had given them nothing. Worse still, Francesca found that she was expected to saddle herself with financial liabilities that had been incurred before they had so much as crossed its doors. The Scalabriniani had piled up a large debt, on which interest had to be paid; and they took it for granted that Francesca would pay—pay what was due from them. By skillful management, the Sisters had managed to cut down expenses, at the same time finding five thousand dollars for some improvements. But Father Morelli was making demands of a kind very obnoxious to the sound business sense that Francesca was rapidly developing.

What she did was to refuse to pay the old debts except on the condition that she should have ownership of the property. By the spring of 1892, however, things had gone too far even for that. A foreclosure threatened and did occur during that summer. After that, there was some argument between the Fathers and the Sisters as to whom the furnishings of the place belonged, on account of the salaries that had been unpaid for a year. Such letters as exist about this do not make things very clear, but at least they are not at all acrimonious. What does emerge from them is that a parting of the ways had been reached.

The anonymous nun who has written Francesca Cabrini's life says that the Fathers carried the case to Archbishop Corrigan and that he ordered Francesca and the nuns to leave the hospital within ten days. This does not seem to be borne out by the letters from Mother Cabrini to the archbishop that are in the New York archdiocesan archives. Nor can this biographer be correct in giving October 17, 1892, as the date for the foundation, as by then Francesca was in Italy. The fact would seem to be that in May Francesca, seeing that the state of affairs was quite hopeless, decided to wash her hands of them and to start a hospital on East Twelfth Street. Whether or not she actually got into that house in May, she was certainly already preparing to move by then. And on September 17th, she wrote to the archbishop telling him, "Now the Sisters are all at Twelfth Street, poor indeed, but tranquil."

❦ ❦ ❦

Another error—one of no great importance, perhaps, but still an error—appears in this biography. There it is stated that Francesca started her new hospital with two hundred and fifty dollars made up of two gifts, one of a hundred and fifty dollars and the other of a hundred dollars. It is only due to Archbishop Corrigan's memory to say that he started off a little subscription book for Francesca with fifty dollars. At the same time, he gave her the names of four well-to-do Italians in New York, whom she could approach with his authorization. It was each of these four men who gave her fifty dollars. With that sum, she started her Columbus Hospital.

Nothing more clearly shows that Francesca was a woman who, once she had put her hand to the plough, kept it there firmly and drove straight ahead. Anybody with less strength of character than hers would have been disheartened by her experience. Had she wanted to find the most perfect of excuses for retiring from a work she had never wished to accept, it was available now. With what is somewhat smugly called a "good conscience", she could have given up hospitals forever.

She did not do so. Her brief contact with the hospital of the Scalabriniani Fathers had revealed to her the possibilities for good that had opened out. Instead of abandoning this work, she rented two adjoining houses on Twelfth Street, and there she transferred ten of her patients, the other fifteen going to public institutions. Their condition was too grave for the experiment she was about to make.

One wonders how she had the courage to attempt it at all on two hundred and fifty dollars, which was just enough to pay the rent for a month and to buy ten cheap beds. The mattresses were homemade. Francesca herself cut out the sheets from a bale as the most economical way of providing them. For the first week, the hospital was without water or gas for cooking, and the Sisters had to buy food from a restaurant around the corner and heat it on a coal stove in the center of the large room that served as a ward. There the Sisters could make soup, but this was as far as they could go for the moment in the way of cooking. Their pharmacy consisted of a dozen bottles of medicine. A Dr. Villari gave them a writing desk and a set of surgical instruments, and somebody else donated an ambulance. As the Sisters had no money left to buy beds for themselves, they slept on the floor.

The opening of a hospital in such a style not unnaturally aroused a good deal of criticism. Today the health authorities would at once step in, for it is obvious that, from the point of view of efficiency, nothing could have been much worse. The compensation was that the lack of efficiency—in the sense of having appliances at one's command—was more than balanced by the devotion of the Sisters. They had had very little training and were not able to employ nurses. But such was their self-sacrificing ardor that other defects were hardly noticed in the midst of an enveloping kindness.

If the Sisters had allowed themselves to think about what they had taken on, they would surely have felt dismayed. But the kind of obedience they had learned to practice forbade even so much as a personal judgment regarding the commands of their superior. They had become extremely proficient in doing what they were told to do with a complete interior assent, and not merely as the external performance of the assigned duty. They all had perfect confidence in their Mother. Like her, they placed their whole reliance in God. With radiant faces that showed how much they rejoiced in their opportunity to serve, they labored for their patients. Again there was the renewal of an idyll.

Francesca Cabrini now had a brilliant inspiration. "Listen, Sisters," she said, "this year is the four hundredth anniversary of the discovery of the New World by Columbus."

Not knowing quite what that had to do with their hospital, they assented.

"But don't you see? The Italians here are very enthusiastic about Columbus. Well, we'll call our hospital the Columbus Hospital. *He* was the first Italian immigrant. If we call it after him, all the Italian immigrants will know that this is their hospital."

One Sister asked whether it would not be better to call it by some religious name.

"Oh no!" Francesca was quite positive. "You know what happened to the proposed Garibaldi Hospital. The name itself was a challenge. Now we do not want to give a challenge of another kind. Not even the most anticlerical will object to Columbus. Under that name all the Italian factions can unite."

The New York hospital accordingly became the Columbus Hospital, and the same name was given to the other hospitals Francesca was to found. Her inspiration turned out to be as brilliant as she thought it to be. With a sure popular instinct, the Italians even began to call the nuns the Sisters of Columbus.

Those who were first received were so poor that they could pay nothing at all; everything had to be provided by the Sisters out of their own poverty. But their example was contagious. Dr. Keane, the head physician, not only gave his services free but was so indignant with some doctors who tried to charge fees that he dismissed them from the hospital staff. Doctors as charitable as Dr. Keane—several of them Protestants—joined him, and when they had private patients who could afford to pay, they sent them there, thus providing the hospital with an income. Donations of equipment and money were given. And seven thousand dollars—all that was left of the twenty thousand collected for the Garibaldi Hospital—was handed over to those who could put it to some use. This was brought about through the instrumentality of General Cesnola, the husband of the contessa. By degrees, criticism died down. Instead, there was a wondering praise that so much had been accomplished with so little.

Even so, few people could have foreseen how much was to flow from this absurdly tiny beginning. Francesca Cabrini herself did not live to see the Columbus Hospital as it is at present on East Nineteenth Street—one of the smaller hospitals of New York but also one of the best appointed. But she did live to supervise the plans for its construction. Like the hospitals she was to found in Chicago and Denver and Seattle, everything came from her intrepid decision to start a hospital with two hundred and fifty dollars.

Chapter Eleven

INTERLUDE IN ITALY

Normally the General of a religious order or congregation remains most of the time at Rome and from that point directs operations. This was not Mother Cabrini's way. She must be unique in her practice of going in person—often in advance—to whatever part of the world she intended to open a mission. Officially the center of the institute was in Rome; actually it was wherever the General happened to be. And Francesca was always on the move; nothing would content her except to be a missionary herself.

The advantages of this method are obvious. She did not have to depend merely on reports; she saw with her own eyes what the local conditions were and how best to meet them. By being on hand when a new house was established, she could deal with the difficulties as they arose. Furthermore, she could encourage those she had under her and who, had she not been with them, might have become bewildered or even dismayed. By this means, she was able to deal, in her decisive style, with whatever problems cropped up. When she was there, there seemed in fact to be no problems at all. Had she been in her room in Rome, months would have elapsed before she could have been consulted and have determined upon a solution. A local superior is inclined to be somewhat afraid of exceeding her authority and in every important move feels it necessary to explain things to the head of the congregation. But in the case of every foundation made by the Missionary Sisters, the local superior had her general at hand; no time was lost, no mistakes were made. Mother Cabrini never left her nuns to their own devices until she was sure that the new mission was going well. The instant she was satisfied as to that, she was off to some other place.

Though she spent the greater part of her life after 1889 traveling about the world, she knew that it was necessary to make periodic visits to Italy. If there, too, she was constantly moving from place to place, it was at Codogno rather than at Rome that she usually was to be found. For it was at Codogno that the largest group of her nuns was gathered; it was at Codogno that the novitiate was established. And the formation of the novices, filling them with the spirit of humility and obedience and missionary enthusiasm, was all-important to the life of the institute.

The training of the young nuns was, of course, by no means neglected during Francesca's many long absences— for it was entrusted to those already trained by her and upon whom she could depend. Moreover, even when she was away, she seemed to be present. To an almost unprecedented degree, she had an intimate personal contact with every one of the rapidly increasing number of Sisters, of whom there were now two hundred. "Mother" was everything to them and became, after God, the soul of their work. So thoroughly did she succeed in impressing herself upon them that even today, twenty-seven years after her death, the Missionary Sisters—even those who never knew her—speak of her as though she were in the next room. Never, perhaps, has the founder of a religious order given or drawn forth the same affection. Every one of the Sisters was utterly devoted to her; every one of them was certain she had a special place in Francesca's love. She was not only their General; she was their Mother.

Yet she saw most of them rarely, and this became all
the more the case as their numbers increased, until at the
end of her life she had over fifteen hundred nuns in her
congregation. This, however, did not prevent her from
keeping her finger on the pulse of each. They realized that
she was much too busy a woman to reply to their letters;
they also knew that the letters she insisted they write to her
regularly were carefully read and that nothing they told
their Mother was ever forgotten. For hours she would sit
poring through a magnifying glass at their delicate Italian
script. By writing to her, they drew near to her. It was
almost like praying to one of the saints in heaven; one was
sure one was heard, even when no answering sign came.
In a special sense, everybody depended on her. It was the
secret of her astounding success.

Or rather, it was part of that secret. The other and more
important part was that even while immersed in endless
administrative details, Francesca kept recollected in God.
Though always immensely busy, she was never ruffled,
never in a hurry, never in a state of anything but detached
peace. Only in such clear, cool calm could she have managed affairs as she did. Her activity was nourished by her
mystical life. Even her practical decisions derived their
soundness from this source. And in the light of her spirituality, she learned best how to employ the loving and
beloved daughters whom God had given her.

One would suppose that an undertaking like the founding
of the Columbus Hospital would have held Francesca in
New York for several years. But she was so swift a worker
that she might appear to be a streak of lightning had she
not been so serene. Quietly and efficiently she dealt with
what looked like insuperable difficulties. In September

she got the work well started there; in October she was in Rome.

The year was that of Leo XIII's jubilee. Fifty years before he had been consecrated a bishop at the age of thirty-three. He had still ten years of active life ahead of him, but he was already so old that everybody supposed he must soon die. The jubilee was therefore thought of as a farewell. The whole Catholic world was celebrating the occasion, and congratulations were pouring in upon him from the heads of all civilized countries. Francesca Cabrini as a personal friend did not want to be absent.

But she had also another reason for this visit to Italy. She felt it necessary from time to time to retire to the quiet of the cloister, for she not only needed to form her young nuns but to renew her own spirit. From these intervals of retirement, she came out refreshed, ready for new intrepid enterprises. As her own spiritual life deepened, she felt, with one side of her nature, a hunger for withdrawal. Essentially a mystic, the Martha in her had to be sustained by Mary. The resignation of office, to which she looked forward as soon as she had built up her organization, she knew was still a far-off dream, and in fact it was never permitted her to retire and give herself wholly to prayer. Yet as she also knew that her work could not be permanently fruitful unless it was built upon an interior communion with God, she was seeking a kind of spiritual holiday at Codogno.

Even so, she managed to perform several important pieces of business in Italy. At the suggestion of Colonel De Maria of Genoa—whose daughter, who became Sister Xavier, was about to join her, and in fact is the author of the anonymous biography—Francesca founded a house in that city. She planned to send her nuns to America in the future from this port. At Monte Compatri, in a picturesque

old castle above Frascati, she also obtained a vacation residence for the Sisters.

Francesca was nearly two years in Italy, and during this
period she saw the aged Leo several times, each time the
pope receiving her in private audience and treating her
with affectionate intimacy. During one of these audiences, he held his right hand over her in benediction.
He then placed it on her head while with his left hand he
drew her to him. She said afterward, deeply moved, "It
was like the Church opening its arms to the Missionary
Sisters in an embrace."

In spite of her awestruck reverence for the person of
the pope, she felt a perfect freedom with him. On one
occasion after she had been to see him, Cardinal Rampolla, the secretary of state, asked her, "Mother, is there
any particular thing that you would like me to request of
His Holiness on your behalf."

She thought a minute. Then she said. "Yes, there *is*,
Your Eminence—if you don't think I am too daring in
what I am going to say."

He smiled at her and returned, "I don't think you would
be likely to ask anything that the Holy Father is likely
to refuse."

"Well then, His Holiness has been very kind to me. But
I have sometimes thought I would like to have him give
me something for my work—not out of the general fund,
but from his private purse."

"*That*, Mother Cabrini," said the cardinal, "is something we shall have to see about."

She had been thinking of only a "token offering"—a
little personal gift as a bond between friends. When next
she saw him, the pope said, "I hear that you want some of
my own money. Here is a trifle I have for you." It was a
gift of a thousand dollars.

In the summer of 1894, she went again to see the pope to say goodbye to him before leaving for the United States. He had discontinued the usual audiences at that time, but he sent Francesca word through Cardinal Rampolla that if she would be in the Clementine Hall on the afternoon of June 11, at the time he returned from his daily airing in the Vatican Gardens, he would see her then. As soon as he caught sight of her, he ordered his litter-bearers to halt and gestured to Francesca and the nuns with her to come to him. He was old and weary but his eyes were shining brilliantly in his worn, rugged, and yet delicate face. When she told him that she was soon to sail for New York, he blessed each of the kneeling nuns, placing his hands on their heads. Then he dropped all formality, and with that bonhomie that was his—as he could also display a certain tartness on occasion—he said to Francesca:

"Let us work, Cabrini; let us work. Then what a heaven will be ours!"

Francesca smiled, "But I *like* work so much, Your Holiness, that I sometimes wonder whether it gives me any merit. Will work get me to heaven?"

"Certainly it will", Leo returned at once. "Heaven is for those who work like you. Courage, Cabrini. Go on working until the end."

He said this with immense vigor and emphasis. And when he gave the signal for the sedan-chair to be carried to his private apartments, he turned back and called once more, "Let us work, Cabrini; let us work!"

She sailed on September 13, 1894, from Genoa, accompanied by fifteen Sisters, among whom was Colonel De Maria's daughter. The colonel's private launch, crowded by many of the nuns who were remaining behind, went out, side by side with the liner, far into the sea. As the liner gathered speed, the launch was obliged to begin to drop behind, and though Mother Cabrini and her companions ran back to the stern of the liner, the last farewells had to be made. From there the goodbyes were called and handkerchiefs waved until the launch was only a speck in the distance.

The sea was so blue while they were still in the Mediterranean that Francesca found it not easy to distinguish it from the sky. Even off the Azores she thought those islands looked like bits of sky dropped into the blue Atlantic. They had passed Morocco the previous day, and a mere fleeting glimpse of that land was enough to inflame Francesca's missionary ardor. She dreamed at once of carrying the Gospel to Africa. She never saw a country—she could hardly think of one—without immediately longing to go there to save souls. Indeed, the world was too small for her.

As the journey was so uneventful, much of her letter written at this time was given over to exhortations. We can gather how Mother Cabrini spoke to her nuns from the way she wrote to them when absent. "The Kingdom of God has no limits; its limits are those of the globe itself. Come, and let your glory be the glory of your celestial spouse, the working out of that celestial talent—the sublime vocation of cooperating with Christ for the salvation of souls. Come, for in the Vineyard of the great Father of the Family we are to gather rich and copious sheaves. There are some who think they are too poor, ignorant, and weak to undertake such work. Do not fear; mistrust yourselves and confide in God, for as I have already said, *Omnia possum in Eo qui me confortat.*" No wonder those in Italy were burning with desire to be chosen for the missions, and disappointed when they were not.

There were, by way of contrast with this, a few little family jokes. Sister Alexandrine, who had started out by keeping a diary, had written nothing in it for two days.

"So we shall run the risk of losing our bearings", commented Francesca. And they were all told to consult Sister Frances if they wanted any information about ships. "She will explain either out of her own knowledge or by reference to ancient and modern works on the subject. I see quite a library of such books spread out in her berth. I was advised to ask Sister Xavier for information, as she knows something of these things, but she replied, 'Those who want to know about the sea had better come and find out for themselves.' Sister Ignatius also set out to give you a very full and learned account of everything, but so far she has written not more than about four lines." A convent is a place so full of innocent gaiety that such small jokes are received there with laughter. From them Francesca turns at once to her edifying reflections, and then back again to her jokes. It was in this way that she passed the time on the voyage.

❦ ❦ ❦

She found the Columbus Hospital emerging successfully from its first difficult period. It became known that when an Italian warship arrived in New York with two sailors on board suffering from typhoid, they were received by the Sisters after they had been refused elsewhere. When Admiral Manghi himself came to visit them, the hospital received a lot of useful publicity. Then the consul general, Giovanni Branchi, made an arrangement with Mother Cabrini under which any sick Italian sailor on a merchant vessel was to be received by her for a flat sum. It meant official recognition. The poor Italians resident in New York had already decided that they much preferred the Columbus Hospital to any other. Though its financial resources were still very limited, it was always crowded to the doors.

That it was going to be a success was now apparent. Looking round for the larger quarters that had become necessary, Francesca found them in the old Post Graduate Hospital on East Twentieth Street. It was a municipal institution, and the price at which it was offered—sixty thousand dollars—was so low as to be virtually a subsidy from the city. With a loan given by Dr. Charles Lewis, the secretary of her medical board, and another from the Emigrant Savings Bank, Francesca was able to buy it. She now had beds for a hundred patients.

But having bought the hospital, she saw that it needed some renovations. These, for the sake of economy, were supervised by the Sisters themselves—the chief foreman being that same nun whose first experiments in building, fourteen years earlier at Codogno, had resulted in the Building Commission stepping in. This time, as the nuns did not attempt any actual bricklaying, leaving that to the workmen employed, their efforts met with more success. A considerable saving of money was effected by these means, but only because unattached Italian laborers were employed. The labor unions would today promptly stop anything of the kind.

※ ※ ※

It was at this time that Francesca's old friend Monsignor Serrati died at Codogno, after a brief illness. She had had a presentiment of it, and for this reason she had been praying for the graces she believed him to need. When last writing to him, she spoke ardently of spiritual perfection. On the night on which he died, she was unable to sleep and so got up and prayed, holding her crucifix in her hands. At last the feeling was so strange that she was impelled to rise from her bedside and go to the chapel to continue the prayers for him there. Yet she had had no intimation that he was even unwell. The way she wrote about him afterward shows her admiration and gratitude and affection. Equally it shows that she did not quite rank him with that other great friend of her early years, Bishop Bersani. Monsignor Serrati she considered a very good man; but there was a difference between being a good man and a saint.

❦ ❦ ❦

While the renovation of the hospital on Twentieth Street was going on, the Sisters occupied the attic of the building as their dormitory. That the rain came through a hole in the roof did not greatly trouble them; they looked upon such discomforts as signs of blessings in store. Nor did those blessings fail to come.

One form they took was that the Italian community in the city organized subscriptions and arranged for celebrations for the raising of funds. Francesca had been quite right; the name of the Columbus Hospital made a powerful appeal to all the Italian factions. She was, however, unwilling to seek favor at all costs. The mere fact that one large donation had been raised at a meeting held on September 20, the day of the fall of Rome in 1870, was enough to make her refuse it. She did not feel that a loyal daughter of the pope could compromise herself even to that extent. It was something soon forgiven her by the Italian liberals. By way of making amends, a little while later they sent Francesca several truckloads of groceries and canned goods.

In March 1895, there came something much more important than these presents, welcome as they were. It was then that the State of New York gave the Columbus Hospital its formal approbation, legal incorporation being made on the 26th. This was decisive and silenced the last of the criticism. After that the hospital's future was assured. As soon as this recognition had been obtained, Francesca Cabrini set out for South America.

PART III

GOD'S GYPSY

Chapter Twelve

ACROSS THE ANDES

When Francesca established the Missionary Sisters in Nicaragua, in 1891, she had thought of that country as a connecting link between the two continents of the western
hemisphere. She had always intended to drive farther
south as soon as possible. Yet that she should so much as
think of doing this before her work in the United States
was fully consolidated struck many people as rash. Prudent
men—those to whom prudence means a timid and tepid
caution—were often to be alarmed by her impetuosity and
feared to be implicated in it. They now seemed to have a
justification for their misgivings—for the Nicaraguan convent had been forcibly closed by the government.

When opening the house at Granada, Francesca had
been well aware of the Latin American propensity for revolutions. Yet that one had occurred, and had apparently
ruined her work in Nicaragua, did not deter her from
making other foundations in South America. After all,
though Granada itself had been lost for the time being,
her nuns still had a "bridge-head" in Central America;
upon being expelled from Granada, they had settled at
Panama. Francesca meant to visit them there before going
on to the Argentine.

As she also wished to see how her mission at New Orleans was progressing, it was from there that she sailed. A

glance having satisfied her that all was well, she remained only a day or two. The only thing that was a little disturbing was that the Sisters at this mission seemed to have so few difficulties to contend with. "If all our foundations", she wrote in a letter, "were as easy as this one at New Orleans, I would fear that they were not sanctioned in heaven, for a little tribulation is very good and serves to form our souls and make them grow in the imitation of Christ." Francesca always used this yardstick for measuring the chances of success.

She was able to use this yardstick now, if only in a small way. The rain poured in such torrents on the morning she left the convent at New Orleans for the docks that the horses of her cab were almost blinded and there appeared to be a likelihood of her not getting to the boat before it sailed. And this would have happened had not Mr. Fallon, the local agent for the steamship line by which they were to travel, made sure that the boat would wait for her by himself arriving late. He did even more than that; he gave Francesca and her companion a free passage to Limón. It was one more instance of the unlooked-for favors from strangers that were showered upon her.

There were other favors. The captain of the boat put up an awning on the deck specially for the Sisters and instructed his personal attendant to see that they got everything they needed. Amid so much kindness, and on so smiling a sea, life seemed good indeed. Rather, to Francesca, the calm and beautiful weather in the Gulf and on the Caribbean appeared, as it always did to her, an image of the serenity of a soul obedient to God. When storms came, she was able to accept them as a trial sent by God for which she should be grateful; on blue, glittering seas she was grateful for God's blessings. With these considerations she pointed the moral for her daughters when she wrote to them.

Everybody on board was so very friendly that she even had hopes for the conversion of the Swedish crew. She saw that they had excellent qualities, being sober and industrious and respectful. It caused her regret that she was unable to talk to these efficient and reliable men. But she gave them religious medals, telling them that these had been blessed by the pope, and noted approvingly that they put their emblems away carefully so as to be able to use them in times of danger.

Everything glowed on that gentle sea under that benignant sun. In the sanguine mood that she felt, she expressed her confidence that Protestants would soon be coming in large numbers into the Catholic Church. A trifle naïvely, she accounted for the continuance of Protestantism on the ground that its ministers had to keep things going so as to secure their own "huge salaries". Particularly did she have great hopes for England, thinking of the High Anglican movement. But her hopes were hardly less rosy for the United States. "I have personal proof of this," she assured the Sisters to whom she was writing, "for the best news I could give the twelve doctors of our hospital in New York was that I had the blessing and encouragement of the Holy Father. So also a number of pious objects blessed by the Holy Father were the gifts most appreciated by some Protestant people. It seems as though we are in a new era, an era of peace in which many people will bend their heads to the Cross and Gospel of Christ." And so no doubt it would be if the world contained more people like herself. It delighted her to observe how attentively the crew listened to the nuns when they sang the *Veni Creator* and the *Ave Maris Stella.* "Poor things!" she commented. "What a pity we cannot instruct them."

❦ ❦ ❦

At Port Limón, an uncle of the president of Costa Rica suggested that while they were waiting for the coastal vessel to take them to Colón, they ought to seize the opportunity of visiting the capital of the country, San José. He told them that Limón was unhealthy and that he had a sister at San José who was wealthy and pious and who would be glad to receive them into her house; thus they would be spared hotel expenses. As Francesca was always anxious to see everything with a view to possible future operations, she accepted this invitation. To facilitate the matter, Mr. Fallon, who had already been so courteous, saw to it that the nuns got a free passage to San José.

Then, just as they were on the point of leaving for that city, an emissary from the governor presented himself. After florid compliments, he came to the point: "I am sorry, Mother," he said, "but I am under instructions to forbid your entrance farther into our country. You must remain here."

Francesca's eyes flashed; she was never inclined to accept such orders tamely. She insisted on knowing why.

He explained. "Are you not the Missionary Sisters of the Sacred Heart?"

"Yes", she admitted.

"Then that shows that you are closely associated with the Jesuits. Jesuits are excluded from Costa Rica. That is the law."

Francesca threw back her head and laughed heartily. She saw her institute was being confused in the official mind with the Religious of the Sacred Heart. But she did not bother to explain the distinction to one who would probably not have understood it.

She did, however, call on the governor, as he lived near the hotel where they had spent the night. He was courteous and apologetic and told her how she might get around the regulation. Again Francesca flared up.

"No, Your Excellency," she said, "I am not going to crawl into your country on a subterfuge." With that quiet decision which, when she displayed it, was quite implacable, she added, "I don't believe I really want to see your country. You boast of your progress and yet have laws quite contrary to the liberty of which you boast."

He tried to soothe her with compliments and explanations, but she told him, "In my case, your laws are most inhuman. My companion is making her first visit to a torrid region; yet you compel us to remain here where the climate is so unhealthy instead of letting us go to San José."

The poor governor—a large, fussy, puffy man—was greatly embarrassed on being talked to like this by the fiery little nun, so he called a meeting of his council that night. In the morning, he came with word that it had been decided that she might go to the capital. But by now Francesca thought she had a good opportunity of showing the authorities that she was not dependent upon the favor of anticlericals. When she told him so, he and the local politicians were all very much upset, as they saw that they had created a bad impression that they could not remove.

Content with her tactical victory, Francesca remained on the low shore of Limón instead of going to the high lands of the west where the capital was situated. She noted that, though the Costa Ricans claimed to be more purely Spanish in blood than any other of the Central or South American nations, religion was almost completely ignored by them. She set this down to the Masonic influence among their leading men and to their superstitious regard for what they liked to describe as progress. When she and her companion went to Mass on Sunday—it was

Whitsunday, a special day with Francesca because of her
devotion to that "most valiant and tender of friends, the
Holy Ghost"—almost the only other worshippers present were some West Indian Blacks who had settled in
Costa Rica.

These, however, were very pious, and she had pleasure in talking with them after Mass—the French she had
learned at school now being useful. A still greater pleasure was hers that day. The month of May, dedicated
to the Blessed Virgin, was closing with the crowning of
the statue of Our Lady by a little colored girl in a white
dress. After that all the women there led up their children,
each of whom laid a flower before Mary's image. It was
a charming scene, made all the more picturesque by the
bright dresses and gay kerchiefs on the heads of the Black
women. The faces of these people, she thought, might
be black, but their souls, shining through their eyes, were
white with candid innocence and simplicity. "Mary", she
wrote, "seemed to rejoice and extend her heavenly mantle over them." She remembered that Our Lady was the
Mother and Foundress of the institute: "Under her aus-
pices, we have an abundance of grace that she continually
showers upon her children."

The enforced idleness of those days in Limón was harder
to bear than the scorching heat. Francesca never was able to
sit doing nothing. But the two nuns found the balcony of
their room in the hotel, from which they could gaze over
the sea, a good place for meditation. Some of the things
she thought of there she passed on to the Sisters in Codogno. "Very often," she told them, "our prayers are imperfect and deserve to be rejected by God; but the loving
heart of Jesus rectifies and adjusts them. He Himself asks
for us what He sees will be for our greater good and com-
passionately covers our unworthiness with His merits."

And she quoted Christ's saying to Saint Gertrude: "Here is my heart; avail yourself of it to make good what is deficient in your prayers." By jotting down such reflections, she felt she might do some little good while waiting for the boat.

Just before it was due, two representatives of the president arrived with copious apologies. One of them was thin and silent, the other rotund and loquacious. "It was all a mistake," his loquacity explained, "an unhappy misunderstanding. You may go to San José and anywhere else you wish, and everywhere you will be very welcome. Look, Mother, we have brought you a free railway pass, good for anywhere in Costa Rica. Now you stay awhile—yes?"

Francesca was rather touched and might have relented had not all this come too late. She was impatient to get to Panama. She explained this to her visitors and added, "But please thank the president for his courtesy. As the ticket has been made out in my name, I will keep it as a souvenir." With that the diplomatic incident ended.

In the diary-letter she wrote about this time, Francesca gave an account of the expulsion of the nuns from Granada. At first things had gone very well. In fact, on July 2, 1892, she had written to Archbishop Corrigan to let him know that she had just received word that the government of Nicaragua had agreed to pay all the expenses of an orphanage. But it seems that shortly after the Zelaya revolution, a young society woman had been converted and wished to enter the institute. As permission had first to be received from Francesca, the prospective postulant went to stay in retirement with Doña Elena Arellano, the benefactress of the convent. Her friends and relatives were annoyed at this and accused the Sisters of having brought undue pressure upon her. Their charges were used as the pretext of the expulsion, though President Zelaya had promised that he would protect the nuns.

He seems to have been an extremely slippery person. For when the local superior called on him to protest, she was received with every mark of esteem and fresh promises of protection. The next week the president even sent the Sisters a case of books that they could use as prizes for their pupils and a letter assuring them of his good will. Despite all this, the next month—on August 22—the convent received a visit from the newly appointed governor of the city and the prefect of police. The governor, wearing the worried look of determined incompetence, told the nuns that they had to leave at once. A steamer was waiting for them in the harbor to deport them. To expedite their departure, they were sent not by way of Corinto, but by the river route to San Juan del Norte.

The superior exclaimed, "But we cannot go just yet! Two of our Sisters are ill in bed."

The prefect of police was immovable. "I'm sorry, madame, but I cannot extend the time. You must go now."

The convent had been surrounded by soldiers to prevent any appeal being sent to the president. None of the pupils was allowed to leave until the nuns had departed. And when their parents came to protest, the officer in charge of the soldiers told them that he would give the order to fire if there was any disturbance. One by one the nuns were counted and passed out, to make sure that none was overlooked.

It was a scene of wild hysteria on the part of the children and their mothers, only the soldiers remaining cold and grim, only the nuns remaining undisturbed. The Sisters were given just two hours to get ready and could do no more than pack a few articles of clothing in suitcases.

Then the prefect of police bundled them into carriages, and between two lines of soldiers they were taken away. It was all very different from the guard of honor they had been given on their arrival, though the soldiers were the same men.

A large crowd followed them to the boat crying out that for this the wrath of God would descend on Nicaragua. The demonstration did no good. When they arrived at the port, a cordon was thrown round the carriages to prevent the crowd approaching. Then the Sisters were taken out and again counted one by one. So as to try to justify an anticlerical outburst on the ground of the alleged abduction of the young woman who wanted to become a nun, the chaplain of the convent and the parish priest were exiled to Corinto. Even Doña Elena had to leave the country. But the authorities were most careful not to institute any kind of legal proceedings.

There was one amusing incident. One of the Sisters, just as she was about to get into the waiting carriage, remembered that she had left her slippers in her room. The procession had to be held up until she had retrieved them. That became a family joke often recalled. Whenever Mother Cabrini wished to remind her nuns not to forget anything she used to say, "And be sure that you don't leave your slippers behind!"

Two things more consoling happened. The Indians of the village of Rama sent the Sisters what was for them a large sum of money, and one of the parents of some children at the school, Don Constantino Motonco, made it his business to collect whatever bills were owing the nuns from other parents who had children there. His conduct stood out in resplendent contrast to that of the boorish administration.

But there was something even better than that. A Don José Pasos, a man well-known for his anticlerical sentiments, was one of those who helped to expel the nuns. Sitting on his horse, he watched them pass in single file, pale but collected and each one carrying a crucifix. He then overheard one of the children say to a nun, "Mother, you are not crying! You are leaving us so calmly. It is *we* who are desolate." The answer came, with a gesture toward the crucifix; "We arrived with Him, and we are leaving with Him." This so touched Don José that he spent the whole of that night in thought. Next day he took all the certificates and decorations he had received from the Masonic society and handed them over to the bishop of León. Eight months later, Francesca was able to report of him that he was still exemplary in the practice of his religion, rising at four every morning to pray and going to Mass and Communion at six.

The government soon became ashamed of its treatment of the Sisters. But though the president himself wrote begging for their return, Francesca decided that a man of this sort was not to be trusted. Moreover, it would be as well to give the Nicaraguan anticlericals a lesson. They had lost the best school at Granada, and now at leisure they might repent their loss. The Sisters had reestablished themselves at Panama, and they were not to be lured back. When in 1912 the request was repeated, Francesca replied that she would be glad to go back—but only on condition that the Sisters receive adequate compensation for the treatment they had received. It was not until after her death, and then through the diplomatic efforts of her friend Pope Benedict XV, that the Missionary Sisters again went to Nicaragua. Then they settled not in Granada, but in Managua, where instead of an academy they opened a college.

When Francesca reached Panama, she was enthusiastic in her descriptions of the new convent. It overlooked the sea and was lovely, she said. "One could imagine oneself to be on board a steamer, because on the south and southwest it is surrounded by the sea, whose proud waves beat against the walls of our garden, throwing a spray of water whiter than milk, with small pebbles that the children think look like sweets. The room the Sisters have prepared for me is surrounded on two sides by large orange trees, the fruit of which touches my window sill. One looks out on a path leading to the sea and its beautiful isles that seem to be playing in the bay.... In our garden we have six kinds of palms, bananas, and coffee-trees and various kinds of fruit, the names of which I do not know." It was all a riot of exotic color.

In a letter written a little later, she appears to be making some reference to the unfortunate Nicaraguan venture in saying: "If sometimes things were not so successful, it was because I acted too much on my own initiative." But Jesus and Mary, who had seen her through thousands of difficulties, were not going to abandon her now. If there was any touch of self-reproach in this, it was hardly necessary. The Sisters were better off at Panama than they had been at Nicaragua. And so far from having really failed in Nicaragua, Francesca had prepared the way for the great work she was to do in the Argentine and Brazil. What is surprising, however, is that she—an Italian and the head of an order that was so far wholly made up of Italians—should venture to establish schools in countries where Spanish and Portuguese were the native languages. For though she did not neglect her compatriots in South America, it was not primarily for their benefit that she went there. Francesca's Central and South American schools were of the select sort attended by children of well-to-do families. One concludes that it was her deliberate intention not to be confined to one particular type of educational work.

On the Panamanian isthmus, Francesca felt herself to be at the very apex of the world. "The position of the house is such", she wrote, "that I imagine I can see every part of the world in this immense space of water in front of me." The sight of the sea made her wish to take the first ship she could get and set out on a mission. So consuming was her ardor that she wanted to be at every part of the world at once. "The calls are many," she added, "and as I cannot go to all the places where we are needed, as commanded by Rome, I will do my best to comply with obedience so far as this lies within my power."

She had already decided, however, where she was going next. This was to Buenos Aires, where she had been invited to open a school by its archbishop. Her plan was to strike down the coast of South America to Chile and from there cross the Andes to the Argentine. With Mother Chiara as her traveling companion, she set out on October 11, 1895, after four and a half months at Panama. It was to be the longest and the most adventurous of all her journeys.

Her parting from the Sisters and the pupils at Panama, which she was never to visit again, was sad to everybody. But by now Francesca was eager to be off, as she was satisfied that things were going well. She had enjoyed her stay in this beautifully located house, even though its peace had been slightly disturbed by the fact that thirty girls practiced the piano every day and twelve others had singing lessons. "You can imagine our eardrums!" was her comment. Even so, the girls had endeared themselves to her, and she to them. Everybody who went on board to see her off was in tears.

The students of the academy were able to go on board the ship itself for the goodbye because the father of one of them, Don Ernesto Icaso, had put his private launch at their disposal. He was one of the committee of parents who, before the evening of Francesca's departure, came to assure her that they would continue to give wholehearted support to the school. As a final touch of courtesy, Don Ernesto gave the nuns tickets he had bought for them. They were for communicating cabins opening on the deck.

Mother Chiara went to bed immediately after supper, though first having said some prayers with Francesca. Then the General of the Missionary Sisters sat alone on board looking toward the lighthouse of Panama and fancying that, if she turned her gaze a little to the left, she could see the nuns at their recreation gazing in her direction. She also fancied she could see all five lamps burning in the chapel, three before the Blessed Sacrament and one each before the altars of the Blessed Virgin and Saint Joseph. It seemed to her that the lamps themselves wished to unite with the Sisters in praying for a good voyage. Hardheaded and practical as she was, she liked to indulge now and then in such pretty sentimentalities. They were a kind of relief in a life so full of realistic considerations. When at nine thirty that night the boat began to move, she continued to stay on deck, straining her eyes to the left of the lighthouse. But soon there was an impenetrable blackness, and Francesca retired to her berth.

A few days later, she crossed the equator for the first time. To her astonishment, she found the weather so cold that she thought the ship must be nearing the North Pole. Everybody had to put on winter underwear and to sleep under mounds of blankets at night. But Francesca did not mind this inconvenience, for off Ecuador she was on a line with the birthplace of Blessed Mariana of Quito, to whom she was praying hard for the success of her South American mission. The passengers, too, were in high spirits, being much amused at a lady who wished to see the line of the equator. To make sure that this would happen, a wag on board gave her a pair of binoculars across whose lenses he had put a thread. "Why, I can see it quite plainly!" she exclaimed, greatly to their delight.

The ship stopped at Guayaquil, but Francesca did not go on shore; she was content to look at the town from the ship. "Having at present no business in Ecuador," she curtly comments, "I simply pray the Blessed Mariana to obtain that it may again be illuminated with the light and faith of former days." Of all South American countries, Ecuador was then perhaps the most addicted to revolutions and new constitutions. Since the assassination of Gabriel Garcia Moreno, the so-called "Jesuit President", at the beginning of his third term of office, a "liberal" reaction had set in, and that meant confiscation of Church property and the expulsion of all religious. Francesca had met a group of ejected Ecuadorian nuns in Panama. At this time, the country was without a president at all, for the contending parties were still fighting it out.

Yet even at Guayaquil she was invited to stay. Some priests came on board to see her and were followed by the governor of the province and the mayor, both of whom were lavish with promises. In spite of the unsettled state of the country, they thought this a good chance to get a good school for their daughters. But Francesca could do no more than give them her address and say that perhaps at some future date she might be able to make a foundation there. When a flock of white birds whirled around their heads, Mother Chiara asked what this could mean. "Oh," said Francesca playfully, "they are inviting us to Ecuador as the birds did three years ago at Panama. We will go there when we can." At that time she was not willing to land even to hear Mass and receive Communion.

The slow journey down the coast was dull, for there were no trees or grass or rivers to be seen from the ship—nothing but parched hills and deserts of scrub. But the former geographer seized the opportunity of writing a little lecture, as though for the classroom, on the real wealth of these lands—the guano deposited by millions of seabirds. And when she did see anything that was unusual—such as the barrel-like contrivance with which passengers at the port of Salaverri were taken off or put on board—that went down for the entertainment of Codogno. She watched a huckster who had managed to get upon the ship ejected by being put into a sack and dumped on the wharf. He was evidently accustomed to this sort of thing, for whereas those in the barrel went pale with fright, he got out as fresh as a rose.

🍂 🍂 🍂

At last they got to Callao, and Francesca took advantage of what was to be a long stop to make a visit to Lima. There the two nuns went at once to the Dominican church, where Saint Rose was buried, for Francesca had made a vow to receive Communion in this very place. She was delighted that at the altar where they heard Mass there was a statue of the Infant Jesus. He seemed to be smiling at her and saying, "It is here that I have waited to favor you, through the merits of my dear Rose, whom you have come to honor."

The Dominican Fathers took them around afterward, and they prayed at the altar where Saint Rose's head was venerated. It was contained in a silver urn, placed above another urn that held the remains of Blessed Martin de Porres, the Black lay brother. But Saint Rose was somewhat

gruesomely distributed in bits over that church and another.
In one of the chapels was the crucifix the saint had used,
and on each side of its altar was one of her arms.

Francesca was inclined to be a trifle critical of Spanish-
American modes of piety, especially of the gaudily dressed
images in the churches; but she made no comments aloud,
reserving them for her letter. When she saw some women
praying in turn with their fingers over the mouth of a
leaden pipe that was enclosed in the column where the
holy-water font was placed and asked what they were
doing, she allowed herself to show no surprise when they
replied, "Don't you know that if you say an Our Father
with your finger there you can get a soul out of Purgatory?" Not to embarrass them, she also said an Our Father
for the Holy Souls with her finger on the pipe. But for the
benefit of those in Codogno she remarked, "I never heard
of any such devotion!"

Francesca also visited other parts of the city, but partly,
as she said, in order to have something to write about to
her daughters in Italy. In one church—the only one she
saw in which there were no dressed-up statues—she found
an image of Saint Margaret Mary, one of the patrons of
her order. That pleased her, as did the cordiality of the
Jesuits and the Religious of the Sacred Heart. But though
she wanted to see the cathedral, she was advised not to go
there; she was told that it had been half ruined by the can-
non fire directed against it during a recent revolution. She
explained: "One of the first acts of these revolutionaries is
always to attack the cathedral of a town, and the first of the
two hostile parties who gains its possession is considered
the victor." That may have been an over-simplification,
and she charitably concludes, "Perhaps their intentions are
good, but those who are declared the victors have the good
fortune to secure the sanctuary for themselves. However,

we cannot deny that they deface God's temple and destroy the most beautiful monuments. They say *adelantados mucho*, which means very enlightened, but to tell the truth their customs and manners are those of the aboriginal Indians."

Again there was a dull stretch of coastline after they had rejoined the ship. But after that there began the coast range of the Cordilleras, mountains rising abruptly from the sea, low enough as compared to the main Andes running parallel in the interior, but still very impressive. Concerning this geographical feature we are given another informative lecture. Stopping frequently and taking its time, the ship made its way to Valparaiso; and from there the two nuns crossed the plains to Santiago at the foot of the Andes. It was from this point that they had to make the passage of the mountains.

The archbishop assumed an authoritative tone and told them that they had better stay in Santiago for several months. They needed rest. Meanwhile they could look around and settle on a place in which to make a foundation. It was from him that they heard that the archbishop of Buenos Aires had recently died, so he argued that there was not much use in Francesca's going there now. A political leader of Chile put the matter in a somewhat different way. He had a little girl of four and would be soon wanting a school for her. He said to Francesca, "So you're going to Argentina, Mother. Well, you had better be back within two years; because if you're not, we shall make war on the Argentinians and take you prisoner. Then we shall *make* you open a school here."

Mother Cabrini laughed. She found these Chileans very friendly, but to have to wait twenty-five days in Santiago seemed to her sheer waste of time. The fact that the archbishop of Buenos Aires had died made her all the more anxious to reach that city. He had invited her, and she wished to find out what kind of a welcome she would get from his successor. However, there was nothing for it but to wait. The Andes were blocked with snow, and the first caravan of the season would not start till later. Even so, she was warned that this first crossing was likely to be extremely dangerous. Such warnings were useless: Francesca felt that nothing could induce her to continue her inactivity. Any difficulty and danger rather than that!

One day while she was praying at a chapel of Saint Philomena the Wonder Worker—a shadowy figure of ancient times about whom nothing definite is known, but who is celebrated for the answers she gives to prayer—Francesca heard a gentle voice whispering in her ear, "This is only a small offering." She was so absorbed that she thought at first that the voice was only in her imagination. Then the words were repeated, and she turned around and saw a little old priest, who turned out to be Canon Pereira, the guardian of the shrine. He was holding out a gold coin and saying, "Take this small offering in honor of Saint Philomena." The saint had begun to help before Francesca had finished asking for help! Afterward the Canon gave her a picture of Philomena and told her: "Keep it in your pocketbook, and you will never be in need of money for your order." From that day, the Missionary Sisters had a new patron.

❦ ❦ ❦

According to her custom, Francesca had selected as her traveling companion a nun who would be of little use elsewhere but who would equally be of little use to her. Mother Chiara was a sick and timid woman, and one is sorry for her being taken on such a journey. But Francesca gave her the choice of going round Cape Horn or of crossing the Andes, and each time—even at the last moment—she said she preferred the mountains a hundred times to the sea. So on November 24 they set out to cross the Andes.

The first stage of the journey was made by train. It wound around the mountains by the edge of enormous gorges. One of these, called the Soldier's Leap, which they traversed by a bridge, was so deep and narrow that they could not see the bottom. Only the faint rumbling of water could be heard in the fearful depths below.

Shortly afterward, the train reached what was then the farthest point of the railway and the passengers were transferred to clanking coaches, each drawn by six mules. These followed the course of the river along a winding road that had a sheer drop into the chasm where the water swirled and foamed. There was no vegetation except here and there some pines of harsh dark green. This was the beginning of Cumbre Pass, over which the volcano Aconcagua rose nearly 23,000 feet above the level of the sea.

Francesca pitied Mother Chiara when they sat down to a badly cooked supper, but so much had the air sharpened their appetites that they ate it and the black bread as though it were the daintiest food. Again when Francesca asked her if she would not have rather gone by the Straits of Magellan, she got the answer, "No, this is a thousand times better!" And Francesca said to herself, "All is well."

So for the moment it was. After they had eaten their meal, they went into the brilliant moonlight. The mountains appeared to touch the sky and to be covered with a beautiful blue mantle. Francesca noted that the earth had the color of the sky, while the spaces between the mountains wore a blue of a darker shade. The night, she thought, represented the beauty of Mary, *pulchra ut luna*,

who had come as a mother to comfort them. "We wanted
to prepare the points for our meditation," she wrote; "but
nature had already prepared them for us." Happy and at
peace, they went to the inn where they were to sleep.

To their surprise they found a bed with good springs prepared for them. And a kindly old muleteer, who they decided looked like Saint Joseph, showed them how they
could bar themselves in for the night. He told them, too,
that if they wanted anything, they would find him in the
mules' stable. The night passed in a moment, so tired were
they, and they woke at half-past three when they heard
the mounts being saddled. The nuns prepared themselves
for the crossing by putting on long brown hooded capes
lined with fur given them by the ladies in Santiago. They
fancied they now looked like Capuchin friars.

It was then that the worst part of the journey began. Immediately after breakfast they set out. And when Francesca
saw a couple of fine mules saddled for women riders, she
supposed that these were for an opera singer and her companion who were in the party. Not at all. The superintendent of the Transandine Company had sent orders that the
best mules were to be given to the nuns. To that, however, there was a drawback; it meant that they would have
to head the cavalcade and mount first. This was something
Francesca would have preferred to see somebody else do
before attempting it, as it was outside her experience. The
Saint Joseph of the previous evening came with clasped
hands to put under her feet to hoist her into the saddle,
but she refused his help. The tiny Francesca had to be got
there by means of a chair.

For an hour, the road looked so easy and the cavalcade
so much like a religious procession that Mother Cabrini

was just on the point of taking out her rosary and inviting everybody to join her when the beaten path suddenly disappeared and they had to push their way through deep snow. Two muleteers went on in advance to show the way, as this often went along the very edge of a precipice. Francesca did her best to drag her mule's head away and shouted at it such Spanish words of warning as she knew. It was in vain that she tried *"Suficiente! Lentamente!"* The mule, which seemed to know that it had an unexpert rider on its back, would take no notice, however hard the reins were tugged, but placidly looked over the precipice and made its own way ahead. Its feelings were a little hurt when the terrified Francesca attempted to alight. As for poor Mother Chiara, she simply lay like a sack of flour on the back of her mule.

Gradually they went higher and higher, and then the muleteer who had gone ahead called to them that they were all to alight. Something was the matter. Mother Chiara was too frightened to say a word, but Francesca knew that she was now repenting for having chosen to go by the Andes instead of Cape Horn. Francesca herself felt uplifted by the magnificence of the spectacle—an immense abyss on one side, a wide expanse of glittering snow on the other, and farther ahead the jagged heights they still had to climb.

Just in front—this was why the muleteer had shouted to them to dismount—was a long deep crevice, which looked quite ready to swallow them all. By way of making a test, the men managed to get some of the mules to jump across and then told the travelers they would have to do the same. As Francesca was at the head of the cavalcade, she had to make the first jump, and in order to encourage the others, she was perfectly willing to do so. She was sure that she would get across easily.

But this did not happen. The intense breathless cold had
drained her of strength, and, no sooner had she jumped,
than she felt like a feather that, however hard it is thrown
forward, does not move unless it has a wind behind it. She
would have gone clear down the chasm had her muleteer not been watching. He contrived to throw his body
across and catch her before she fell. Then with the aid of
his staff and that of his comrade, he succeeded in straight-
ening himself up and drawing the frightened nun to the
other side. She had such a shock that she thought she was
dying and fell fainting into a snowbank. When she came
to, she found that all her companions had made the leap
without mishap, and her muleteer was waiting to help her
to mount again. But she still refused to do it by standing
on his clasped hands. Her fastidiousness, her *casto pudore*,
would not permit this. As the chair was not available, a
boulder had to be found from which she could get back
on her mule.

Francesca soon recovered from her fright and was admiring the grandeur of the scenery with a pleasure as keen
as before. But when she was given clouded glasses to protect her from the glare of the snow, she preferred to be
without them so as to be able to see better where her mule
was going. The glasses were more often on her forehead
or her chin than her nose.

They were by now so high up, though this was a pass,
that they felt almost able to take in the whole wide world
at a glance. Here was the boundary between Chile and the
Argentine. From that point they began to descend, but
through falling feathery snow, to the inn where they were
to have their lunch. An employee sent by the Transandine
Company took the bridle-reins of Francesca's mule and
led it down the path. Everybody was very much surprised
that, when she was asked to write something in the visitor's

book, she actually found something enthusiastic to say. She was the first person, they said, who had ever spoken well of the crossing. It was all the more remarkable because the writer was not a man, and the journey had been made at the worst time of the year. But Francesca had thoroughly enjoyed the adventure. "The fact is", she noted in her letter, "that I was very pleased to have ascended such high mountains, which gave me an inducement to incite myself to ascend the heights of spiritual perfection, a peak much higher than any in the Andes."

❧ ❧ ❧

Yet there was a final bit of unpleasantness. At Punta de Vaca, where they were to spend the night, they found that all the beds in the inn had been taken by a cavalcade coming from the Argentine side. There was nowhere for the nuns to sit but the bar, which was full of men drinking hard and, as the night wore on, getting very tipsy and noisy. When the innkeeper was appealed to, he said all he could give them was a bed in the hall, which of course they could not accept. They resigned themselves to sitting up all night, but did not relish the prospect in such company.

Fortunately there was an American from San Francisco in their party, and the nuns begged him to sit with them for the sake of protection. Like them, he had been unable to get a bed. But though he got none for himself, he found a means—possibly by using a few good American dollars—to get one for them. Two ladies who had obtained a room and had a small boy sleeping with them were persuaded to take them in. The boy was put into the bed in the hall, and Mother Cabrini and Mother Chiara fell upon their bed, where they lay exhausted and motionless until the morning.

Chapter Thirteen

THE INTERNATIONAL SCOPE

Francesca Cabrini concluded the long diary-letter of her journey with the words, written after her arrival in Buenos Aires: "Prayer, confidence, and total abandonment to God will always be our arms. We are good for nothing.... But I can do all things in Him who strengtheneth me." The Pauline maxim that she had made her own was her sole support now.

She found herself in a city where she was completely unknown. The archbishop who had invited her to come had died; the new archbishop was a stranger, and she had no reason to suppose he would be favorable to her. She had, it is true, been given some letters of introduction in Panama and had received others at different points on her journey. These were her only credentials. She had no idea whether they would be accepted or how she would be received. When she arrived at the capital on December 1, after a train journey across the Pampas, she fortunately remembered that there was a Father Broggi there who had once said Mass at her convent at Genoa a couple of years previously. At once she took a cab and went in search of him. By making enquiries at several convents and churches, he was located after a couple of hours.

He welcomed the two nuns kindly, gave them an excellent dinner *à l'Italien*, and took them to see the new archbishop, Ladislao Castellano. Upon him of course everything depended.

On his part there was no lack of cordiality. He received Francesca like a father and said he would be delighted to give all the support that his predecessor had promised, adding that he was glad he could begin his episcopate with a foundation of a house of the Missionary Sisters.

His vicar-general, Monsignor Espinosa, who was present at the interview, was equally encouraging. By way of doing something practical, he gave her a number of his visiting cards with permission to present them to prominent families of the city; and when Francesca asked, "Would you not write something on them as an introduction, Monsignor?" he answered, "Mother, you may write anything you like."

The two nuns had reached the episcopal palace at a moment when it was full of priests, who were visiting Buenos Aires to join in a procession about to be made to the shrine of Our Lady of Lujan. This was in honor of the new archbishop of Chile and to celebrate the peace that had just been effected between his country and the Argentine. Because of this, Mother Cabrini met on the very day of her arrival all the most influential clergy of the diocese. It was very fortunate for her; these men took to her at once, and they were the men in the best position to be of help.

The help she needed, or the promise of it, came at once. Francesca's famous charm, something of which she was altogether unconscious, again brought everybody under her spell. These new acquaintances came forward with offers of service. The forlorn condition of the two Italian nuns in a strange city made an appeal to their chivalry. It was even a little comical the way they told her, "Mother, don't look so timid and troubled; we'll see you through!" or "Courage, Mother; we will help you!" She may have

seemed slightly bewildered that day, but never had she
lacked courage. These priests had met Francesca Cabrini;
they had still to get to know her.

Father Broggi was especially useful. For that night he
found them rooms with an Italian family, and the next
day he got the Sisters of Mercy to take them in until they
were established in their own convent. Then every day he
used to conduct them around the city, introducing them
to such people as it might be well for them to know.

In a case like this, it was Francesca's practice to visit
all sections of a great city before deciding upon the quarter that would be best for her purpose. In Los Angeles,
some years later, she trudged on foot the whole length
of its enormous boulevards—not so endless as they are
now, but already very long—so as to make quite sure that
she had seen everything. So now she went out each day
in Buenos Aires, coming back to the Sisters of Mercy in
the evening very tired and with her shoes soon worn
into holes. Sixty possible houses were inspected by her
before she picked out one at the center of the city for
her school.

As soon as it was known what she was about to do, a
number of the ladies whom she had got to know through
Father Broggi and the vicar-general called on her. They
were all volubly emphatic. "But Mother," they protested,
"you are making a great mistake. That place is much too
expensive. We know conditions, and you must allow
yourself to be guided by us. For the first couple of years,
you cannot expect to get more than six or seven pupils.
So you had better begin in a small way and go slowly. If
you rent that house, you'll be ruined."

Francesca listened to them and then said, "It's very kind
of you to tell me all this. But I have a secret inspiration for

which I cannot account. I have decided to take that house at any price."

They threw up their hands and gave her up as a hopeless case.

Her decision, however, turned out to be very shrewd. As was so often true of her, what seemed to be rashness proved to be acumen. "The courage", she was able to write later, "shown in undertaking a difficult enterprise made a good impression on the people, so much so that the principal families brought us their children; and this went on so well that, when we left, the academy was already full and I had to arrange for a second and larger house." That anybody—especially that any woman—should show such energy and enterprise was astounding to the Argentinians.

Father Broggi was not only astounded at Francesca's audacity; he was dismayed by it. When she showed him the cables she was about to send to New York and Italy ordering Sisters to come immediately to Buenos Aires, he exclaimed, "Mother, what *are* you doing? I simply cannot understand on what you are counting. You have not only taken that expensive house but now you send for Sisters without waiting to see how things are going to turn out. Please, please wait, and don't do anything so rash."

Francesca merely smiled. "Don't worry, Father", she said. "If I were to think too much about procuring the means, the Lord would withhold His graces. Just send the cables for me."

That was always her method; she did make her calculations, but they were not always of the kind that she could explain to people like Father Broggi. When she saw a piece of work that needed to be done, she prepared to do it, without waiting to include in her preparations everything that she knew would eventually be necessary. She was sure that what she needed would be forthcoming, and she refused to delay merely because it was not at hand at the outset.

On Christmas Day she took possession of the house. The Sisters of Mercy did their best to keep their guest with them at least until the Feast was over. But Christmas seemed too good a day for Francesca not to make a start then, and nothing could hold her back. All she would take with her was a little hamper of food. She wanted the founder of her first South American establishment to be the Infant Jesus, before whose image she had prayed in Lima. She used to say that he was the cardinal protector of her institute. Its patroness was Saint Rose of Lima, the first canonized saint of the New World—a happy choice, as Saint Rose is also the patroness of the Americas. That, too, made a splendid impression on the people of Buenos Aires.

She and Mother Chiara lost no time in setting to work to get the house ready for the Sisters for whom she had sent. One day the archbishop called, and Francesca let him in. He did not recognize her at first—or pretended not to—with an apron on and a broom and duster in her hands. "I should like to see your Mother General", he said.

"Certainly, Your Excellency", Francesca replied. "Please take a seat in the parlor and I will call her."

A few minutes later she returned, minus her broom and apron, and with face and hands washed. How the archbishop laughed!

It was much the same thing when the Sisters arrived from New York, a few days before they had been expected. They found her with a market-basket over her arm and one of the orphans she had already picked up walking by her side. She kissed them cordially—and at once set them to work, while she hurried off to buy groceries. Never was she the kind of superior who would allow herself to be let off her share of domestic duties.

As the Sisters had got to Buenos Aires three days before the announced schedule, she decided that she would open the school two weeks earlier than she had intended. Though one cannot quite follow her arithmetic, it was things like this that explain her success. The easygoing Argentinians gasped before her decision and energy.

She was a witness, just after her arrival, of the strikingly Christian fashion in which Chile and Argentina settled a boundary dispute. War had threatened but had been averted. Now the archbishops of Chile and Buenos Aires made a pilgrimage together to the shrine of Our Lady of Lujan. With them went the minister of the interior, who was acting for the president. The vicar-general of Valparaiso made an eloquent address that was frequently applauded. The cheers were especially loud when he said that, as Chile could give nothing worthy of the Blessed Virgin, whose statue was already covered with gold from head to foot, he thought the best offering he could make was the flag of Chile as a sign of peaceful accord. Francesca felt slightly scandalized at the loud shouts of *Viva Maria* in a church, as though a political meeting were in progress, but sensibly concluded that this was, after all, a good way to handle disputes, "for it leads the rulers to decide the destinies of the people in God's own sanctuary." She made allowances for the fact that the South American temperament was different from the Italian. The settlement is now commemorated by the famous statue of the Christ of the Andes.

The preparations for the opening of the school were hurried on. Though Francesca knew very little Spanish, she nevertheless set herself to produce the necessary prospectuses until a priest came to her rescue. She furthermore insisted on a musical program being got ready, although there were as yet no students enrolled. "But Mother," protested the music teacher, "how can we even begin until we have the girls?" The answer was, "You prepare the songs, and the girls will come."

Francesca was right. The girls did come. The academy was opened on March 1, with the wife of José Evaristo Uriburu, the president of the nation, acting as chief sponsor. The mayor of the city, Señor Euoje, sent the public gardeners to decorate the house and the altar of the Sacred Heart with flowers and wreaths. And the head of the Catholic Club had men put up curtains and lay down carpets. The archbishop pontificated at Mass and his vicar-general delivered the sermon. Nothing more could have been done in the form of official recognition.

The success of the school was assured from the first day, when fifty students were enrolled. Francesca waited only to be perfectly certain that the new foundation was operating smoothly. As soon as she was satisfied about this, she sailed for Italy.

❧ ❧ ❧

One constantly has to look in dumbfounded wonder at Francesca Cabrini. That she should have accepted a mission among the dispersed Italians of the United States is understandable; this was something that could only have been undertaken by somebody like herself. But that she should have immediately afterward established select schools in Spanish-speaking Argentina—and soon after that in Portuguese-speaking Brazil—would appear to be well-nigh incomprehensible. Perhaps a few of her nuns in Italy knew a little Spanish, and those who had been in Nicaragua had learned that language after a fashion. But one would suppose that the giving of a general education—especially to girls of wealthy families that demanded the best—would have been utterly beyond them. The explanation that there were a great many Italians in both of these South American countries, and that they had prospered better there than elsewhere, hardly suffices. For though some of the students enrolled came from Italian families, the majority of them did not. The truth is that schools were so badly needed in South America that Italian nuns, who were otherwise highly competent, were very welcome for the purpose.

Even so, Francesca thoroughly understood that another sort of competence was also desirable, indeed indispensable. That was why, when on her way home, she tried to find out from those on board all that she could about Spain. When passing through the Straits of Gibraltar, where she could actually see Spain, her questions multiplied. The Spanish officers of the boat, she remarks in the letter she wrote on this voyage, "were pleased at my being so interested in everything, little realizing perhaps that for me everything is important, as my thoughts spread over all Spain. For I desire to open a house in that country, not only to do good but to obtain vocations among the Spaniards. They would help in the work in Spanish America, which needs so much help and worries me so much, as I have no Spanish Sisters to send there." This house in Spain was, in fact, to be opened before long. Reckless as Francesca may have appeared to be in Buenos Aires, she was really working with a very definite plan in her mind. From this period on, her outlook was more and more international in its scope. The United States had led to Central America, and Central America had led to South America; now South America was leading her back to Europe to obtain the necessary recruits.

But she did not end even there—at least not in her desires and ambitions. In the Straits of Gibraltar she could see not only Spain but Africa. So she burst out with: "The demands of these missions are devouring me! I shall never be content until I have given the aid they need.... Now and again at times I turn toward the west coast of Africa and Morocco, as I have inspirations to go there also. I should love to fly and save souls there, but this cannot be done during my lifetime, because there is so much to be done in the Americas." The zeal of God's house had eaten her up. She put no bounds to her work.

The voyage from Buenos Aires was uneventful, and the main importance of Francesca's diary-letter is the account it contains of her first South American foundation. But we hear also that she had an Argentinian postulant with her; that they stopped at Montevideo and the Canaries to hear Mass and receive Holy Communion; and that Francesca became a professor of modern languages by giving lessons in Italian to President Uriburu's sister-in-law, who was a fellow passenger.

That she was again charming everybody on board comes out from her saying that she and "that little angel, the postulant", when they tried to find a quiet corner in which to pray, were never so much as able to finish the rosary because of the people who gathered round wanting to talk to her. The "little angel" seems already to have become inflamed with missionary enthusiasm, for when, just north of the equator, they passed a large rocky reef named Piñedo de San Pedro, she asked Mother Cabrini, "Is there any chance of our going there one day to establish a mission?"

"Why yes," came the reply, "if you wish to convert the birds!" Then fearing that her jest might have sounded somewhat sharper than was intended, Francesca added, "Well, of course we do want to convert the whole world. And as you seem to be like Abraham, who wanted his children to multiply like the sands of the sea, perhaps you will find something to do even here." The little South American angel might not be very strong on geography, but at any rate she was showing the heart of a missionary. Francesca was pleased with her.

Italy detained Francesca longer than she had expected, though she was impatient to set about carrying out the plans she had made. The delay in extending her work to other European countries was due solely to a rather trivial lawsuit. That Francesca fought it through to a finish was characteristic of her—as characteristic as her desire to work. Yet even work had to wait when it was a question of loyalty to a dead friend's memory.

The matter deserves further mention. Bishop Gelmini of Lodi, during the first days of the congregation, had given the Missionary Sisters six thousand lire, but on condition that they pay a small pension to two aged Ursuline nuns. They were now dead, and Bishop Gelmini was dead, too, but the Ursuline Order claimed that what had been a gift was really only a loan and so should be refunded. Francesca was perfectly ready to do this, so as to avoid litigation, until the thought crossed her mind that the bishop's action might be misunderstood, as might also the connection of the Missionary Sisters with the transaction. To defend the bishop's memory, to defend her institute from the slightest imputation that might be brought against it, she was willing to suffer a long delay at the very moment when she had her greatest projects in mind. Francesca was a lioness in things of this sort. Here was an affair of honor she felt she could not decline.

The episcopal court of Lodi pronounced in her favor, but, as so often happens when issues of this sort are at stake, an appeal was made; and for the sake of the trumpery sum of six thousand lire, litigation dragged on for a couple of years. In the end, Francesca won, when the case was decided on July 4, 1898, by the Congregation of Bishops and Regulars in Rome. But how much precious time had been wasted! She had now to work all the harder to make up for what had been lost.

❧ ❧ ❧

No sooner was the lawsuit settled than Francesca knelt before Leo XIII to receive his blessing and to say goodbye. She was leaving that night and, as she had already received the pope's blessing through the Brazilian legate, and as she knew that he was not very well, she had not expected to be admitted to an audience. But Leo sent her word in the afternoon that she was to go to him. She had already seen him several times during this period, and once to a couple of her nuns the pope had said, "Mother Cabrini is truly a saint!" It was with great joy that she hastened to the Vatican—just before catching her train.

She was with him half an hour, and he asked her all kinds of questions about her institute and her plans. He also confirmed her commission—to go all over the world as a missionary. The venerable old man—he was now eighty-eight—understood her perhaps better than anybody else did, and he realized that, though he had sent her to the United States, she could not restrict her activities to any one country.

He could not but notice that she was in poor health. "How is it", he wanted to know, "that you can do so much work? I am much older than you, but I am much stronger than you. And I could not work as you do."

Francesca smiled and said, "Holy Father, I am your spiritual daughter. That is what gives me the necessary moral strength. I am not going to lose my health by serving that dear Jesus who made me a Missionary of His Sacred Heart."

At parting he did not merely lay his hand on her head in blessing; he took her head between his hands. Both of them must have thought that they would never see one another again. "Pray for me, Cabrini," he said, "and get all your nuns to pray for me. I am very sad these days."

With a full heart she promised the prayers the pope had asked, and he blessed her again. With that blessing she felt that she was ready for anything. "The pope has spoken!" she exclaimed afterward. "God has spoken through him. I shall go everywhere without fear. Oh, how powerful is the blessing of the pope!"

Three weeks later she was in Paris. For seven years she had been dreaming of opening a house there.

❧ ❧ ❧

At Paris, the pope's blessing at first did not seem to do her much good. Archbishop Chapelle, who had recently been appointed to New Orleans, but whom Francesca had not met so far, was waiting for her at the railway station on her arrival. The pope had asked him if he knew Mother Cabrini and had said, "Oh, but you must meet her!" So here he was. But he had no authority in Paris, and those who did have authority were in the beginning decidedly unfriendly.

The archbishop, Cardinal Richard, was away and his vicar-general, Monsignor Thomas, refused to give Francesca permission to make a foundation there. She would have to wait until the cardinal returned.

"But Monsignor," she explained, "I'm afraid I *can't* wait. My plans call for a visit to London and getting

back to the United States in November. You see I have to
act quickly."

"I can see that you would *like* to act quickly," he retorted,
"but a matter of this sort is not to be hurried. You will just
have to be patient until the cardinal gets back. I don't feel
that I can give you the permission you want."

For the meanwhile, Francesca and her companion—a
young Irish nun named Sister Frances—went to live
with a Madame de Mier whose sister was in the school at
Panama. In her house they saw nothing of their hostess
except at meals. Then she would sometimes come to sit
with them, but never to eat, for she was in poor health.
Left to themselves in the midst of this external grandeur,
and having nothing to do except wait for the cardinal-
archbishop's return, the nuns were almost able to make
a convent of Madame de Mier's magnificent house.
It turned out to be fortunate for this lady that she had them
there, for at the end of those few weeks, she returned to
the practice of her religion, which she had neglected for
many years, and then suddenly died.

Francesca was now without a place to live and without
permission to establish a convent in Paris. But as Madame de
Mier left her some grand furniture in her will—something
not at all suitable for a religious establishment—she proposed to put this to use by opening a boardinghouse for
ladies at 20 Rue Dumont d'Urville, between the Étoile
and the Trocadero.

It was a desperate expedient, and not at all what Francesca wanted. She thought of it as being merely a temporary solution of her problem. Somehow or other she
meant to get a foothold in Paris, if only for the sake of
obtaining French vocations. French nuns would be invaluable in her schools.

The vicar-general made difficulties even about that
much, and when Francesca presented to the nuncio at

Paris the letter of recommendation she carried from Cardinal Rampolla, he said he was sorry but he could not go against the vicar-general. His suggestion that she conduct her boardinghouse as a private person was something she refused to accept. "No," she told him; "we are religious and we intend to live as such." The only thing to do was to refer the whole matter to Cardinal Richard, who was on vacation in the Riviera. On September 8, his answer came; she might establish herself in the parish of Saint Pierre de Chaillot—the very parish, as it happened, in which the Rue Dumont d'Urville was situated, the site of her ladies' boardinghouse.

After that, all was plain sailing. On September 29, the seven Sisters who had been summoned from Italy arrived in Paris, and the house was opened. The only trouble now was that, though eminently suitable for the reception of well-to-do ladies, it was too sumptuous for a convent. The nuns were especially embarrassed by the many enormous gilded mirrors, which, they said, multiplied them to no practical advantage. In their own section of the building, these therefore had to be covered with sheeting. For the rest, they occupied the servants' quarters and turned the coach house into a refectory. The *conciergerie* was their community room.

The grandeur was, however, useful by way of attracting the kind of ladies they hoped for. On October 1, the first of their paying guests took up residence with them. She was somewhat mysteriously styled by Francesca in her letters as the Countess Spottiswood Makin, "an American lady of excellent disposition and a big heart". She did all that she could to bring the convent boardinghouse to the notice of her wealthy and aristocratic friends and organized a concert for their benefit under the patronage of the ex-queen of Naples, the Countess d'Eu, the Duchess of Vendome, and the Infanta Eulalia. It was through this last contact that the

Missionary Sisters were invited to Spain the following year. Had it not been that circumstances had forced Francesca to open the kind of establishment in Paris that she had no wish to conduct, this would never have happened. It meant that when she did go to Madrid, she was able to do so under the patronage of Queen Maria Cristina.

One turns, however, with a sigh of relief from all this splendor and these royal and noble names to something simpler and sweeter. Walking one day through the gardens of the Tuileries, Francesca sat down to rest on a bench. At that moment, a flock of birds came winging from the trees nearby and clustered around her. They were at her feet and on her shoulders and her lap. Everywhere there were birds, and Francesca caressed the little creatures as Saint Francis would have done. It was a scene straight out of the *Fioretti*.

Francesca always had a special love of birds, and her thoughts were full of the imagery of wings. At West Park, when the fruit trees were plucked, she always had one tree left intact for them. They now seemed to show that they recognized their friend from the way they gathered around her. She frequently imagined that birds had a private message for her—even the seabirds at Panama, who had seemed to represent the souls the Missionary Sisters were destined to save. This time she took what happened as a symbol of the orphanage she was soon to found at Neuilly. She had never thought of the grand house near the Etoile as anything more than a stepping-stone to that.

With England, seen for ten days, Francesca was enchanted.

Arriving at Victoria station early in the morning, she and Sister Frances, the young Irish nun who was her companion, started by going to the Jesuit church at Farm Street to receive Holy Communion and to give the superior a letter of introduction. He tried to lodge them in a convent, but before one was found that could take them in, Francesca's tired legs gave out under her, though she tried to sustain herself by thinking of Mary and Joseph seeking shelter in the inn at Bethlehem. At this point, she took a cab with the intention of calling upon Bishop Bourne, the future cardinal-archbishop of Westminster, who was then at Southwark. She had no conception whatever of the immense distances of London, so it was two in the afternoon before the two nuns reached Bishop Bourne's residence. He was away, and it was late in the day before his secretary at last succeeded in finding a place for them to stay.

Poor Francesca, whose eyes were now dropping out of her head, wanted to go to bed at once. But the good Sisters who were her hostesses were so eager to talk about Rome and the pope—for they had a friend of the pope's among them—that before anybody was aware of it the time for supper had come. When Francesca was at last allowed to go to bed, she was too exhausted to sleep at all.

These English nuns were kind but appear to have been a little imperceptive, for as Francesca did not come down to the community Mass in the morning they supposed she must be ill. One of them coming into her room, drew up the blinds and exclaimed, "She is just like a baby asleep!"

Francesca accepted the pretty compliment, but explained that she would like to rest a little longer and then receive Communion. "After that," she said, "perhaps I could hear Mass at some chapel nearby." She did just that, but still found herself too worn out to do anything else all day.

One might have thought that this not very satisfactory start might have given Francesca a bad impression of

England. Moreover, she had another unfortunate adventure
when she and Sister Frances got lost in the underground
railway, whose system of inner and outer circles they did
not understand. But her little mishaps served to make Francesca discover how polite and helpful the English can be.
When she asked the way, people offered to carry their bags
and umbrellas and, when they could not accompany the
nuns, apologized for this. "In other countries," Francesca
exclaimed enthusiastically, "they speak of nobility and courtesy; in London they practice them!" If this was how nuns
were treated in Protestant England, she concluded, God
would certainly bless the country and give it the grace of
entering the one true Church. "I was astonished", she wrote
again in this letter, "at the courtesy shown me and inwardly
implored blessings on this country of England, which I
should love to call, if possible, the 'Land of Angels'."

However, she had not gone there merely to make the
acquaintance of the English. Her purpose was that of
establishing an orphanage, one specially for Italian children. It was to explore the possibilities for one that she
was in England, and though this project had to wait several
years, it was ever afterward in her mind. That was why
she had called on Bishop Bourne; she wished to make her
foundation in his diocese.

Thinking of this Italian orphanage, she and her Irish
companion went among the Italian restaurants of Soho.
While Sister Frances rhapsodized over the wonderful
Milanese bread, Francesca ate a spiritual food. She was
delighted to discover that the Faith seemed very much
alive in these exiled compatriots of hers; their exile was
therefore less devastatingly complete than it so often was
in the United States. Certainly she must return to England.
This admirable country would prove, she thought, a field
golden at its harvest.

Chapter Fourteen

THE SOUL OF A SAINT

If a saint can be annoyed, it is at being called a saint.

He may know that he has a close union with God; he also knows that, however close it is, he cannot be satisfied with it. A greater perfection always lies ahead, never to be completed in this life. The saint refuses to believe for an instant that he is a saint; at most he can hope that he may become one. Meanwhile, he does his best to hide the fact of his holiness.

Of no saint was this more true than of Francesca Cabrini. When one questions the nuns who knew her: "Did you know that she was a saint?" some answer with admirable candor, "No, I did not suspect it at all. I knew of course that she was a very good woman, and a very kind woman. But a saint—no, I did not think of her in that way." She would have been pleased with the answer; she had always tried to seem as little out of the ordinary as possible.

On the other hand, some of those who say that they always knew that Francesca was a saint may be unconsciously coloring their answer with subsequent knowledge. But it is also certain that there were at least a few whose spiritual insight made them aware that they had a saint among them. They watched her closely for some sign of her sanctity; they never caught her off her guard. What they did see, however, was something that confirmed their suspicions—that she was most careful to drop a veil over her interior life and that she was trying to throw them off the scent. So as to prevent their noticing her absorption in the divine, she would deliberately do some little fussy act, even if this was only adjusting the veils the orphans wore in chapel. But she could not hide her face, try as she might: when she knelt in prayer, it often became like an alabaster lamp in which a light has been lit. There were times when she passed into a state of ecstasy. One nun who was kneeling beside her and whispered something to her, upon finding that Francesca was oblivious, ventured to remark on this afterward. She was never again allowed to kneel anywhere except in the pew ahead, where she could not notice anything.

Yet from the first years at Codogno, incidents occurred that the Sisters could not but believe were miracles. When food and money were found where food and money had not existed a few minutes before, it was in vain that Francesca attempted to dismiss the matter by saying, "You did not look well enough."

There was another device she used. She used it when at West Park the Sister in charge of the wine cellar came up with the bad news that three barrels of wine had turned sour. Something had to be done about it. This time Francesca said, "Well, I'll tell you how to set everything right. You take a little rice and parch it. Then divide it into three equal parts and put each part into a bag. Then let down a bag into each barrel."

Wondering at so strange a method of turning vinegar back into wine, the Sister obeyed. A week or two later she returned greatly excited, crying, "Mother, Mother! The wine is perfectly all right now."

Francesca smiled. "You see, Sister!" she said. "You have obeyed, and God has worked a miracle through your obedience." Yet even her studiously casual manner at such times never quite convinced the Sisters that this was the complete explanation. An inexplicable thing had happened—and their Mother had brought it about.

Faith, simplicity, humility, obedience—these Francesca believed to be the sources of all spiritual power. She was never tired of assuring her daughters that the only mortification they needed was that of observing the Rule perfectly. By that means, they would all become saints. Not by doing extraordinary acts they were not asked to perform, but by carrying out ordinary duties wholeheartedly—that was the way for them. And early in her career, after a retreat made in 1891, she set down in her little private notebook that she had asked the Blessed Virgin to prevent her ever telling the nuns to do anything that she was not fully resolved to practice herself.

Her own obedience was so perfect that once, toward the end of her life, when a priest, after she had gone to confession, wanting some matter for absolution, asked her to accuse herself of some sin of her past life—suggesting a sin against obedience. "But, Father," she exclaimed, "how can I accuse myself of disobedience when I never have been disobedient!" The *Advocatus Diaboli* tried to make a point of that during the process for her beatification. His objection was ineffectual; Francesca was only telling the truth, and truth had to be told.

Obedience: she was always telling her nuns that the true missionary never asked, "What duty will be given me? Where shall I be sent?" Instead, she was to accept everything under obedience—whether to be superior general, to teach in a classroom, or to sweep the stairs. The proper response should be: "If they place me on a hilltop to pray,

or as superior in a city, or forget me in a village, I desire
only to do the will of God and to serve the order."

Hers was an institute dedicated to the most intense and
strenuous work. But precisely for that reason it was also
dedicated to prayer. This was, however, mostly prayer of a
simple and communal sort, devotions adapted to busy people. And Francesca's own devotions—that is, of the external kind, for about her mystical communion with God she
said nothing—were those common enough among Catholics. First of all, of course, there was her devotion to the
Sacred Heart. But she also had a special love for the Infant
Jesus, and with that went a love for Our Lady and Saint
Joseph. So intense was her love for Mary that once, having
quoted a line of the Litany of Loreto, she could not stop
herself, but went right on to the end:

> *Turris Davidica,*
> *Turris eburnea,*
> *Domus aurea.*

She recited the whole litany, her eyes shining, her lips
moving but hardly audible.

There was also her devotion to the saints of the institute,
its patrons—Saint Francis de Sales, Saint Francis Xavier,
Saint Margaret Mary. This, too, was ordinary enough, for
most Catholics have particular saints to whom they pray,
their private friends in heaven. Equally ordinary was Francesca's devotion to the souls in Purgatory. It was all something commonly taken for granted.

Nor is there anything unusual in the fact that she liked
to have relics of saints in her possession, though perhaps
she went to unusual lengths in carrying around no less
than forty-two such relics, which she called her "Cru-
sade". But if she always carried them, she never burdened
herself with a prayerbook on her travels; she would use

the first prayerbook—any prayerbook—she came across. And because she was so constantly on the march, she was not able to have a regular spiritual director, but made her confession to the first priest who chanced to be at hand. When she was a child at Sant' Angelo, Don Bassano used to say to her, "Go and tell that to Jesus." That was what she went on doing for the rest of her life. "The soul learns", she wrote in one of her letters, "that there is no necessity to look for her Beloved outside her own being and that she can find Him within herself, as in His own throne and in His tabernacle." In this we hear the voice of the authentic mystic, though hers was a mysticism of a very practical sort. She proceeded immediately from prayer to action.

❧ ❧ ❧

Candid herself—"If anyone wants to know what is in me," she used to say, "let him look at a glass of water"—she liked open manners and detested affectation in her nuns, especially the kind of affectation to which pious people are sometimes addicted. Slyness or evasiveness of disposition she could not tolerate, but she was always willing to make wide allowances for the outbursts of vivacious temperaments, believing that such people had much good in them. She wanted her daughters to walk with their heads held high, even though they kept their eyes downward. It displeased her to see one of them carrying a rosary unless she was actually saying it.

Complaints of any sort—even about the weather—also displeased her. Despondency was the great enemy of the soul. She could not bear to hear any of her nuns speak about her "cross". What were they in religion for except to bear the Cross of Christ and to rejoice in it? But though she spoke her mind plainly, she always did so very gently— and was all the more effectual because of her gentleness.

But gentleness did not mean softness. "Robust, vigorous, strong, masculine"—these were the words she used to describe the spirituality she demanded. Instead of giving orders, she generally used to make requests—and she was promptly obeyed. Though she had to rule a large congregation, she did not relish being styled its General. Once when she was ill and a Sister had to write in her name to Pope Pius X, she objected to the phrase, "The order of which I am the head." Forgetting how sick she was, she sat up in bed to declare vehemently, "That letter will not do. 'Head of the Order,' indeed! Nothing of the kind!" The letter had to be rewritten.

At recreation with her nuns, she would put herself on an equality with the youngest among them. If there was one of them who seemed to be shy or neglected, Francesca would seek to draw her out. She shone in the community herself because she was such good company, such a good storyteller, so vivacious and kind. She was, however, a poor hand at cards and never won, except when her opponents saw to it that she did. This, however, was not enough to stop her from playing or from inviting others to play. "But Mother," one of the Sisters said, "I have forgotten this game." "So have I", Francesca returned, shuffling the pack. One would give much to have seen the saint considering the deck she had received.

If there happened to be any candy or fruit for these recreation periods—at which times she liked to see the nuns enjoying themselves like children—she always took care that those whose duties kept them away did not suffer. Their share of the little treat was always put on one side for them to enjoy later.

She knew every one of her daughters intimately—if only by letters—and every one of them regarded her not merely as her General but as her Mother. Yet it was

characteristic of Francesca that she never kept a list of the
members of her order—though they were between fifteen
hundred and two thousand at the time of her death—nor
could she have told anyone just how many houses she
had under her direction, constantly as the needs of every
house were in her mind. There was nothing of the cold
statistician about this great organizer. She did, indeed, say
that her nuns were like so many pawns on a chessboard
and that she could move them anywhere. But nobody
was ever less of a drill sergeant or martinet. She governed
by love. And she used to say that good manners were a
part of holiness.

It was her courtesy that made her so patient, that even
made her put up with people who imposed on her. In the
Argentine, a servant girl of fifteen arrived one day bearing a message from her mistress. Having delivered it, she
remained to chatter for two hours without ceasing, and
Francesca let her go on. When the girl had left, a Sister
present, who was worn out by the visit, asked Francesca,
"How could you put up with this for such a long time?"
Upon which Francesca smiled and said, "Didn't you see
how she was enjoying herself? I was not going to deprive
her of this pleasure. Had she been a person of importance,
I would probably have dismissed her quickly. But this
servant-girl, no."

Francesca's sense of humor made her a bit whimsical
at times, though even here she often contrived to put
humor to a practical purpose. One day she told a young
Sister to sow grass seed on the lawn at West Park, and the
next day she sent an older Sister—one who was an expert
gardener—to see whether the grass was coming up yet.
When the reply came, "Yes, Mother, I'll do it at once",
Francesca was delighted. She wanted to discover whether
the nun had an unquestioning obedience or whether she

was going to argue. In this sort of thing she was rather like the whimsical Saint Philip Neri.

Another time, when being visited by the superior of one of her convents, Mother Cabrini told her she wanted her to stay till the next day, as a very distinguished lady was to arrive then. "You'll have to help in the reception", she said.

"But Mother, I talk English so poorly. Don't you think you had better get somebody else to receive this lady?"

"Oh, that's all right. She understands Italian very well."

Even so, the anxious superior did not get much sleep that night, for she was not used to grand functions. But when in the morning she noticed who the caller was, she said to herself, "Here I am worrying over nothing! Why, I know that lady quite well."

Francesca laughed. "I don't mean her. Get ready, because the lady I mean is waiting in the parlor."

Then all the Sisters of the House were assembled and, headed by Mother Cabrini and the visiting superior, they went in. There was a newly arrived statue of the Blessed Virgin. And Francesca like a mischievous child clapped her hands and laughed because of all the excitement she had caused.*

❦　❦　❦

These incidents are, of course, illustrative of no more than a certain playfulness of disposition, but perhaps they are worth recording if only to correct the popular picture of a saint as a somewhat solemn if not actually grim person. The picture exists only in the minds of those who think

* This incident is also related of Monsignor Serrati in the anonymous Sister's Life. I have obtained it, as related of Francesca, from a manuscript collection of incidents compiled by her daughters. Both may have happened. Let it be supposed that Francesca, many years later, repeated the Monsignor's practical joke.

of the practice of exalted virtue as a terrifyingly difficult thing, not being aware that it gives lightness and gaiety and a sense of freedom. But Francesca indulged her sense of fun with a purpose: those who worked as hard as her nuns needed some relaxation, and she was careful to provide it in this way, though usually it bubbled out of her spontaneously and was not planned.

The main relief from work, however, was prayer and then more prayer. In the little notebook in which she jotted down her resolutions—the *Propositi*—she wrote: "I would become weak and languid and risk losing myself if I were to occupy myself only with exterior things, however good and holy these may be; or if I were to be without the sleep of prayer ... in the heart of my beloved Jesus. Give me, O Jesus, an abundance of this mystical sleep." Though it has been somewhat cynically remarked that Mary was able to sit at the Master's feet only because Martha was willing to do her sister's share of the housework as well as her own, in Francesca's case it was the contemplative Mary who gave the necessary energy to Martha. Francesca's intense activity—and that of her daughters— would, she knew, be impossible unless it was continually fed by their spiritual life.

She had little leisure for reading, though the many apposite quotations she makes offhand show how well she remembered what she had read and how well she could apply it. These come almost entirely from the Scriptures or spiritual books. She was not a student, but a woman of action. As she had her work to do, she was obliged to put from her, almost as though it were a kind of temptation, her longing for the purely contemplative life. One day she confided to one of her nuns: "If I followed my secret desires, I would go to West Park and there, far from all distractions, do many beautiful things for the institute.

But because I see that the Lord does not wish this of me for the time being, I forget solitude and attend to the affairs of the Order. In this way I carry out God's will, even on the street, on the train, aboard ship—everywhere I feel as though I were meditating in my cell."

Work was a sovereign specific also for the nuns. If she visited a convent and observed an air of discouragement or moodiness, instead of asking what was wrong, she would immediately start the Sisters on some occupation that would keep them bustling around. In this manner, she made them forget themselves. It operated like magic. A few days later, she would see nothing but smiling faces.

Her own serenity and cheerfulness never failed. "Difficulties, difficulties," she would exclaim with gentle scorn, "scarecrows to frighten children!" However great the turmoil around her, she was never flurried, never even hurried. Whatever her activity, she radiated a profound peace.

None of her nuns ever heard her speak of any troubles she might have; she made it a cardinal principle to speak to them only of pleasant things. Though she was frequently worried—or rather, though she frequently had cause to be worried—she kept it to herself. Indeed, at such times she showed herself more than ordinarily cheerful. This cheerfulness was not assumed as a mask; she really did feel cheerful, for then she would draw all the closer to God. If a trial came, she thanked God—and was sure to find it a sign that a blessing was about to follow.

When she said, as she often did, that enemies were to be regarded as friends, she spoke out of personal experience. Had she not begun her own religious life under the eccentric Antonia Tondini? Now she saw how providential had been that dark period which had seemed the end of all her hopes. When she subsequently encountered opposition, she told her nuns that this gave her an opportunity for putting her trust all the more completely in God.

She did not escape spiteful acts, and these she freely forgave. At Codogno, soon after the foundation there, an incendiary started a fire in the shed where the whole year's supply of wood was stored. She knew very well who had done this, but she refused to accuse him to the police. Instead, when he died a few months later, she got the community to offer prayers for the repose of his soul—prayers that he presumably badly needed.

At the same time she could be, when the occasion demanded it, quietly devastating. A young nun who was to accompany her to America stood on the dock at Genoa telling her parents who had come to see her off how willingly she was making this great sacrifice. Francesca listened to the outpouring of complacent self-pity as long as she could stand it; then she said: "My daughter, God doesn't expect such enormous sacrifices from you. You should feel joy, not that you are making a sacrifice. You had better stay in Italy." And though this nun's berth was ready for her on board, she was left behind. It was not merely a question of giving that particular Sister a lesson; everybody was given a lesson. But it should be added that nearly all those chosen for the missions regarded themselves as specially favored. Though well aware of hardships ahead, they accepted these as a privilege.

It has often been remarked that sanctity gives a special sort of psychological insight—what is called the discerning of spirits. The nuns had many opportunities of learning that Mother Cabrini knew their secrets before they ever spoke of them. Generally this was a consolation to them. But there was an occasion now and then when a Sister found it rather disconcerting. Thus one young nun who was with the others in the chapel for the examination of conscience, feared to go out with the rest when the signal was given, as she knew that she had not been keeping the Rules very well. So she waited in her place until Mother Cabrini would leave. As Mother Cabrini did not stir, the frightened Sister moved to the front pew and then to the altar rail, as though she wished to say some more prayers; and still Mother Cabrini stayed where she was. At last the young nun crept into the sacristy and tried to make a dash for it by the side door. The moment she got to the end of the hall, there stood Mother Cabrini waiting for her.

"Why are you running away from me?"

Embarrassed and nearly crying, the Sister held down her head and said nothing.

Mother Cabrini looked at her with sweet, dominating eyes and went on gently: "My child, live like a good religious, and you will never have to fear the glance of your Mother." It was all that needed to be said.

This gift was more embarrassing to Francesca herself than to those whom she governed. In fact, it became such a torment to her that she prayed to be released from it, and to some extent her prayers were heard. Having so great a reluctance to reveal her own soul, she did not wish to pry into the souls of others.

Just where ordinary psychological processes end and a supernatural insight begins is a nice question. Perhaps it is safest to suggest that psychological perceptions are sharpened by the spiritual life. They can, however, be sharpened to such a degree as to seem prophetic. Gabriella, the daughter of Mother Cabrini's first friend in America, the Contessa Cesnola, could testify to this on her own account. She wanted to enter the institute, and Francesca allowed her to try her vocation, though telling her from the outset that she did not have one. Gabriella had other reasons for believing that Francesca possessed what were at least extraordinarily acute sensibilities. Thus in New York one day, they went together into what they thought was a Catholic church to pray. This High Anglican chapel looked like a Catholic church, having even a tabernacle on the altar. But as soon as Mother Cabrini got inside she exclaimed, "The place is empty! The Blessed Sacrament is not here." At the door as they went out, they met the sexton and asked him, "Is this a Catholic church?" "Yes," he answered, "it is a Catholic church; but it is not a *Roman* Catholic church."

There was another happening of this sort. In 1900, two young women, one of whom intended to join the institute, went to see Francesca. The other girl had already arranged to enter the Franciscan community that conducted the parochial school at Saint Anthony's parish on Sullivan Street. The prospective Missionary Sister contrived to draw Mother Cabrini into a corner. It was only for a moment or two. Soon Francesca went up to her other visitor and said, "Your friend here does not have a vocation, but *you* have one."

The girl answered, "Yes, I know. I have been accepted by the Franciscans."

At this Mother Cabrini shook her head. "No, young lady. You are going to become a Missionary Sister." And so it proved to be. In the same way, Francesca once pointed to a girl, unknown to her, who was crossing the courtyard. "See that girl!" she said. "She will be one of us." At that time the girl had no intention whatever of entering religion. As superior at Buenos Aires she testified many years later to what had happened.

Francesca often startled members of her community by her intuition. One Sister who was troubled by some interior difficulty was advised by her confessor to tell Mother Cabrini about it. As soon as she did so—bringing herself to the point with great reluctance—she got a smile and the assurance, "I have known all about this for some

time. Now there are no secrets between us. Don't worry
about it anymore." Yet Francesca would rarely bring
such matters up herself. When the confidence was made,
she would answer, "I cannot violate the secret of your
conscience. But if you come to me, I will always try to
help you."

These difficulties were as a rule those small scruples
that beset the religious life. One Sister in 1892 spent most
of her meditation trying to decide whether her spiritual
condition was such that she could go to Communion at
the Mass that was to follow. As soon as Mother Cabrini
came in, she went straight up to the Sister and whispered,
"Don't waste any more time worrying about this. Just go
and receive Holy Communion and promise Jesus that you
will not do it again." There we have something that seems
to be a good deal more than psychological perception.

On the other hand, what some people took to be fulfilled prophecies might well be nothing but shrewd infer-
ences. A case of this occurred when Archbishop Corrigan
was being talked of for the cardinalate. Francesca said,
"No, Archbishop Corrigan will never be made a cardinal.
But that little Monsignor Farley, he will become one."
Others with no claim to sanctity might have said the same
thing, for Archbishop Corrigan had put himself out of the
running by some unhappy involvements in ecclesiastical
politics. He was therefore passed over. But as John Farley
was his auxiliary, it was not particularly hard to foresee that
he would obtain the red hat that normally the archbishop
of New York receives.

For the sick, Francesca had a special solicitude. If she ever
thought that one of the Sisters was looking a little pale
or tired, she would give an order. Then the Sister would

have an eggnog handed to her with, "Mother says you are to take this." But she discouraged all self-pity. To one nun who left the chapel before the others one morning and who told her afterward that it was because she was not feeling well, she said, "Is that any reason for you to let your face become so woe-begone? Next time when you have to go out, say to Jesus, 'I am not feeling well. But I thank You for letting me suffer a little for You.' Then you will go out with a smiling face." Novices who were afraid that they might be dismissed on account of poor health were comforted with, "Your Mother never sends anybody home for that reason. I am satisfied with your good will and docility." She could not fail to remember that she herself had been refused by two religious orders because she was so delicate—and that she had lived to found one of her own. Nor did she forget that she was always expected to die—and did a prodigious amount of work in spite of everything.

She worked even when she was ill, but for that she had graces of her own. Once when in a high fever, she saw Saint Joseph in a dream and said to him, "I am longing to receive Holy Communion. If you would let me be free from fever—if only for an hour—I could go." She awoke without her fever, and though she had been seven days in bed, she went to the chapel to communicate. An hour later, her fever returned, though in a milder form. Within a few days she was up again and about her duties.

If sickness could be turned into a blessing by those who received it in the right spirit, almost anything could also be turned into a blessing. One nun—young then and now old and a superior in the institute—asked her what to do when her prayers were not answered. "Do?" Mother Cabrini replied, "Thank God all the more!" It was her practice to say at such times, "I thank Thee, dear Jesus, that Thy

will and not mine has been done." She was supremely
confident that all her affairs were under God's guidance.
If she had an important letter to send, she would leave it
for some hours under the altar cloth before the Blessed
Sacrament—and not mail it until then. The Articles of
Testimonial Proof drawn up to guide the process for her
beatification credit her with "a simple prudence and a
prudent simplicity." But though she was always prudent,
as the outcome of events showed, she frequently acted
with an intrepidity that alarmed her advisers. The truth
was that she never acted until she had prayed; then she
acted with startling decision. That was the simplicity of her
prudence—an unshakable trust in God's Providence. She
was really so far from being rash that she kept a watchful eye
upon the smallest details. "How am I to buy new houses
and provide for them unless you spend no money except
what is absolutely necessary?" she would ask the treasurer.
Generous as she was, she was also careful not to waste so
much as a button or a pin. Everything was put to use.

Nobody could have been less of an introvert than herself.
In her opinion, there might be as much vanity in looking
too much at one's soul as in looking at one's face in the
mirror. The first was only a more subtle form of egotism.
If she could serve God in spite of her physical weakness,
she believed she could also serve Him in spite of her spiritual shortcomings. Confessing these, feeling deep compunction for them, she yet refused to brood over them. By
committing them to God, they could be made to redound
to His glory. All this was the more remarkable in her case
because a doctor who examined her said that tempera-
mentally she was inclined to melancholy and that such sufferings as those she constantly endured should have turned
any woman, whatever her temperament, into a neurotic.

Francesca has been called an essentially silent soul, and the description is correct. She was obliged to talk a good deal, and, though she had no writer's itch and not a particle of ambition for authorship, she did in fact put many words to paper. But all these words, whether spoken or written, were only a form of action or a means of inspiring others to action. By them she made her daughters feel that they were greater than their own capacity. She gave them wings. Even her prayer was hardly separable from work.

Asceticism, as it is popularly understood, she had long ceased to practice. Actually every year there grew in her soul the asceticism that means self-abandonment and self-conquest. The two boards on which she had slept at Vidardo were given up in favor of a comfortable bed, and the mortification she stressed was that of keeping the Rule, for she said that diligence in little things was the road to holiness. "Animate or inanimate creatures", she wrote, "must all help me to serve God better. I shall use them or renounce them according as I see that they help or impede the service of God and my sanctification." These are the words of one completely detached—the consummate ascetic. Though she was very sparing in the amount of food she ate, she did not go to such extremes as to injure her health. While eating like a bird, she declared she took all that her constitution needed and that coarse food best suited her. It was the same with regard to sleep. She was up an hour before anybody else for an additional hour of meditation; but what she got sufficed. Her sleep was the sleep of a child.

Her detachment extended even to the matter of a home for herself; she had none. All the other nuns in her institute belonged to this or that particular convent: she belonged nowhere. Her headquarters were wherever she happened to be. And wherever she stayed, it was only as a lodger—one who might remain some months but who would certainly be soon on the move. So as not to allow herself to feel that even her ring or her cross were her own, she would exchange them now and then with others. And as one young nun was exactly her size, she and Mother Cabrini used indifferently to wear one another's clothes. But she was so detached that she only now and then remembered to do this; and then it was mainly to teach others, not to mortify herself.

Above everything else was the force of love—of her love for God and her love for God's creatures. "The holy passion of Jesus", she wrote, "pursues me so much that I cannot resist." It was the theme of "The Hound of Heaven". Another cry was, "Come what may, I shall close my eyes and not lift my head from the Heart of Jesus." But this, so far from being a sinking down to rest, was rather a propulsion to fresh activity. "Rest!" she used to say. "We shall have all eternity in which to rest. Now let us work." By work she manifested her love. Whatever she was doing— traveling, talking, laughing, even while administering necessary rebukes to her daughters—she showed her love, to them and to Christ. Her own words were: "Neither science nor speculation has ever made, or ever will make, a saint. Better to be an idiot capable of love, because in love he will sanctify himself."

Only in such chance remarks do we get a fleeting glimpse of her soul. She did her best to conceal God or, rather, her relations with God. This most candid and affable of women lived in an impenetrable reserve. What she could not hide was the love of God that made her face luminous.

She had, as all the saints had, the compunction that makes them call themselves the worst of sinners—and that makes them really believe they are precisely that. This sort of self-accusation has often struck ordinary people as strained and exaggerated, though one would suppose that the relationships of human love would offer an analogy helping comprehension. "Are my sins great or slight?" she asks in her private notebook, and she answers, "Immensely great." Yet on another page she wrote: "We must not be surprised at our faults, because surprise springs from pride." In humility she accepted the fact that she had her faults, or what seemed to her such, and added: "An imperfect but humble soul is dearer to God than one that is innocent and self-disciplined but full of self-confidence in its own strength and its own practices and disciplines." While grieving, she could also rejoice in her imperfection as giving grace something to work upon.

Love and sacrifice—these words run through her life and are often the burden of her *Propositi*. But here again an effort at understanding should be made. "The science of suffering is the science of the saints", she noted. But this does not merely mean resignation to whatever God sends, but that love of its very nature is the spring of suffering, even if suffering blends with and sometimes becomes the same thing as gladness. It is what Francesca called her "sweet martyrdom". "The good I expect is so great that every pain is a joy to me. I abound in happiness in my sufferings." These sufferings with her were not by any means solely compunction for past or present faults, but an almost intolerable ache that she did not have an infinite love with which to respond to the Infinite Love. "I feel myself consumed with love for You," she tells Christ, "and this is a great torture to me, a slow martyrdom at not being able to do something for You." Again she writes: "My book will

be the crucifix, and I will always keep it before my eyes to
learn how to love and to suffer.... The Missionary Sister
who does not wish to suffer should give up the name.
Whoever assumes the title of the Sacred Heart must always
suffer by looking at the thorns that intertwine around the
Heart of Jesus.... How beautiful it is to suffer for Jesus,
with Jesus, and out of pure love to be consumed by suffering for Jesus." Again she cried, "O Jesus, Jesus, I grieve
with love for You. I am languishing and dying; why don't
I die for love of You?"

It is at the same time clear from these words, for the most
part addressed directly to Christ, that her union with Him
had always existed and had never been interrupted. "From
the first moment I became acquainted with You," she tells
Him, "I was so enchanted by Your beauty that I followed
You." But that is also the source of her grief. "The more
I love You, it seems the less I love You, because I want to
love You more. I can bear it no longer. Expand, expand
my heart!" And in the same notebook she wrote: "Convert me, Jesus, convert me completely to Yourself, for if
You do not make me a saint, I will not know how to work
in Your vineyard and will end by betraying Your interests,
instead of rendering them successful."

She tells Christ that He seems to be "madly in love"
with her, and she can respond only by crying: "O Jesus,
Jesus Love, help always Your poor miserable one, Your
miserable little Bride, and carry her always in Your arms."
But in the end she can find nothing to say but a stam-
mered, "I love You, I love You so very, very much." The
words are lame because there *are* no words. Francesca was
once more the child Cecchina.

Chapter Fifteen

THE WIDENING FIELD

Francesca spent the greater part of the year 1899 founding schools—most of them in or near New York—for
poor Italian children. This work was not of course new
to her, for the very first thing she did upon her arrival in
the United States was to open just such a school at Saint
Joachim's. And since then she had sent Sisters to teach in
Brooklyn and the school attached to the church of Our
Lady of Pompeii on Bleeker Street. But now Francesca
laid a special emphasis upon schools of this type.

The problem before her was indeed large enough to
engage her attention for nearly a whole year, and because
it was so pressing, she did not feel that she could wait any
longer. She had to do what she could at once, inadequate
though it might be. The neglected children of the immigrants needed her help, and needing it, they got it.

Francesca never supposed that she and the handful of
nuns she had at her disposal would be able to solve the
whole problem. It was much too large for that. But they
did address themselves to the situation as they found it,
and they were almost alone in doing anything at all. One
merely had to take a glance at conditions in the Little Italies to see that the children running wild there were not
only likely to be lost to the Church but were even likely
to become very unsatisfactory members of society unless

they were taken in hand. Among the immigrants there were criminal elements, and though many a man who had been a bandit in Italy settled down to a reasonably respectable life when his transference to America gave him a chance to do so, many another man did not. In a case like this, America's capacity to organize crime, as it organized everything else, hardened the casual thief into the gangster. And the gangster found recruits among the young Italians growing up round him. These had to be rescued before it was too late.

Nor was the problem much less as it concerned the Italian girls. Many of these found an easier and more profitable way to live than toiling in the fetid air of the sweatshops. Their pretty faces, their charm, and their complaisant good nature were all dangers to them. This aspect of the situation had been startlingly brought home to Francesca during the first April she had spent in New York when she had gone out searching for a place in which the Sisters teaching at Saint Joachim's could live until the Roosevelt Street house was ready for occupancy. Then she had gone into a furnished house that was for rent in Little Italy—and found that its character was revealed by its lush gaudiness. The Sisters with her—simple-minded young women— had exclaimed, "Oh Mother, isn't this wonderful? It's just the place for us!" And some of them never quite understood why she had hurried them out with, "No, it's the very last place!" She was nearly as ignorant of the wicked world as her daughters, but her shrewdness had made her avoid that house—and prefer to it the dreary desolation and discomfort of the one she took on White Street. This was why Francesca had not confined her activities to children but had established classes in Christian doctrine for the adults. It was also why she opened an embroidery school in the basement of the church of Our Lady of

Pompeii, for by giving girls a skilled trade, she was helping to preserve their virtue. As many of them came attended by small brothers or sisters, she even provided a crèche for their convenience.

There was still another factor to the problem—that of the proselytizing that went on among the Italians. Francesca counteracted it in all her schools but especially in the mission she founded at the Five Points, where, since 1855, there had existed a very active Protestant mission. This did not have a great deal of success among older Italians, for even the most seemingly indifferent—even the most anticlerical—among them had Catholicism bred in the bone. It did nevertheless win over a few by offering tangible inducements for the profession of what was represented as the American faith. And by employing evangelists who used the vulgar Italian dialects, more comprehensible by the illiterate than the language of educated men, it had a certain appeal.

With it cooperated the so-called Children's Aid Society, an agency that set itself to bring in the waifs of the streets who had left their native country too young to remember it or those born in the United States. As such children very seldom had had much religious instruction, they were often an easy prey. Their quick minds saw that Italians were despised largely on account of being Catholics; now they were being promised a material advantage in turning Protestant. In many instances, their parents—to whom formal apostasy would have been unthinkable—were not unwilling that their children should go the road that they themselves would not take.

Francesca had long been aware of all this. Though she was far from happy about the spiritual condition of the adults, she knew that few of them would sever all connection with the Church. Even those who had not gone to Mass or frequented the sacraments for years could always be counted upon to turn out when it was a question of celebrating a *festa*. Then the image of the saint whose day it was would be carried through the decorated streets, and there would be a noisy and happy holiday, even if it was not quite a holy day.

To that extent, nearly all the immigrants remained faithful to their religion. Of their hundreds of societies, the majority bore the name of some saint—usually the patron saint of the town from which the people forming the society came. It was a tenuous thread, but it held. The children, however—both those who were being lured away by the Five Points mission and those who were attending the public schools—were coming to regard such things as "Italian superstitions", whereas they were rather the scraps and remnants of the Catholic tradition. As they had no means of connecting these festivals in their minds with the dogmatic content of faith—about which, through no fault of their own, they were rather vague—they were growing ashamed of being Catholics. To meet the challenge of the Protestant mission at the Five Points, Francesca established her own mission at the very place where the challenge was offered.

She had already established several parochial schools, and at Chicago and Scranton she now established others. In a parish she had, of course, some equipment and support given her. But there were other places where she saw a school to be necessary in which she had to provide everything herself. Later, it is true, the Italian government, having been brought to recognize how important a work was being done for its dispersed people, granted some subsidies; at this stage, Francesca had to operate on her own all but nonexistent resources.

At Newark, already a thriving manufacturing city of well over two hundred thousand inhabitants, she opened a school in a couple of empty adjoining stores, where the classrooms were divided only by glass partitions. In these large rooms—intensely hot in summer and without heat in winter—the Sisters set to work with sixty cents as their sole capital. Yet four hundred children were gathered there, children for whom until then nothing was being done.

Similarly two large stores on 105th Street in New York were turned into a school. A year later this was moved to an abandoned factory on 105th Street. In their new quarters, the Sisters felt almost luxurious, as there were four stories and a yard for a playground and an assembly-hall that was used on Sundays as a chapel for the Italians in the Bronx. Schools like these got the neglected Italian children off the streets and—though Francesca was concerned with rather more than that—it was acknowledged that she was doing much to solve the problem of juvenile delinquency and so helping to restore the good name of the Italian people. Even those who attached slight importance to the religious instruction given by the Sisters had to admit a value to society.

❧ ❧ ❧

Now for the first time Francesca opened in the United States a high-class boarding school for the children of Italians in well-to-do circumstances. These were often in still greater need of her help than were the poor, as they were liable to abandon the practice of their religion in order to climb more quickly up the social and business ladder. Yet they demanded an Italian school, and an Italian school was the best means of preserving the faith of their daughters. Accordingly, on 190th Street and Fort Washington Avenue—at that time so far out of town as to be a wilderness—Francesca established the Sacred Heart Villa. There, too, for a time the American novitiate was set up, following a period when it functioned at West Park. It became for Francesca the nearest thing she was ever to have as a settled home.

The Sacred Heart Villa no longer exists as an academy but, known as the Mother Cabrini High School, takes girls of all nationalities; and it is in its chapel that the saint's body now reposes in a crystal reliquary under the altar. The surging development foreseen by Francesca's keen eye has recently flooded past that district [as of 1945—EDITOR]. Now from the George Washington Bridge there runs the Cabrini Boulevard, which, as it comes to the school, opens out on a magnificent view of the Hudson and the Palisades. Where the Cabrini Boulevard starts, there are new tall apartment houses that give an impression in some ways more startling even than that of Park Avenue, for the boulevard is narrow enough to give the feeling that one is looking up a canyon. It is in this way that New York has perpetuated the memory of the forlorn Italian nun who arrived there on the last day of March 1889 to work among the Italian poor.

The year 1899 had been a strenuous one for Francesca, and the series of foundations she made in rapid succession at that time called for an energy and courage that are astonishing. Then came several weeks of whirlwind work, as Francesca had to make plans for the alteration of the buildings at the Sacred Heart Villa before sailing for Europe. On the very day that she signed the deed for the property—it was September 2, 1899—she embarked on the *Touraine*, so exhausted that she dropped into the nearest deck chair as soon as she had finished waving her handkerchief to the Sisters who had come to say goodbye. There she lay stretched out, at first in a kind of daze, then fast asleep. When she awoke, it was to head the diary-letter begun at once with four lines of the verse she composed so easily. And her first reflection was, "How lovely and sweet it is to undertake a sea voyage when one is tired and worn out with the labors of the missions!" She was now sure of a week's rest. To smell the salt of the sea, even to smell the faint sickly smell of white paint and the spit and polish of a great liner promised a complete holiday. During the two days just passed, she had been obliged to work night and day in order to take this boat. No wonder she had fallen into a sleep as of the dead.

The rainy weather in which they set out, she confessed, made her sad. But instantly she checked herself; even such mild and casual complaints could not be permitted, however weary she was. Therefore, she added, "I ought not to let sadness take hold of me. So I entered into the Heart of Jesus, where I saw all the Sisters, and though I could not speak to them, I asked the Sacred Heart to tell each of them what I had forgotten or what I had not time to say."

A few days later, she was in high spirits, and with good reason. The captain of the *Touraine*, a large luxurious boat, was, she thought, like a king or a father. He took Francesca and Mother Virginia, her traveling companion, out of the cabins they had engaged and gave them instead a most luxurious suite opening on the deck. It had its own lounge, which nobody could enter except at the invitation of the nuns, so they had perfect privacy. Hard as Francesca's life often was on land, people went out of their way to wrap her in every possible comfort the moment she set her foot on a ship. Well might she say, "I'm like a fish—I feel better on sea than on land, and eat with a better appetite." These journeys were the only vacations she ever got, and she needed them badly. They renewed her strength for the toils of the missions.

They landed at Le Havre, and no sooner had they got to Paris than they found that Spain was now open to them. The Infanta Eulalia had already met Mother Cabrini. She was empowered by Queen Maria Cristina, who was acting as regent for her young son Alfonso XIII, to invite the Missionary Sisters to Madrid. What the queen had in mind was a school for the children of the nobility and military officers. It turned out later that she also wanted a nun who would live in the Escorial and act as governess for the royal family. Mother Cabrini would be most welcome in Spain.

Francesca immediately set out for the country she had so long thought of as a nursery for her order. From Spain she hoped to obtain recruits with whom to staff her South American schools. Under the royal patronage she might expect to secure just the material she needed—young women of good families and high culture. They would give those schools prestige, and though Francesca was never the kind of woman who relies too much on such things, she was also practical enough to use them for what they were worth.

At the frontier, she and her companion found, when their baggage came to be examined, that orders had been received from the queen to pass it unopened, under the diplomatic privilege. Francesca's characteristic comment was, "It's only fitting that Brides of Christ should be treated in this way!" And in Madrid, Maria Cristina showered favors upon the newly arrived nuns. She took them herself into the royal furniture depositories. "Now, Mother," she said, "if you see anything here that is going to be of any use to you, just take it for your school."

Francesca gazed bewildered upon the gilt and satin furniture and the heavy brocade that the queen suggested as appropriate for the purpose. "I think I'd prefer something a little more plain and simple, Your Majesty", she returned. It was not very easy to find anything like that there, but in the end she selected some of the least ornate and pretentious articles. For the little aristocrats whom she was going to educate, a certain amount of gorgeousness would not be out of place; for the rooms to be occupied by the Sisters it was rather hard to select anything in consonance with their profession of poverty.

The queen then broached her other plan. "I am going to ask you, Mother Cabrini," she said, "to lend me one of your nuns to teach Italian to the princesses."

"Do you mean, Your Majesty," she asked, "that she would have to live in the palace?"

"Of course."

Francesca shook her head. "I'm afraid that's impossible, Your Majesty."

"Impossible! Why? She would have her own room and her meals all by herself."

Francesca explained. "I'm afraid that's out of the question, Your Majesty. In a school—in however aristocratic a school—the nuns would still be free to live their conventual life. This could not be done in the Escorial. In the atmosphere of the court, the religious spirit could hardly be maintained. I'm sorry, but I must disappoint Your Majesty here."

The queen gave her a swift, sharp, imperious look, but saw at once that the smiling little woman before her was not to be moved even by the demands of royal personages.

Accustomed though she was to getting her own way, the queen recognized that it would be best to acquiesce, to take the school and to forego a nun as governess.

Francesca had long been given to look upon obstacles at the outset as a sign that God's blessing was to follow. That this time the way was being made so smooth was for her almost ominous. However, she did not have long to wait for the expected difficulties. A revolution in Madrid and in the Basque country, where she had established a house at Bilbao, soon gave her all the opposition she needed. At Vitoria, in fact, the archbishop, his eccentricities having increased with age, threatened to expel the Sisters and did succeed in preventing them from opening any institution. In a magnificent house they lived in extreme poverty, and only because of the intervention of Cardinal Rampolla were they permitted to have the Blessed Sacrament reserved in their chapel. The favor of the queen counted for nothing in the face of the Basque jealousy of all things Spanish, and not until June 1900 was Francesca able to come to terms with his Excellency of Vitoria. Only with some difficulty were the foundations in Spain maintained. But they were maintained. Madrid got a college as well as a school—and later an orphanage as well; and at Bilbao two orphanages were founded. These fully served their purpose: they not only did a great deal of good locally, but—more important still—they became a reservoir for Spanish America.

❧ ❧ ❧

If 1899 was the year in which Francesca established the greatest number of houses in the United States, 1900 was the year in which she established the greatest number of houses in Europe. After leaving Spain, she busied herself with extending her work in Italy. At Turin she opened a boarding school and a rest house for her nuns, at Città della Pieve and San Raffaele convents, and at Rome a school and a church—that of the Holy Redeemer—on the site of the demolished Villa Ludovisi. She even departed from her policy of establishing herself only in cities when Cardinal Satolli, whom she had known when he was apostolic delegate to the United States, asked her to open an orphanage in his native Marsciano.

That year, in which the ninetieth birthday of Leo XIII was being celebrated, there were several meetings between Francesca and the pope. Usually he gave her a private audience, but there were also times when, in her desire to have sight of him, she went with a large crowd of visitors. The aged pontiff was still remarkably vigorous, but of course was showing his years. That was why Francesca thought for a moment, when he singled her out from all those kneeling in his presence and spoke to her with so very affectionate a cordiality, that he might have mistaken her for somebody else. She was used to his being like this toward her in private, but hitherto in public he had invariably maintained a stately reserve. She was afraid that perhaps his eyesight was failing him, or else his memory. She did not want to have him embarrassed by going on too long and then discovering his error.

"Are you sure, Holy Father," she asked diffidently but smiling, "that you know who I am?"

"Of course I know who you are," he exclaimed; "You are Mother Cabrini." Then it was a thrill to her to find that he had meant to show her this intimate friendship before all the other people present.

When she parted from him at the end of the year—again supposing that she would never see him again—he again affirmed her commission. "Ah, Cabrini," he said, "you have the spirit of God. Now carry it to the whole world."

She was always upheld by the thought that she was acting under the personal orders of the Vicar of Christ. Though it was he who had sent her to the United States eleven years previously, he had often made it plain that he wished her to go wherever she felt God's service called her.

On December 2, 1900, she embarked at Genoa on the *Alfonso XIII* for Buenos Aires. Some of the pupils of her Genoa school came on board and, taking possession of the piano in the lounge, proceeded to give an improvised concert in honor of the captain. He was so delighted that he invited the nuns who had come to see Francesca off to stay the night, as his ship was not to sail until the morning.

At dawn the next day—it was the Feast of Saint Francis Xavier, the patron of the institute and her own patron saint—she had a special desire that Mass be said. But the priest who was to have celebrated it could not find the key to the case in which he had his vestments, so was on the point of giving up and going to breakfast.

"But Father," Francesca pleaded, "please look again. We do so much want to have Mass today." Upon this he made a further search and found the key—which Francesca took to be a special present from Saint Francis Xavier to herself.

Captain Decampa, who was in charge of the liner, was a most pious man, always at any Mass that was said on board and always praying very fervently. And Francesca's table companions were Monsignor Isaza, the coadjutor bishop of Montevideo, and some other South American priests. They all knew a little Italian and liked to hear it spoken. In return, they used Spanish so as to help Francesca and her nuns to learn it a bit better—a very pleasant and profitable arrangement.

Two days later, while the ship was waiting for passengers and stores at Malaga, Francesca had the chance of visiting the city. As everybody was buying the famous raisins, she also bought some, though she got hers thriftily from a man who was coming down the hill with a pannier-laden donkey, whereas the other passengers bought at fancy prices in the smart shops. That evening at dinner, one of the priests produced some Malaga wine, and Francesca remembered that she had a hamper in her cabin—supplied by the superior at Genoa. She sent one of the Sisters to get a bottle of its Piedmont vintage. When the bishop asked, "Is this Malaga wine?" Francesca laughed and answered, "Well, I suppose we *could* call it Malaga wine while we are still in the port." It was probably nothing very choice, but the bishop and the priests drank some with the nuns and politely told Francesca that they could hardly believe Piedmont produced anything so good.

It was in this congenial company that she made her long voyage. The best part of it was that she was able to hear Mass frequently. It was the first time that this had happened during her many sea trips, for though priests were often on board, on previous occasions they had neglected to bring the utensils of the altar and their vestments. On the Feast of the Immaculate Conception—December 8—she was able to assist at no less than seven low Masses, which were followed by a High Mass and a sermon by Bishop Isaza. All this set Francesca off into several pages of rhapsody about the Blessed Virgin. She never wanted her nuns to forget who was the real Foundress of the institute.

❧ ❧ ❧

The next seven months were spent in the Argentine, partly in the capital, where her school was flourishing mightily, but partly also in the pampas, where there were many scattered groups of Italian laborers.

She had also to see about the finding of new work for the Sisters whom she had left five years before in Panama. Their lot had been hard. Ejected from Nicaragua by a revolution, they now had to withdraw from Panama because of the outburst of another civil war. The treatment they received was exceptionally scurvy, because at the outbreak of yellow and typhoid fevers and the bubonic plague, which occurred at that time, they had closed their school and had turned themselves into nurses, going among the sick and those wounded in the civil war. In spite of this, they received orders to leave. In Latin American countries, political upheavals were nearly always complicated with an extraneous anticlericalism. At such times defenseless nuns were the easiest of targets.

Mother Cabrini was not in the least disturbed, though she pitied her daughters. These trials, she told them, were sent by God and were for the benefit of their souls. Incidentally, they were also of benefit to her schools in the Argentine. She put all the ejected nuns to work there, and she welcomed the stream of South American novices that had begun to arrive. As the houses in Spain could not yet supply the badly needed recruits, these young women from the Argentine were invaluable.

It was just like Mother Cabrini to purchase a large house at Flores, which was at that time a not very well settled suburb of Buenos Aires. People told her that she was making a mistake, that there were not enough inhabitants there to make a school possible. Disregarding their advice, she not only bought a house for a school but a large amount of land, as this was going cheap. She seemed to have an eye for the way populations make their trend. Within a very few years, Buenos Aires extended in that direction, and this district became one of the most select of its suburbs. Real estate men would have given much to have had her acumen.

Another foundation was that made at Rosario in the Province of Santa Fé. It was a great inland port on the Paraná River. There, in spite of a good deal of local opposition, offered by the so-called liberals who were in power locally, she established her Collegio Internacional del Rosario.

At Villa Mercedes, far back on the pampas, another house was opened. After a fatiguing journey of sixteen hours on the train, Francesca went out within an hour to look for a place that she might occupy as a convent. She found it, and on Whit Sunday—three days after her arrival—she took possession of it. On that day, as she came toward the house, she met a boy selling a couple of white doves. These she bought from him as a symbol of the Holy Ghost. Practical as Francesca was, pretty things of this sort always made a strong appeal to her, and the memory of them is cherished by the community. She has every right to be permitted these charming touches.

Villa Mercedes, a town of fifteen thousand souls, was used as the center of a wide sphere of operations. From there the Sisters could strike in all directions into the pampas, and on the pampas—within that part of it they regarded as their special field—there were seventy thousand people, many of them Italians, scattered so thinly in what was considered a Catholic country that few of them were ever reached by a priest. This was a new kind of a mission—but every mission of Francesca's had distinguishing features of its own, for Francesca's work was always adapted to the needs of each locality to which she went. One gets a little dizzy looking at her during these years, so much does she flash about. One would think of her movements as lightning, were they not entirely free from all thunder. Unobtrusively she came and went, very calm but also very efficient. And wherever she passed, she left a new foundation behind. That she was so intent on getting so many new establishments operating would seem to indicate that she felt her death to be near. The night was coming in which no man can work.

She had been thought to be almost at the point of death when she started her institute in 1880. Nine years later, when she was at last able to begin her missionary career, warnings had again come that her health could not stand the strain. She had smiled each time, caring nothing for herself, only believing that God had called her and that He would supply the strength that was needed. But she had more and more frequently to admit that she was ill, even when she passed it off lightly. Buenos Aires had, she wrote, proved far from being "good air" for her. But though intermittent fever—a familiar visitation of hers—forced her to bed, she took it mainly as a warning that she should bestir herself all the more afterward. The moment she was up, she threw herself with even greater energy—an energy born not of a vigorous constitution, but of the force of her indomitable will—into the enterprises she had in mind.

An indication of the weariness under all the display of driving force appears in the diary-letter she wrote on board between Buenos Aires and Genoa. Though the voyage was very long, the letter is very short. It was as much as the weary woman could do to write even these few lines.

She opened it with one of those scraps of verse she seems to have been able to turn out with such facility. But she followed that immediately with the admission: "We embarked on August 22, but I have not begun to write until today, the 28th.... The day I left Buenos Aires I was not feeling very well, and your farewells and that of the children had really overcome me, and I have remained in this exhausted state a good while." She had left New York two years previously all worn out; she was even more tired now—tired and ill.

Yet she managed to recover with that resiliency she seemed to have at command. At Santos, a little south of Rio de Janerio, she went on shore to hear Mass and receive Communion, though it was raining so hard that a sick woman should not have gone out at all. That the High Mass was accompanied by drums and trumpets instead of an organ gave her a novel experience. And when somebody spoke to her in Portuguese, she was delighted to find that she understood him fairly well and decided that that language came between Italian and Spanish, of which tongue by now she knew a little.

Even about Rio de Janerio she does not say much, though she visited it. In reading what description she does give of it, one has a feeling that her pencil went with some effort over the paper. Yet she must already have been thinking of establishing a house there, the one that was actually established in 1908. Of São Paulo, where she did send Sisters within a year, she says nothing at all except that everybody had told her that it was beautiful. Apparently the whole of her brief letter was written on one day—the 28th. She admitted having been too tired to write until then, and we must infer that she was too tired to write afterward.

❧ ❧ ❧

In Italy she arrived so ill that she had to go to bed at once. Her life was now despaired of, and in expectation of death she began to give instructions as to the government of the institute after she had gone. This was in the spring of 1902. Already she had appointed delegates—not provincials, as in the case of other orders—to represent her in the various countries in which the Missionary Sisters were at work. Even if she lived, she now felt she must have some assistance. Until then she had been shouldering the whole burden of government alone.

Suddenly she recovered. She was in Rome, and on March 19 there arrived a basket of oranges sent her by Leo XIII from the Vatican gardens. For several days she had been unable to take food, but she considered herself almost under obedience to eat one of the pope's oranges. "Delicious!" she commented, sitting up in bed. "That has given me back all the energy I had lost." Those beside her thought she took the fruit as though it had been picked in paradise. When she went to see Leo again soon afterward, the blessing he gave her was the last she was to receive from him. During the summer of the following year, Francesca Cabrini's great friend and patron died, ninety-three years old.

Work first had to be done in Europe. The convents in Italy—there were now many of them—all had to be visited. So, too, had those in Spain, where Francesca had managed to straighten things out with the somewhat crusty old bishop of Vitoria and had founded an orphanage near Madrid. In Paris the grand boardinghouse had been given up and an orphanage founded instead at Neuilly, which was afterward transferred to Noisy-le-Grand. But the main project was to settle Sisters in London.

Francesca had set aside very little time for this. On August 5, she left Paris, and she was due to sail from Liverpool on the 23rd. But that time was enough for a woman like herself.

On the way from Dover, she and the Sisters with her saw one of those rich, tender, golden sunsets that do sometimes come in England, and she was delighted. In her fancy, the shining clouds formed a throne—the throne of the Queen of the Angels. As she said in the letter she wrote about it: "I then saw our Blessed Lady wearing a beautiful diadem, with the Child Jesus on her knees stretching out His arms in protection over us.... It seemed to augur a special protection from heaven for our foundation in London."

That protection was given. Francesca wished she could spend more time among the English, with whom she may be almost said to have fallen in love on her earlier visit among them. But time was pressing, and she could set aside only a couple of weeks for her dear England. That time, however, sufficed for what had to be done. Bishop Bourne, who was still at Southwark, expedited her plans. A house was found at Brockley, a southeastern suburb in his diocese—from which afterward the Sisters transferred themselves to Honor Oak, not very far away—and the necessary decrees were obtained from Propaganda immediately upon request. The dispatch shown by the authorities was equal to her own. When Francesca left England, she knew that all the ecclesiastical formalities had been complied with. It was with an easy mind that she sailed for the United States.

Chapter Sixteen

FRANCESCA RIDES WEST

Four years were now spent in the United States. Though during that period Francesca by no means neglected her foundations in Europe and Central and South America, she directed them from a distance. Her concentration on the northern continent may be regarded as a return to her original plan. Leo XIII had, after all, commissioned her to work among the Italian immigrants, though he had soon come fully to recognize that she should not be restricted to that undertaking. But now that it had been made clear that the whole world was the scene of operations for the Missionary Sisters, she felt free for the time being to give most of her own efforts to the section of the world with which she had begun. The outposts had been sent out and were holding firmly. Italy was still the country from which she drew most of her recruits. The United States was again the main center of her work.

If during these four years she founded few houses as compared with 1899, these were also the years of the most important of her foundations. She was so busy that, when in 1902 the Missionary Sisters established themselves in São Paulo in Brazil, she was not able to go herself. This was the first time that such a thing had happened, for it was Francesca's habit to deal with all problems on the spot and to accept all responsibility. But it was impossible, even for her, to be in two places at once, and it was not too difficult a matter for some of the nuns in the Argentine to move a little farther north. She left them—she had to leave them—to their own devices.

Now for the first time Francesca struck to the Rocky Mountains, evidently with the intention of eventually carrying her work all the way to the Pacific Coast. In the spring of 1899, she had sent Sisters to staff a school at Chicago—the one on West Erie Street attached to the Servites' Church of the Assumption; but a far greater work than this was awaiting her there. Francesca's immediate objective, however, was the mining fields of Colorado.

In that state, the Italians of the dispersion suffered somewhat less from economic exploitation than their brethren in other sections of the country, but the good money they made in the gold and silver mines was in itself a danger, because it tended to become an all-sufficient end. Segregated from their families, as they usually were, and with no priests near them, many of them forgot country and God. Perhaps they, most of all the Italians in America, needed such spiritual aid as the Missionary Sisters could bring.

As was generally the case with her, Francesca began in a small way. The city of Denver in which she settled was to see a large, well-equipped orphanage conducted by her nuns, but she was content to start with a poorly equipped parochial school on Palmer Avenue, a school that would deal with the problem of children who had little or no parental attention.

Denver was also the *point d'appui* for what she meant to do in the mines. As the miners were scattered in camps throughout the state, the only way of reaching them was by going to them. This meant journeying in rough country, visits to the dwellings of the miners (which were

often underground), and, more frequently, the plunging
in cages or bucket-like contrivances hundreds of feet into
the depths of the earth. From there the Sisters sometimes
had to walk miles along the galleries before they came to
the men at their work. Then the conversation had to be
very brief, during a moment's pause in the toil with pick
and drill or during the lunch hour. But it meant much to
these miners, isolated and buried and forgotten. Italy and
the Church were coming to them in the persons of these
smiling, kind-faced nuns.

The superintendent of the mines, aware of the good
effect of such visits on the morale of the men, provided
a room for the Sisters, and there they would sometimes stay for several days, in the evenings talking in the
dining-shed or in front of the bunkhouse to the hands.
It was from these contacts that Francesca discovered how
urgent was the need for a hospital and an orphanage.
The miners were often badly injured in their dangerous
work, sometimes fatally so, and then their children were
left destitute. When accidents occurred, the men, helpless on account of their illiteracy and their ignorance of
English, were frequently defrauded by the more unscru-
pulous mining corporations—which meant that they
could make no provision for their dependents. Though
Francesca could see no immediate means of opening
the institutions that she saw to be necessary, she at once
began to plan for them.

❧ ❧ ❧

When she did return, to give what was so badly needed,
there occurred again an instance of that insight which, in
its daring, was really more prudent than the caution of
her advisers. She proposed to buy a large property on the
straggly outskirts of the city, but the bishop—Nicholas

Matz—said, "No, you mustn't go there, Mother. You will be completely isolated. Get nearer the center."

Francesca shook her head. "I have been studying the map, Your Excellency", she said. "I know the very place for me."

She was a great student of maps and used them as a general does in his campaigns. Central America, the Argentine and Brazil, the strategic spots she had already occupied in the United States—and those she was to occupy—were all carefully selected. Yet they often appeared to be chosen at random, or from an "inspiration" that came from nowhere. It was an inspiration that invariably turned out to be of the kind that real-estate speculators would give their eye-teeth to possess. Francesca had an extraordinary faculty for gauging population trends. She did not buy property, of course, because she saw it would go up in value; but she was able to buy property because she was in advance of everybody in seeing what was going to happen. She therefore picked up bargains and got well established in the right location by the time that the extension of a city caught up with her.

When Bishop Matz raised his objection to the outlying place she thought of purchasing, her immediate argument was, "There I shall have a large orchard and vegetable gardens. These will help me feed my children. And in the country air they will have a healthy home."

"But who will look after the orchard and farm?" the Bishop wanted to know.

Francesca had her answer ready. "Why, *our Sisters* will look after them. They are nearly all young women from the country and know about such things."

He smiled and gave his permission. She did not tax his credulity too much by adding to her other reasons for the purchase of this property that she clearly foresaw Denver developing in that direction, with trolley-lines laid down

to thriving, hiving suburbs. But when all this happened
her choice was doubly justified.

The bishop of Denver, like the archbishop of New Orleans,
became Francesca's firm friend. The two men were alike in
many ways. Again, Confirmation was sometimes adminis-
tered in the open air, with the bishop taking a tree stump
as his episcopal throne. To the older Italians who attended
these occasions, it was a scene very different from an ecclesiastical function in one of the glorious cathedrals of their
native land, with their rich glass and lapis lazuli altars and
golden baldachins and columns of rose and forest-green
marble. But the sacrament was the same and made the
children who received it soldiers of Christ.

Sometimes afterward, the bishop would say sadly,
"These poor people! They should never have left Italy.
Here they make good money in the mines but ..."

And Francesca would reply, "Your Excellency, these
people really had no choice. No doubt almost every single
one of them as individuals would have been really better
off as a *contadino* in Italy than a miner here. But as a group,
no. They *had* to come to the United States to earn a living.
What breaks my heart is to see how often they think of
nothing else."

Francesca's work in Denver, however, was not confined
to Italians, or even to Catholics, though it was mainly done
for them. One day a Mr. Young came to Francesca, bringing with him his daughter Leslie. Would the Sisters accept
her? He would willingly pay. He explained that he had
married again and that the girl did not get on very well
with his new wife. Francesca agreed to take the child, but
the Sisters soon found that Leslie was of a difficult temperament, and they were for sending her home. It was Francesca
who would not allow this. "Keep her", she said. "You will

see; she will not only become a Catholic herself, but her father will be converted as well." As though that were not enough, she added, "And I'll tell you something else. One of these days Leslie is going to become a Missionary Sister." All of which proved to be true to the letter.

❦ ❦ ❦

While the Denver project was maturing, Francesca left a group of Sisters at work in Colorado and swung back to New Jersey to found Saint Anthony's Orphanage at Arlington. It was between Newark and Passaic and so had the advantage of being near a thickly settled industrial district; it had the other advantage of providing a large rambling house in wide grounds for the children she was to rescue. Buying it cheap, she established herself where she could reach out to a populous center and still be removed from it. Again she showed a very sound judgment.

There was then, and there remains to this day, something of a mystery as to how Francesca managed to finance these undertakings of hers. From the Italians she begged assiduously, but from them she could as a rule obtain only very small doles. To get the larger sums necessary, she had to go to wealthy men, whom she seemed to pick at random but usually with success. Going to one of them, a Mr. Wentworth, she had to lie in wait around the corner of the passage from his office, as he had several times refused to see her. When at last he found himself trapped, he tried a bit of bluster. "What is it you have got to sell?"

"Sell, Mr. Wentworth? Sell? Only children."

He stared at her dumbfounded. He gasped when she lectured him in her high-pitched little voice: "When you began as a business man, Mr. Wentworth, you had dreams. You *must* have had dreams to have been successful in business. Well, I have dreams, too. Different dreams from yours, perhaps, but still dreams."

She got a sizable check from him. But for that matter, she generally got a sizable check from such people. They found that it was almost impossible to refuse the bright-eyed, smiling, passionately convinced woman. And though begging went against the grain of her temperament, she was a wonderful beggar. When it came to the point, she used to tell them plainly, "In asking you for something, I am conferring a privilege upon you. You have a chance to do some good. You should be grateful to me for coming to you."

Upon which the hardheaded business man would gulp and stare—but end by drawing out his checkbook.

Even so, she often had to fall back upon what she called her bank of heaven. When there seemed to be no way of obtaining money, she would tell a Sister, "Why not look in that drawer over there?"

"In that drawer, Mother? There's nothing in it."

"When did you look last?" she would ask, tossing the question over her shoulder as she went on writing at her desk.

"Yesterday, Mother."

"Supposing you look today?"

This was a method used only as a last resource, but it was always available. The Missionary Sisters knew that in their darkest hour their needs would be supplied.

Francesca was accustomed to say, "We have nothing, yet we spend millions." It was true. Millions were needed, and millions were forthcoming—nobody was ever able to say from where, unless it was from the bank of heaven.

The Columbus Hospital in New York had flourished. After the old Post-Graduate Hospital on Twentieth Street had been taken over, three houses on Nineteenth Street were bought, so bringing the capacity to two hundred beds. It was here that the present Columbus Hospital was to rise. Now at the end of 1903, Francesca went to Chicago to found a hospital. Pressure was being brought to bear upon her from several quarters—from the Servite Fathers at whose school her nuns were teaching, from Archbishop Quigley, who had just been transferred to Chicago from Buffalo, and from a young Italian doctor named Lagorio who had been in practice there since 1879 and who was at this time in charge of the Pasteur Institute. It was at his house that Mother Cabrini and two young nuns stayed for three months while they were looking for a suitable place for a hospital.

There was much to be done before a hospital could be opened. Funds had to be raised, and to get these the three nuns went out every day begging. Usually they would start very early in the morning, coming in from Mass while Dr. and Mrs. Lagorio were still asleep, and get their own breakfast in the kitchen before going on their rounds. In the evening, they often dragged themselves back so worn out that they were glad to slip off to bed early. But there were evenings *en famille* with the Lagorios. Then Sister Xavier, the daughter of Colonel De Maria and the anonymous author of the chief biography, would sit at the piano and play one operatic score after another, delighting her hosts. To the tired Francesca, this music was often a means of refreshment.

All this was delightful, but the money came in slowly. And Mother Cabrini certainly would have made a bad mistake had she not been under the advice of Archbishop Quigley, who had just arrived in Chicago to take over his charge. Her idea was to open an orphanage, and she thought of buying the old hospital of the Alexian Brothers, as it was going cheap. Fortunately the archbishop insisted on going to have a look at it. Dust was thick on the rotting floorboards. Cobwebs hung from the ceilings and across the dingy windows. And though many of the panes were broken, the air was dank and miasmic. The plaster was off in great patches of the walls; in other places damp showed. It was a scene of depressing desolation. After his inspection Archbishop Quigley sent for Francesca.

"Do you know", he asked her, "the condition the place is in?"

"Yes, Your Excellency", she told him. "It's not, of course, just what we would like to have. But after we have cleaned it out ..."

"Cleaned it out! You will never be able to clean that place out. Why, it swarms with rats and cockroaches and bedbugs! Even if you could get rid of them, it would not be suitable for you. Your Italians need something better than that. And they need a hospital more than they need an orphanage."

Again Francesca started to look, and one snowy April day she came upon the North Shore Hotel that fronted Lincoln Park with the lake beyond. It was a grey stone building of six stories and had been one of the most fashionable hotels until ruined by bad management. The site was one of the best in Chicago and since that time has been made still better by the reclamation of much land from the lake. For the price at which it was going—a hundred and sixty thousand dollars—it was a bargain.

But how was Francesca to carry such a deal through? When she told Archbishop Quigley that she had collected a thousand dollars, he threw back his head and laughed. "Mother, Mother! A thousand dollars is not going to get you very far!"

She knew that already; she regarded the whole thing as impracticable. However, she went out collecting again, this time with a definite project to offer the Chicago

Italians—the North Shore Hotel at a bargain-basement price. Even so, it staggered most people, and though at last she gathered ten thousand dollars—here a hundred dollars, there a dime—it was only out of obedience that she decided to follow the archbishop's advice and take such a huge burden as the North Shore Hotel on her shoulders. "Left to myself," she said, "I would never have made such a blunder. I have always made my steps accord with the length of my legs. But if the archbishop wishes it..."

This time obedience served just as well as insight; the buying of the North Shore Hotel was perhaps the shrewdest of all her business deals.

❦ ❦ ❦

The policeman on the beat at Lakeview Avenue saw a strange sight in the dim five-o'clock light that morning. Two nuns were prowling outside the empty hotel. Every now and then, they bent double and held something to the ground, before making a mark on the sidewalk, jotting down a note in a little book, and then moving on a little farther to repeat the performance. The policeman's hat got pushed back on his head, and the policeman scratched his crown without getting any nearer to solving the mystery. He had never seen nuns do anything like this before, and had they not been Sisters and he a pious Irishman who had been brought up by Sisters in a parochial school, he would have walked over without hesitation and asked, "What do you think you're doing?" Instead he slipped around the corner and signaled to his sergeant.

"Sarge," said the policeman, after they had stealthily looked round the edge of the building, "what do you suppose they're up to?'

"Search me, Clancy! Looks like they're measuring the hotel."

"With bits of string, Sarge?"

"Yeah. That's what they're doing, Clancy. They must be some of these Eyetalian Sisters who are going to buy the hotel."

They were. Francesca had got with a wave of the hand an indication from the owners of the extent of the property. At the same time, she had somehow felt a distrust of these people. To guard against being cheated, she had sent out the two Sisters who had been her companions at the Lagorios to find out the exact measurements of the lot on which the North Shore Hotel stood.

Later that morning, Francesca met the owners to sign the documents of the sale. She looked at them, with eyes sharpened for one point. Then she laid the papers down. "No", she said. "You told me I would have the whole length of the block. But you are not giving me that. You have cut off a strip twenty-five feet wide at the end."

That was just what the owners had done. Such a strip would have enabled them to have built two houses back to back and still have left room for a yard for each. That would mean not only the loss of those building lots but a serious decrease in the value of what was left.

The owners tried to assure Francesca that she *was* getting the whole length of the block. She looked at them calmly and said, "I have had it measured. If you like we will measure it again."

They hastily agreed that that was unnecessary.

And there were others who tried to cheat her. She was a woman and a foreigner. What could she know about business? As she had to go somewhere else, she left Sisters in charge of the renovations that were necessary to turn the hotel into a hospital, and their inexperience proved nearly fatal. The contractors suggested so many improvements, where a few slight changes would have sufficed, that the building was almost completely gutted. Then huge bills began to be presented, and the Sisters had to wire to Francesca to come to the rescue.

She returned at once and saw Archbishop Quigley the same day. "Yes," he told her, "I saw that the Sisters were getting themselves into a hopeless mess, so I said they had better send for you. Another day or two and there would have been a foreclosure—and then your nuns would have to sleep in Lincoln Park. But you are here now."

"Yes, I am here now."

"And not a moment too soon! Now what are you going to do, Mother?"

"That's what I shall have to find out, Your Excellency."

On going to what was to be Chicago's Columbus Hospital, Francesca found that all the plaster work in the rooms was being torn down, that the heating-plant, the flooring, and even the supporting pillars were being ripped away. Already practically nothing remained except the shell of the building. "The ruins of Jerusalem!" she exclaimed, gazing upon the devastation. And the charges for all this were two or three times what they ought to have been. The contractors imagined that the nuns were going to be an easy prey. If work had been stopped, this was because funds had already given out.

Mother Cabrini immediately sent for the contractors. Then facing the heavy-jowled, greedy-eyed men, she said, "You will of course be paid what is just; you will not be paid one penny more. I'm going to take this in hand myself."

They stared at her. One of them asked, "What do you mean, ma'am?"

Francesca serenely turned to him. "What do I mean? I mean that you are all fired. I'm in charge from now on."

Fired they found they all were. Some of them threatened but grew more amenable when Francesca produced
the proofs of their sharp practice or even of their down-
right dishonesty. A few of the better sort were re-engaged,
but under new and more equitable terms.

Francesca herself became the chief contractor and supervised every detail of the work in what now looked like a
shipyard. But though under her energetic direction, the
transformation of the North Shore Hotel into the Columbus Hospital was so speeded up that what was supposed
to need twelve months was done in eight, she managed to
combine a family atmosphere with her efficiency. She
made friends with all the workmen, and several of them
became converted to the Catholic faith while they were
working under her. And that, too, added to the enthusiastic interest they showed in what they were doing.

Though there was a great deal of damage that could
not be undone, many fraudulent bills were repudiated,
so that with this saving and the saving of time brought
about by Francesca's personal presence all day long on the
scene of operations, the hospital at last emerged without
too staggering a loss. Her Congregationalist lawyer, John
Willard Newman, stood astonished at the way she cut to
the heart of every problem and at the decision with which
she solved it. He was so impressed by Francesca that, in
spite of his sturdy Protestantism, he wore a Catholic medal
for the rest of his life.

Mr. Newman was useful to her for the legal advice he
was able to give. For the necessary medical advice, she
always relied on the celebrated surgeon John B. Murphy,
whose name is still attached to a number of hospital appliances. Though he was at the head of the staff of the Mercy
Hospital, he nominally became head of Francesca's hospital as well. She picked her coadjutors with an unerring

instinct for the best. And her courage and efficiency made such an impression upon Chicago that the money she needed, and had so far been able to obtain only in small donations, rolled in in much larger amounts. Just when everything seemed to have been lost, Francesca's efficient hand and brain saved the situation. On April 26, 1905, the hospital was formally opened.

As in the case of New York, Francesca decided to call this the Columbus Hospital, the name she was to give to all the hospitals she founded. For though it obtained many wealthy patients from the outset—its equipment making it one of the best institutions in the city—she wished to show the Italian immigrants that this hospital was primarily their own. The Missionary Sisters today operate three such hospitals in Chicago.

🍂 🍂 🍂

As was always the way with Francesca, as soon as she was assured that one project was well in hand, she went on to another. Though she was suffering from a high fever, she struck to the extreme West and seemed to forget her own condition while admiring the magnificent scenery all around her. She was on her way to Seattle. From there she meant to go to California.

At Seattle she was to found another hospital, but for the moment she was content with a small orphanage and a parochial school on Beacon Hill. For the sake of the Italian immigrants, she ran up a temporary wooden church and, as at first it had no bell, she sent out her nuns in twos every Sunday morning to summon the people from their scattered settlements. Some of those she gathered in this way had not been inside a church for thirty or forty years. Yet of them she could write: "Though these Italians have been so many years away from God, still I found the Faith well

rooted in them, even in their very bones.... By means of
a little kindness and courtesy it is easy to bring them back
to God. It is very touching to see men of advanced years
cry with emotion at seeing an Italian church in which they
hear the Word of God in their mother tongue and are
reminded of the old country, so long left, and the ever-
dear impressions of childhood." Among them were people
who became so pious that while waiting for Mass to begin
they said the Stations of the Cross three times.

When this church was being built, Francesca herself
took a pickax and worked on its foundation, though the
rain was falling steadily all that day. And there, as a kind of
private dedication in advance, she dug a hole in which she
placed medals of all the institute's patrons. She then signed
a paper on her knees and put it with the other objects of
devotion. Over it now lies the cornerstone.

To those who were outside the city, Francesca went
herself or sent some of her nuns. It was all one to her
whether she visited a lumber-camp, a mine, or a prison.
Everywhere the Italians were given a feeling that at last
something was going to be done for them. They were
so grateful that, as Francesca put it, "They follow us like
chicks following the hen."

About her work in the prisons, a special word should be
said. It was nothing new, for she had begun it in New
York, making grey, gaunt Sing Sing the first place of this
sort she visited. She had a great pity for Italian prisoners,
especially because crimes were often fastened upon these
helpless and hapless men. "There," she said one day in a
horrified whisper to a Sister who was walking with her in
Chicago, "do you see that man? He is handcuffed. Perhaps
he is innocent."

Whether they were innocent or not, her compassion went out to men for whom the official chaplains could do little, as they knew no Italian. She therefore made it her business to arrange for Italian-speaking priests to visit the prisons to hear confessions, but also making sure that the Sisters would be there two or three times a week.

Those under sentence of death received the most tender kindness from her. At least once she was able to secure a stay of execution until she had brought the aged mother of one such man from Italy to see him before he went to the electric chair. On other occasions, she was even able to bring about a review of the sentence, for the judges of the courts became very glad to cooperate with her.

At Sing Sing, she gave one Italian, awaiting execution, the promise that his daughter would be taken in her orphanage at West Park. That was a great comfort to him; just after condemnation, he had been so overwhelmed by despair that he had tried to commit suicide. But the Sisters brought him to Christian resignation, visiting him every day during his last week of life and spending almost the whole of his last day with him. As he climbed into the electric chair he handed his crucifix to one of the guards. "Take it," he said, "and give it to the Sisters."

At New Orleans, a young Black man was converted by the Sisters before he was hanged. As he was led along the line of iron-barred cells to the gallows, some of his companions in crime called to him, asking him to pray that they might be set free. "No," he said, "I shall do better for you than that. I shall pray that you may repent as I have repented."

In Chicago there was a still more moving scene. Five men were to be hanged together. The judge who had sentenced them to death himself asked the Sisters to stay with them on their last day. This they did, helping them to

make acts of contrition and of faith, hope, and charity.
The youngest of the prisoners—one hardly more than a
boy—was so terrified that he clung to Mother Antonietta
della Casa, who was destined to be Mother Cabrini's successor as General; and it was she who had to put on the
helmet he was to wear. She stayed by him, holding his
hand, until the last moment. For the sake of giving him
courage, she managed to be calm; after it was all over, she
broke down and was ill for over a week.

This prison work, like so many things done by Mother
Cabrini and the Missionary Sisters, was not designed by
them, but merely accepted because it so obviously needed
to be done. As soon as it could be replaced by a more definite system, it was relinquished, but until then it was performed by those who had a hundred other tasks. They had
one invaluable qualification—a complete understanding of
the Italian religious psychology. The Sing Sing prisoners
were to express their gratitude by sending a beautifully
illuminated address to Francesca on the occasion of the
twenty-fifth anniversary of the founding of the institute.
Those at Chicago did still better; they subscribed to buy a
horse and carriage for the Sisters who visited the prisons.

Never did Francesca say to others or herself, "This is the
work I mean to do. In prudence I must not go beyond
it." Her heart was so large and so warm that she was continually dreaming of starting some work in a new field,
work that she was not always able to carry out. China was
never quite forgotten. When she first arrived in Seattle—
where labors enough awaited her—she began to turn over
in her mind a project for starting a mission in Alaska. Italian miners were going there. But in Alaska there were also
Eskimos, and she had a great hunger to bring the name of

Christ to places where it was unknown. She was wondering what it would be like to live in an igloo, and, realizing that such a mission would be very difficult for delicate women, instead of assigning nuns to it, she asked for volunteers, obtaining twelve, from among whom she selected five. Francesca was perfectly serious about this Alaskan project, for she called upon the volunteers to come forward "quickly, quickly and cheerfully". But the scheme did not seem quite practicable and therefore had to be dropped; there was so much that was crying to be done nearer home.

Yet though Francesca gave up her idea of a mission to the Eskimos, she did not give up all idea of being a missionary to pagans. Her dream was revived when, on her journey from Denver to California in September 1905, she visited the Pueblo Indians in Arizona. That was enough to make her long to work among them. Ever since she had met Indians in Nicaragua, she had been strongly drawn to carrying the gospel to such people. For though here and there among the Pueblo clans that were so doggedly rooted in their mysterious traditions Catholicism was to be found, for the most part they were pagan. When circumstances again prevented her from going to the heathen, she had the sad feeling that a part of her ardor was wasted or unfulfilled in its immediate purpose.

Train robbers were still operating in the West. One night there was an attempt to hold up the train on which Francesca was traveling. A window crashed by her side, and when the conductor came to her, he dug out a nail above her head; it was this that had been used as a bullet.

"Keep still, Sister", he said. "Don't be frightened. We've left those fellows far behind by now."

Then with the train-man he measured the trajectory
from the hole in the window to where the nail was buried;
it was in precise line with Francesca's head.

"Sister," he told her, "there must be somebody who's
looking after you. I don't believe that if that man had fired
right in your face he would have hit you."

At this Francesca beamed and told the conductor that the
"somebody" was the Sacred Heart—an explanation that
he found entirely unintelligible. Her traveling companion
had a dream in which she saw the devil and heard him say,
"Oh, if only I could tear that old woman to pieces!" Upon
which Francesca's mild comment was, "Poor devil! How
he does suffer when we try to take souls away from him."

So rapid were Francesca's movements across the North
American continent at this time that it is a little difficult to
follow them. Nor perhaps need they be followed here in
close chronological sequence. It is enough to say that she
was in New Orleans again in the spring of 1904 and in the
fall of 1905 in Los Angeles. These two points, along with
New York, Chicago, Denver, and Seattle, were the main
centers of her operations in the United States.

At New Orleans, the work begun twelve years previously in such extreme poverty had prospered. The Sisters
were still poor enough, and their orphanage and school on
Saint Philip's Street were now inadequate; but their work
had proved its value, and their settlement was becoming
more and more the pivotal point of Italian life in the city.
Francesca saw how much more she could do if only she
could secure better support.

The patron for whom she had been praying appeared
in the person of a retired captain of the Merchant Marine.
He was a man named Salvatore Pizzati, who, after coming

to the United States, had made something of a fortune
in trade. Though he had been very generous to the Vin-
centian Fathers, up to this time for some reason he had
never given the Missionary Sisters more than a dime or a
quarter when they had come to him on one of their begging tours. Then one day when he happened to be passing
the Sisters' school, he saw the children playing in the yard.
Most of them were Sicilians, and he was from Palermo.
The feeling of kinship that binds Italians from the same
province awoke in him. The idea of building an orphanage for them came to him in a flash.

The same day he called on Francesca. "Mother," he
asked her somewhat inconsistently, "why did you not
come to me sooner? I'd like to do something for these
children." What he was prepared to do was something on
a grand scale.

But as was so often the case in these Italian communities, there were anticlerical factions, and these tried to
get at the captain. They had been planning a hospital, and
they did their best to persuade him that his money would
be put to better use there than in an orphanage. In such
an argument there was enough plausibility for Francesca
to be afraid that the impulsive Captain Pizzati might be
won over, after she had left New Orleans. To make sure
of him, she took the precaution of getting him to sign a
legal instrument. And it was as well that she did so, for the
promoters of the hospital scheme contrived to make him
admit that he would help them if only he were free to do
so. "But I have made a written agreement with Mother
Cabrini, and I can't get out of it."

His visitors clapped him on the back. They felt that
the good-natured captain was now weakening. "But of
course you can get out of it!" they told him. "We'll bring
a lawyer round tomorrow, and he'll show you how to do

it. Have your agreement ready for him. That's only a bit
of paper."

But the lawyer when he came with them next day
to examine it had to say, "I don't think you will be able to
break that agreement. It's made of iron." Francesca had
seen to it that it should be precisely that.

The faction opposed to her had managed to get the Italian consul to join them, and his influence as that of an
official counted for a good deal. Francesca went to see
him, and in his case used very blunt methods. "Just try to
harm this work, and you shall pay for it!" she told him.
He knew that she was a lioness in some things and that
she had come into favor with the Italian government. A
word from her might do him a good deal of damage. He
thought it advisable to withdraw. "One does not fool with
Mother Cabrini", was his comment.

The New Orleans mission was eventually housed in a
new building on 3400 Esplanade Avenue. And the very
fact that work there had already been started was an advantage when in 1905 an epidemic of yellow fever swept the
city, for though the Sisters were unable to use the plant
that still existed only on paper, the certainty of its coming
had given them a standing greater than ever in the Italian
colony. The poor immigrants, living as they did in the
close congestion of the slums, fell victims by droves. The
Sisters now were almost the only people whom many of
the more ignorant would admit into their houses. These
illiterates had vaguely heard of a germ, and the rumor had
been spread among them that it was being deliberately
carried by the doctors and the priests. It was noted that
where they went death often arrived, too. Only the Sisters were trusted.

Yet a Sister was surprised one day to be asked by a
stricken man to give him "the fatal vial".

"What vial?" she asked. "I have no vial."

"Oh, yes, you have, Sister. Please lend it to me. I want to use it on an enemy of mine."

Obviously they did carry bottles of medicine with them, and no doubt the vial was among them. But at least *they* would not use it for lethal purposes. It was also noted that the Sisters did not hesitate to go into places from which doctors and nurses carefully stayed away.

Sometimes the priests were also under suspicion. In any event, there were not enough priests who spoke Italian and so were able to give the consolation of religion to the dying. Time after time a dying man would plead, "Sister, come and hear my confession!" Though that was something they could not do, they could at least help those in their last hour to prepare their souls for the judgment of God.

The city authorities, discovering the aversion of many of the more ignorant Italians to doctors, used the Sisters to break down this prejudice. The medical staff of the naval hospital was placed at their disposal, and every morning a truck delivered medicines and food to Saint Philip's Street. Then when a call came, a doctor would take a Sister along with him in the ambulance, to make sure that he would be permitted to see the patient. Even so, medicine was often refused until the Sister had first taken some herself; only in this way could one be sure that the fatal vial was not being used. And if the doctor insisted on the man's removal to the hospital, the Sister had to accompany the patient, or he refused to go.

The archbishop himself, the same Placide Louis Chapelle who had welcomed Francesca when she went to Paris to open a house there, contracted the fever and died on August 9, after which the epidemic died down gradually. But not one of the Sisters caught the terrible infection, though they had been more constantly exposed to it than anybody else. Later there came from the Italian minister of foreign affairs a letter to Francesca expressing the gratitude of Italy for what her nuns had done at this time.

❧ ❧ ❧

The fall of that year found Francesca in Los Angeles. It was not as yet the immense, sprawling city it has since become, though even then it was growing with spectacular rapidity. As was customary with her, Francesca went on foot along the boulevards from end to end, examining everything before deciding upon the best location for the orphanage she was going to establish. Except when she had a special impulse and picked out a site merely by looking at the map, this was her mode of procedure. It took a good deal of time, but only in this way could she make quite sure that she was getting just what she wanted. Her plan was to do something for the Mexicans there as well as for the Italians. Before she left Los Angeles, she had got the Regina Coeli orphanage in operation on Sunset Boulevard, and she had also opened a school on Alpine Street.

One new form of work dates from this visit, at least in its inception. Francesca had often noticed pale, sickly, undernourished children among the poor and knew that many of them had already contracted tuberculosis or showed a tendency toward it. She also knew that, especially in the case of children, the disease, if taken in time, was easily curable. What was wanted were rest and plenty of good food and clean air—none of which things they could get in their own homes. Therefore when she found at nearby Burbank, where in those days property was still cheap, a magnificent tract suitable for the erection of a preventorium for girls, she bought it at once. A few years later, the dizzy rise of real-estate values would have put the place quite beyond her reach. This preventorium was the first institution of its kind in California. It was useful not only for children there but for tubercular girls picked up by Francesca all over the country.

❦ ❦ ❦

It was during this visit of Francesca's to Los Angeles that the twenty-fifth anniversary of the founding of the Missionary Sisters of the Sacred Heart occurred. Anyone else would have gone back to Codogno for that fourteenth of November, the date on which she and her first little group of disciples left the House of Providence for the old Franciscan friary that became their motherhouse. But Francesca had important business to clear up before she could return to Italy. She said that the celebration would have to wait until she was free to go the following year. She was never much given to turning her eyes back to the past; the future still lay before her—a future of new projects, new work.

But California would not have been California had it allowed such an opportunity to pass unheeded. The priests of the diocese said that it had never happened before in Los Angeles that the foundress of a religious institute was there at the time of its jubilee. They insisted on solemnizing the day with the utmost pomp. For Francesca, it was not at all the same thing as being at Codogno, but as the local celebration would please the local clergy, she submitted to it. The real thing, in which all her daughters could join, was to come later.

Chapter Seventeen

THE CROWN ON THE WORK

At the belated celebration of the twenty-fifth anniversary of the founding of her institute, Francesca Cabrini was able to reflect that it was only seventeen years since she and her first group of nuns had landed in New York to begin their missionary career. Since then, they had spread into eight countries and the number of houses had grown to fifty and the number of Sisters to almost a thousand. It was a wonderful achievement, yet Francesca always said, "I have not done it. God has done it all, and I have merely looked on."

Though hers was still only a small community, Italians everywhere knew of Mother Cabrini. She was now being officially praised by the Italian government and to some extent was subsidized from that source. The Italian ambassador to the United States said very handsomely: "As Ambassador, I consider the illustrious Mother General of the Missionary Sisters a priceless collaborator; for while I work for the interests of Italy among the powerful, she succeeds in making it loved and esteemed by the humble, the infirm, and children." Upon her arrival in Italy, Francesca was received in audience by the queen and decorated. And even professedly liberal—which in Italy meant anticlerical—politicians had to admit that she was doing more for the immigrants than all the other agencies put together. Those who did not like to go so far as to say this openly acknowledged the fact in private.

If in the United States there was a changed attitude on the part of the native-born toward the hitherto despised Italian newcomers, this was in large part due to what Francesca had done. There is no need, of course, to claim that this was solely, or even mainly, due to her. As Italians got on in the world, they won respect from those who measure by the yardstick of material success. But at least it is true that the hope she had brought to the poor increased their dignity and self-reliance. Her schools and orphanages deserved all the praise they received—and even more than that praise, when we recall how meager were the resources she could use. Yet throughout the United States—from New York to Chicago, and from Chicago to Denver, and from Denver to the Pacific Coast, and from there down to the Gulf of Mexico—her nuns were busily at work. The same had to be said of Central and South America and of France, England, and Spain, though in those countries the activities of the Missionary Sisters wore a somewhat different aspect. Mother Cabrini had shot back and forth across the world, and everywhere she went, some new activity sprang up and flourished.

Retiring though she was in character, Francesca had become a public figure. She hated the spotlight and would never allow her picture to appear in the papers—and could be photographed in private only by some affectionate ruse of her nuns; nevertheless, even those who had no idea of her diminutive, vivacious, smiling presence were aware that she was a personage.

One can discern in her at this time the attitude of one who felt that her own work had been done and who was thinking merely in terms of clearing up a few odds and ends before laying down the burden of administration. She had begun as a woman whose health was so poor that nobody gave her more than a year or two of life, and her health had got no better as she grew older. Surely she was entitled to rest as soon as she had given the finishing touches to her design. She looked forward to what she had always desired—a life of contemplation—and meant to leave to younger and stronger women the carrying on of her tasks.

❧ ❧ ❧

Her great friend and patron Leo XIII had died in 1903. With the new pope, Pius X, she did not have the same extraordinary intimacy that she had had with his predecessor. The interests of this simple and humble man—the only pope since the Fifth Pius who seems likely to be canonized [and indeed was, in 1954—EDITOR]—were deeply engaged in a number of reforms and the extirpation of the virus of what was called modernism. But he was not unmindful of missionary concerns, and it was during his pontificate that the Missionary Sisters of the Sacred Heart and their constitutions received papal approbation. This had, indeed, been given in general terms as early as 1888; it was now sought in a more explicit way, and in July 1907, it was obtained.

But though the Rules as finally sanctioned were, except for very minor details, the same as those Francesca had drawn up twenty-six years earlier in Codogno, there was some objection to the use of the words Sacred Heart in the official title of the institute. As such it had in fact been legally incorporated in the United States since 1899; but until that date, the nuns had been variously known as the Salesian Sisters of the Holy Angels, the Missionary Salesians, and the Salesian Sisters of the Sacred Heart. A little confusion had risen on this account, and the precise minds of some canon lawyers wanted to know just what order it was that they were being asked to pass judgment upon. This confusion was easily removed. The other titles had been used only tentatively, and the one with the words

"Holy Angels" had been largely due to a misunderstanding on the part of the lawyer Francesca employed. With the giving of papal approbation, the Rules of the Missionary Sisters of the Sacred Heart were set in definitive form.

The moment had now come when Francesca, even if she had not resigned her generalship, would have been amply justified in governing her institute from Rome, leaving active missionary work to others. But the immediate effect of the approval of the Rules being used by Francesca, far from lightening her burdens, was to increase them. She decided to make a personal visit to each of the houses she had founded so as to promulgate the constitutions in person. Her conscientiousness would permit nothing less. As she was the framer of the Rules, she believed it incumbent upon her to expound their inner significance to her nuns wherever they might be. But this meant—as events were to show—that these visits involved her in the initiation of new undertakings, even while she was trying to wind up her active career. She could not endure the thought of retiring until every last detail for which she was responsible had been tidied up and folded away; and in the process of doing this, fresh opportunities opened before her, which she was not the woman to neglect.

At the end of 1907, Francesca was on her way to Buenos Aires. Her first visit to the Argentine had been made twelve years previously, when she had ridden on muleback across the Andes. This time she went there more comfortably by boat from Barcelona; but only after having founded an orphanage at Canillas, near Madrid, through the generosity of the Marquis of Portugalete. Though she was always ready for hardships, she never sought them out for their own sake; she was far too sensible for that. What needed to be done, that she did; but in the simplest and most expeditious way.

Her common sense was now displayed in a different fashion. She saw that the Buenos Aires school ought to be transferred to a larger and more suitable building; so she did her utmost to obtain one. But when, after three months, she had not succeeded, she saw no reason to struggle further against difficulties that for the time being appeared to be insuperable. She would have preferred to have attended to this herself; but the local superior could, after all, be relied on to carry the matter through later. As for herself, she was needed elsewhere.

Brazil was calling. From the Argentine a group of her nuns had already gone to open a school at São Paulo, and at that time Francesca had been too much occupied elsewhere to supervise this in person. Now she could visit it. She wished also to see the province itself, as it was one in which the Italian immigrants formed one-third of the entire population and had prospered. Moreover, at Rio de Janeiro, where she had once stopped for a day, she was being begged by the archbishop, Cardinal Arcoverde, to open another school. He had said to her, "Mother, I have a million souls to save; come and help me." It was impossible for her to resist such an appeal. As she was now fairly close at hand, she could attend to the matter on the spot. She always had an eye to placing her work, whenever possible, at a country's center; the strategic point was the one from which she wished to operate.

Francesca was getting on to sixty now, but it almost seemed that the energy of her early years returned when at six each morning she took a streetcar crowded with manual laborers off to their toil. Then she would spend the whole day, day after day, searching each quarter of the city in turn for the place she needed. It was an immensely fatiguing process, but it was her way of doing things. She did not like to make a decision until she had investigated all the possibilities. Her observant eyes took everything in. It seemed that she wanted to catch the tone, the color, the atmosphere, the very smell of a new country. She was not one who laid her plans in the cloister's seclusion.

On these days, Francesca took her lunch, wherever she happened to be, at the nearest workingmen's restaurant, and not until evening did she return to the convent where she and her companions were staying. At last on the Praia do Flamengo she came across a house. "A doll's house!" she exclaimed. "But it will have to do for the present. At any rate, it has a nice position facing the bay."

She rented it on the understanding that she would be free to move into a larger house nearby as soon as it was ready for occupancy. Within a month she had the doll's house completely furnished, and on June 25, 1908—which that year was the Feast of the Sacred Heart, an auspicious day—the school was dedicated and opened.

❦ ❦ ❦

The school was eventually to flourish, but it met at the outset with such severe and unexpected trials as to bring it to the edge of disaster. An epidemic of smallpox began to rage and at once brought down several of the nuns. This in itself was enough to ruin everything, for worried parents withdrew their children, and for those allowed to remain the teaching staff was so depleted as to be almost unable to function.

The coincidence of dates appeared very strange. The first of the nuns to be brought down, Sister Gesuina, was attacked on July 12, and that was the first anniversary of the papal approval of the institute. By the order of the Health Department, she was transferred to the Lazaretto, where she died three days later. This was on Francesca's birthday, and Francesca herself on hearing the news murmured, "That's God's birthday present to me!" In any other mouth, the remark would have been bitterly sardonic; all that Francesca meant was that a cross had come for which she should be grateful.

When two other Sisters caught the infection, Francesca met the situation by having them removed to a tiny house a mile and a half away from the main building. By doing this, she hoped that the matter would not reach the ears of the Health Department and that the Lazaretto might be avoided. She nursed the two sick nuns herself, being used to this kind of thing and doing her work so skillfully that not only were their lives saved but no pockmarks were left on their faces. All day long she was making visits to them, and in their retreat she prepared their baths and applied castor oil and whipped cream with a feather to their pimpled skin. Late at night she went to them with a lamp in her hand to light the way. She could think of nothing else but fighting the infection. This was not only life or death to the nuns who had been stricken but life or death to the newly opened school.

One of these Sisters—Maria Pastorelli—was to testify at the process for Francesca's beatification as to the devoted treatment she had received. She also testified under oath that sometime later when she was ill at Rio de Janeiro—this time with gastric troubles and headaches—Mother Cabrini suddenly appeared to her, though she was then in Chicago, and removing the wet bandages from her forehead said, "Why are you lying here, my daughter? Get up and go about your duties!" Upon this Sister Maria awoke and found that her bandages were gone and that she was perfectly well.

Whatever may be the explanation of that incident, it was certainly Francesca's cool, calm courage that carried the school safely through the crisis that threatened it at its very birth. But she spoke her mind very plainly—and in one of the most crowded streets of the city—to a young woman who, while she had used polite expressions of condolence toward her, had also been spreading malicious gossip about the dreadful ravages of the smallpox in the school. Francesca detested nothing so much as double-dealing, and when her blood was up she could be very blunt. Afterward, when she had calmed down somewhat, she explained, "That girl needed a good talking to, not only for her own sake but for that of others." The cardinal-archbishop, upon hearing of what had happened, laughed heartily. To Francesca he said, when next he saw her, "Good, very good! Don't leave Rio until you have put other people in their place."

As a provision for the future, Francesca bought what she called "a hole in the mountains" at Tijuca. The house was little more than a cottage among the health resorts there, but it could be used as a refuge in case another epidemic should come. Modestly as Francesca described this place, it was to be the core of the new academy when it was transferred there from the city, which afterward had only a day school. For small as the house was, it stood in ample grounds. In the end, the onslaught of smallpox turned out to have done good rather than evil.

Such preoccupations held Francesca in Brazil longer than she had intended to remain, and the expenditure of strength required told severely upon her. No sooner had she brought the new foundation through to safety than she fell ill of malaria, and from this she was to suffer for the rest of her life. But just as she had never allowed herself to be hindered by ill-health in the past—"While I am at work, I am well" was her axiom; "I fall sick the instant I stop working"—so this additional burden could usually be forgotten in activity. She was indeed every now and then forced to spend several days in bed—an old story with her—but except for such times, she never paused. The less she was able to do, the more she did; in that way she overcame her handicaps. As soon as she was able to travel—which means that it was long before she was fit to travel—Francesca sailed for New York.

❦ ❦ ❦

This was toward the end of the winter of 1908, and in the United States she was to remain for nearly two years. She required every bit of that time to attend to all that was waiting to be done there. As in Europe and South America, she felt that she should herself promulgate the Rules in their definitive form and consolidate the work now being done in so many important centers. New York had not only its Columbus Hospital but a number of other institutions within the city or not far away. The only rest she took was at West Park, which she always loved to visit, or the Villa on 190th Street, where the American novitiate was now set up. It was this place that she made her head-quarters, insofar as she could be said to have had any.

Yet even as she sat in the gardens of these houses, her active mind was always turning over its projects. She had to be doing something even there; only when stretched out in a deck chair on board a ship was she able to submit to complete idleness. So she pottered around the rosebeds, trimming or transplanting the bushes. Her nuns noticed that her light little body seemed to skim over the ground, skim over the floor. Her nervous energy needed to find some outlet.

It was also noticed that there was no fussiness about her. However small the thing she did, or that she told others to do, the Sisters saw that it was always something that demanded to be done. She got through so much because she was never ruffled; her work was performed in the abstraction of prayer. She was never so still as when in action. But action of some kind was necessary to her.

There is perhaps no need to go exhaustively into the details of Francesca's life at this period. Externally she was engrossed in administrative problems, and such matters are rarely exciting in themselves. The striking thing is that she was able to perform so efficiently while in such poor health. Chicago, Denver, Los Angeles, Seattle, New Orleans— they all saw her again in turn. And from these flights of bird-like directness, she came back to rest a moment on the bough of the Villa and then would be off on a new flight. It was unceasing and without haste and invariably fruitful. But it was work done in repose and the recollection of the contemplative. It was the activity of a saint.

The main fact that calls for mention here is that in Chicago in 1909 she founded another hospital.

The Columbus Hospital in that city, though it still accepted a number of free cases, was now so much frequented by the well-to-do that a new hospital had to be planned—one that should be exclusively for poor people who could not afford to pay. Nor was this hospital to be merely for the poor; it was to be for the Italian poor. The Sisters and the nurses were all to be Italians; the doctors were to be Italians, too; it was to provide what the grand building looking out on Lincoln Park was no longer able to provide so well. On the prosperity of the one the other could be supported. The immigrants who looked upon Francesca as their mother were not to be allowed to feel that she had forgotten them.

Again she went on foot through Chicago looking for the kind of place she wanted. The wild sudden wintry winds from the north sometimes nearly whisked her away as she bent her head against them, and it was in a snowstorm that she eventually came on the West Side to a stop. At a little open space, Vermont Park, the rows of apartment houses ended. Though this did not give Francesca the wide stretch she had in her other hospital, where Lincoln Park spread its grass and trees before the lake opened like a sea, it at least assured her of a site that would never be completely enclosed. It was such a site that she always preferred.

A house stood, solid, spacious, squat, which while now somewhat dwarfed by the new hospital that stands by its side, was then admirably suited to Francesca's needs. It would do for a start, and it had grounds that could later be used for a larger building. Francesca bought it at once.

She pushed the matter through so quickly that the local property-owners were not aware of what was happening until after the deed had been signed. To make up for this, they howled with rage at the intrusion of the Italians. Today that section of the city has somewhat declined, but thirty-five years ago it was considered rather exclusive, and the entrance of the Sisters there was thought to endanger real-estate values.

A storm broke on Francesca's head. When she began to make renovations in the Lytle Street mansion, saboteurs came one night and cut the waterpipes. When the workmen arrived in the morning, the floors were covered by a thick coating of ice. This had to be broken by picks before the men could get on with what they had to do.

That effort at intimidation having failed, another was attempted. A few days later, thick smoke was discovered at dawn to be coming from the basement. Fortunately the building—now used as the nurses' home—had such stout walls and hard woodwork that the fire was slow in getting hold and was put out before it could do much damage.

"What are we going to do, Mother?" the Sisters asked her. "The next thing is that these people will bring in dynamite. They have no intention of letting us get into the place."

Francesca remained serene. "I'll tell you what we'll do", she said: "We won't wait until the renovations are finished; we'll move in now. Our enemies are not going to carry the fight to such lengths as to roast the sick poor to death in their beds."

She started by having sixteen patients from the other hospital carried over. By the same evening, the hospital was half full of patients, and three days later it was crowded to the doors. One wonders whether they would have consented to go there had they known the whole truth about the situation, but Francesca proved that she had judged its psychological factors correctly. All sabotage ceased. She had won.

Again we have beginnings that are pathetic in their inadequacy. But the Italian colony of Chicago was appealed to, and a large number of the many societies among them responded by undertaking the furnishing of a room. Other gifts, especially those that arrived from individuals, were smaller—a few kitchen utensils, a mattress, a dressing table, some pillow slips and towels. Sometimes the towels and such things came only singly; at least one stocking did so. However, they came in large numbers, for Mother Cabrini was now a famous figure, and the mites when added together made up a respectable total. Even the anticlerical newspapers of the Little Italies backed the project as one that had to be admitted as being for the good of all Italians. But still nobody has ever been really able to explain how

the large amount of money that Francesca had to spend
was obtained. It is hardly enough to say that Francesca was
a remarkable businesswoman, for any businesswoman would
have seen that what she so cheerfully attempted was impossible. Once again, like Francesca herself, we have to fall back
upon the "heavenly bank".

❧ ❧ ❧

More and more had Francesca Cabrini impressed herself
upon the consciousness of America, not simply upon that
of America's Little Italies. Here, among other things, was
a glittering success story of the kind that all Americans
love—only Francesca's success was achieved without the
appliances of what is called efficiency, without any seeking of publicity, even without any display of organization.
Yet, of course, there *was* organization—of that effective
sort in which each person worked with well-nigh absolute
anonymity toward a common aim. That fact was not something that could be trumpeted abroad; the world merely
noted that somehow or other a hospital, an orphanage,
or a school had sprung from nothing, as though at the
waving of a magician's wand. Often it was in such a small
way as to escape notice at first, unless the notice of rid-
icule; but while the backs of the scoffers were turned, a
great building would go up—and Mother Cabrini would
be on a train journey of a couple of thousand miles to start
something else.

It was at this time that she became an American citizen.
She had from the outset intended to seek naturalization,
but until now this had been put off—either because she
did not remain long enough in the country to complete
the necessary probation or because she had been too busy
to think about it. The matter could no doubt have been
carried through during the period between 1902 and 1906,

but that was when Francesca was most hard at work, and she had not known that she was going to be in America for so long an unbroken time. It was in Seattle in 1909 that she at last took her oath of allegiance to the United States.

This would make her the first citizen of the United States to be canonized. The seventeenth-century martyrs, put to death with hideous tortures by the Indians, were French missionaries, very French indeed. And there was, of course, no question then of any naturalization or any new nation to which one could attach oneself by personal choice. So also with the great missionaries of the early nineteenth century: most of these also were French and remained so. Blessed Philippine Duchesne, who was beatified in 1940 and is scheduled to be canonized, is a case in point. There will no doubt be other American saints, and probably before long, as the cause of several is now well advanced. But Francesca will be the first of our own citizens upon whom the honor of canonization is conferred.

That Francesca Cabrini elected to become an American is, under the circumstances, worthy of remark. Her work, at least in its inception, was for Italians, and she herself was Italian to the day of her death. But she never thought of her work as being exclusively for Italians. From the outset, she had taken the whole world as her field of operations—finding it too small a world for the ardors that possessed her. Though she was obliged to make her beginnings assisted only by young Italian women, as soon as she could, she went looking for recruits among Americans, English, French, Spanish—people of any nationality— giving her institute with each year an increasingly international character. This international character, too, is bound to be more accentuated as time goes on and the scope of the Missionary Sisters is extended to lands to which

Francesca was only able to dream of going. And though its
main center of operations may not always be the United
States, the community cannot but remember that it began
its missionary work here. It was in the United States that
Saint Francesca spent most of her active years; Italy after
1889 was for her hardly more than the nest where she gave
strength to her wings. It was in Chicago that she died, and
it is in New York that her mortal remains repose. If Americans think of themselves as specially gifted with the faculty for getting things done with the utmost dispatch, then
Francesca Cabrini—whose life might almost be described
as a quiet whirlwind—was the most typical of Americans.

Chapter Eighteen

THE HOPE OF RETIREMENT

Though Francesca Cabrini had always had a longing for solitude and contemplation, one feels that her activity was, at least to some degree, a fulfillment of her natural temperament. Such an inference, however, may not be quite accurate. Her energy and executive gifts were possibly always latent in her, needing only an opportunity to manifest themselves; but it is as good an explanation that they were divinely infused. However this may be, it was solely in obedience to her vocation that she accepted the government of the Missionary Sisters, and the way she succeeded in her office was a good deal to the astonishment of those who had known her as a shy, demure young provincial schoolteacher. The best explanation of all probably is that grace builds on natural aptitude, but increases it beyond all knowledge.

The kind of life Francesca led—the union of the active and the contemplative—is perhaps the most difficult of all. But in the case of a saint, activity does not smother contemplation. When the Abbé Dufour asked the Curé d'Ars for advice on mental prayer, he got the answer, "I no longer have any time for regular prayer, but from the first moment of the day, I endeavor to unite myself to Jesus Christ, and then I do whatever needs to be done with this union in mind." From which the Abbé inferred that Saint

John Vianney's life was one long prayer. Yet though a saint can remain undistracted in God while immersed in external tasks, a saint would always choose to leave them, if he could, excellent though they may be, for a mode of spiritual life in which there are no intrusions.

It was for this reason that Francesca had frequently spoken of giving up the generalship of her institute. And each time she had renounced her personal wish as a temptation, so clear was it that duty called her to the active life. But now that she was sixty and worn out with her labors and in worse health than ever, she decided that duty had been served and that she might, with a clear conscience, retire and leave the direction of the institute to somebody else.

She had already mapped out the rest of her life. She intended to go to Codogno, motherhouse of the Sisters, and to spend whatever time was left from prayer in writing meditations for her nuns. By way of recreation, she would go into the meadows and gather medicinal herbs. Surely nobody would grudge this rest to her weary bones! She could not have more than a year or two to live.

Sometimes in the past when she had talked about this, the nuns had exclaimed, "But Mother, we are all ready to die for you!" Upon which Francesca would give her little smile and say, "A lot of good that would do me—to have a pack of dead nuns on my hands! Live and work—that's the best thing you can do."

Now the devotion of those who protested that they were willing to die for her strapped the burden all the more securely to her shoulders. As soon as the Sisters at Codogno saw that Francesca was serious in her intention of retiring, they wrote secretly to every one of their houses all over the world, to tell them what was afoot and to invite the votes of everybody on the proposal. The plebiscite, when the results arrived, was complete and unanimous: so long as Mother Cabrini was alive nobody else was even thinkable in her place.

The Sisters did not say anything to Francesca about what they were doing, but they entered into a kind of conspiracy with Cardinal Vives y Tuto, the prefect of the Congregation of Religious; and he prepared a decree that accorded with their wishes and not with Francesca's. To make everything perfect, this decree was to be issued on July 15, 1910, Francesca's sixtieth birthday.

The cardinal summoned her with a delegation of her nuns. She went hoping that this meant that her request was to be granted and that she was to be relieved of office. Then before reading the formal document, the Capuchin cardinal said: "Mother Cabrini, as up to now you have governed your institute so badly, I have decided to give you another chance, in the hope that you will do better in the future. You are to remain superior general."

At the grim joke—somewhat in Francesca's own vein of humor—she smiled appreciatively, though her heart sank. While the cardinal himself laughed at his own pleasantry, the circle of Sisters in the room clapped their hands and laughed with him.

❦ ❦ ❦

Francesca accepted this decision as a supreme act of obedience. It was contrary to her own desires, but as the task had been laid on her again by the Church, she submitted. In one sense, it made her happy: she could not but see how much she was loved and trusted. Speaking to the Sisters afterward, she told them: "If the chapter had been held in the ordinary manner, of course I would not have the signatures of all my daughters as a guarantee of the pledges that have been made." Then she made her own little joke:

"But what about those who were wanting to become Mother General? Now they have lost all hope." As the laughter died down, she added with an exquisite blending of gravity and jest, "Well, your Mother I have always been, and I know I would have remained your Mother even if another superior had been elected. So I shall serve you *in perpetuum*. I warn you, however, that I shall be just as severe as in the past." At which nobody knew quite whether to laugh or cry.

That day, by way of showing them how wholeheartedly she reassumed office, Francesca permitted what she was at other times most reluctant to allow: the nuns could come up and bow before her and kiss her ring. They did so in joy. Nor was her joy lacking; a sacrifice was something to be accepted thankfully.

❧ ❧ ❧

Before she left Codogno, Francesca sent word to Antonia Tondini that she would like to see her. The eccentric old woman who had been superior of the House of Providence was still living at an advanced age, but no longer as a nun, if she had ever been one except in name. On coming into the room where she was, Francesca knelt before her.

"But why do you kneel?" Signorina Tondini asked, after she had found words in her astonishment.

"I want you to forgive me for anything I did that grieved you."

Antonia Tondini immediately softened. She put her arms around the little figure kneeling before her and drew Francesca to her feet.

"No, Francesca, I should kneel to you. I always knew you were a saint."

"Reverend Mother," Francesca used the title as of old, as though Antonia were still entitled to it, "Reverend

Mother, you must not say that. Just tell me that you have forgiven me."

"Child, child!" Antonia's tears were flowing as they embraced again.

"'*Child!*'" A tear was in Francesca's own eye as she smiled. "Call me that again! It's so long since anybody called me anything but Mother General. And that's what I am, though I don't want to be. I was a bad child to you, Antonia."

They laughed and embraced again, and then talked over old times—such hours as would bear being talked about, and there were more of these than either had supposed. They melted in tenderness toward one another.

"Just you and I are left now, Francesca. They are all dead—the bishop and Monsignor Serrati and Monsignor Bersani. And I am over eighty. But you did me good, my little daughter. You saw where the embittered woman was going. You prayed for me?"

"Every day I have prayed for you, Antonia. And now you make me so happy."

"I am happy, too, hearing of all the wonderful things you do in America—all over the world. You always wanted to be a missionary. But if I had been a good nun, you would still be stuck in the House of Providence. You see how God works, Francesca."

"Every day I see that, Antonia. Soon I am going to America once more. That is why I wanted to say goodbye."

"And we shall not meet again, Francesca, dear child."

"Oh, but we *shall* meet again, Antonia—in heaven."

They embraced for the last time and parted.

A new vigor seemed to come at once to Francesca when the burden of office was taken up again. She had been caught somewhat by surprise and so needed a few weeks in which to get ready to leave the Codogno in which she had been expecting to pass the rest of her days. But it was only a few weeks. Then she was off to her last labors.

In August she was in Paris, and there she remained two months walking all over the outskirts of the city looking for a suitable house to which she could transfer the orphans she had at Neuilly. What she obtained was the former residence of the Empress Josephine at Noisy-le-Grand. In London, too, a new house had to be found. But though Francesca showed what seemed a new energy, it came wholly from her indomitable will and not from renewed physical powers. That she was utterly tired was only too obvious, but she did not permit this to serve as an excuse for not spending herself to the limit. She was a little bent now, and on staircases she often had to stop, gasping for breath. When the Sister who was with her looked at her with alarmed eyes, Francesca would merely smile and give herself a little shake as though in rebuke of her own weakness. Then she continued her painful climb. She found what she was looking for in the southeastern suburb of Honor Oak, a fine old house on its own hill, a place very suitable for an academy. On Christmas night, the first Mass was said there. The Infant Jesus was still the Cardinal-Protector of her Order.

Business detained Francesca in London for ten months. Then instead of going on to the United States, as she had intended, she found it necessary to return to Italy for a much-needed rest. But this was only rest of a kind. At Codogno she went through all the documents relating to the founding of her institute and put them all in order. She knew that it would be her last chance to do this and that it needed to be done. She also established a school of domestic science for the local women. These were relatively small things, things that could be regarded as relaxation. It was impossible for her to be quite idle.

Francesca seems to have had a strong premonition that when she left Italy she would never return. Everybody noticed in her a more than usual kindness and tenderness. No need was too small to escape her attention. Thus, as she feared that some Brazilian novices who had recently arrived might find the winter hard after their own warm climate, she saw to it that they got hot-water bottles every night. It was by such small means that she got a chance to manifest her consideration. The quick eyes of her daughters did not fail to observe that she was making a special effort to show her love for them. They knew that she would not put this in words, as that was not her way; but the small silent signals of affection, these they caught.

In December 1911, Francesca traveled to Rome, and there she fell seriously ill. Yet she would not often consent to stay in bed, as so much business needed to be dealt with. Instead, she would lie fully dressed on a couch, ready to drag herself up at any summons. The nuns were wondering whether she would ever be able to leave.

With the coming of spring, she rallied. One day in the middle of March, she suddenly announced, "I am going now. I *must* go. There is so much that I have to attend to in New York. The hospital there needs me."

Only a few days before this, her old friend Dr. Lagorio, on a visit to Rome from Chicago, had called to see her. He was no sooner inside the door of the convent when he heard a familiar voice piping in its tiny treble from the floor above. "Oh, doctor!" it called to him. "I am so glad you have come. I will be down at once. I was expecting you."

The doctor did not know how she knew of his coming, and she did not explain. Instead, she said, "There is something I want you to do for me."

"Gladly, Mother. What is it?"

"Well, you may have heard that I am going to build a new Columbus Hospital in New York, and it's going to cost a lot of money. I wonder if you would mind going to Senator Pantano, the chairman of the Committee of Foreign Affairs, to ask him if he could give me a million lire."

Dr. Lagorio gasped. A million lire in those days was worth about two hundred thousand dollars. "But Mother," he said, "That's an awful lot to ask for."

"It's only a third of what I need, Doctor."

Dr. Lagorio still hesitated. "You know what an anticlerical Senator Pantano is."

Francesca knew all about that. Perhaps she had selected Dr. Lagorio for this task because he was a Mason in those days. And the doctor had found by past experience that when she asked something, it was impossible to refuse her.

She turned her burning eyes on him. "All the same you will go, Doctor, won't you?"

"I'll go", he promised doubtfully.

When he arrived at Senator Pantano's office a little later, he found that he was expected. Mother Cabrini had already rung him up to tell him that Dr. Lagorio of the Pasteur Institute of Chicago was calling to see him.

The senator was taken aback by the request. "But Doctor," he asked, "how can my committee do that? Oh, of course I know that Mother Cabrini has done good work among the Italians of America. But you must know that I am a liberal. For me to try and get her this money—and so much money!—what effect do you suppose that would have on my political career?"

But Francesca had known what she was about in choosing her emissary—one who would make his appeal on humanitarian and not religious grounds. The upshot was that, though the Italian government would not give anything like so large a sum as a million lire outright, it did agree to pay the Columbus Hospital in New York an annual subsidy of five thousand dollars.

❦ ❦ ❦

Francesca had meant to visit all the houses in Italy, as well as those in France, Spain, and England, once more before leaving. But so much time had been lost through illness that she decided she had better go directly to New York. She would undoubtedly have collapsed had she attempted anything else. When she sailed from Naples on March 22, 1911, the sea again acted as a restorative. It was the last time she was to be upon it.

Immediately in New York, she went back to her old life, frailer than ever, but as energetic as ever. Yet despite the fact that she had brought with her a subscription book that Pope Pius X had signed, recommending the Columbus Hospital to public support, she found it difficult to collect much money. Undeterred by this, she determined to make a start with what she had and so called in a young architect to design a ten-story building for her. As it now stands at 227 East Nineteenth Street, one can see that something of a feat was accomplished in crowding so much into the small space available. It was all according to Francesca's own ideas of what a hospital should be. Had it not been for the war of 1914–1918 she would have lived to see it completed. What we now see there is her dream in stone and iron and concrete.

Her usual disregard of her health nearly put an end to her life at this time. One morning in July, when she was visiting West Park, she appeared at the door of her room crying, "I am dying! I am dying!" and then, "Come, O death, come!" But death did not come; her resilience made her bound back to life. As soon as she was able to travel, the nuns got her to go to the Mount of the Holy Cross in Colorado—fourteen thousand feet high and getting its name from the figure in its snow-filled ravines; and there she camped out in a log cabin until her strength—or some of it—returned. She still had a great deal to do.

That same July, the Columbus Hospital in Chicago formally opened its extension. This was the institution the saboteurs had tried to destroy when she began it in a smaller building in 1909. Though Francesca could not be present on the occasion, later in the year she herself supervised the construction of an annex to the house in Los Angeles. As she did not have enough money to employ contractors, she put the building operations under the direction of the same Sister who twenty-seven years before at Codogno had imperiled everybody's lives by her amateur bricklaying. Since then she had learned by experience and had become a first-class foreman. But it was Francesca who stood out in the sun, wearing a large straw hat and leaning on her cane, and took charge of the demolition of Luna Park. She had bought it cheap, intending to use the materials in the new structure. Gleefully the children of the neighborhood worked under her direction, filling pails with nails, locks and hinges—for all these could be used again. Francesca found that she had so much brick and woodwork left over that she was able to ship a great deal of it to Denver, where another building was going up. In her function of contractor, she immensely enjoyed herself.

Early in 1913 she went to Seattle. She had to buy a new orphanage there. So according to her usual practice, she went out to find it, walking over the hills and through the woods on the outskirts of the city. The Sisters with her could see that she was subjecting herself to too great a strain and begged her to take more care. To which she would only answer, "What's the matter? Are you tired?" and trudge on ahead.

This time she did not find anything that satisfied her. So she tried another method. Taking down a map of Seattle, she studied it closely and at last put her finger upon a spot. "You two Sisters go there tomorrow," she said, "and when you come back, tell me what it is like."

"But Mother," one of them protested. "I know that section. There is nothing there that will do."

"All the same I want you to go."

They came back greatly excited. They had seen paradise on earth, they said. There was a large house standing in an estate coming down from Beacon Hill right to the edge of Lake Washington, with a wide view of the snow-capped mountains beyond.

"But how did you know about it, Mother?" they asked.

"You know about my dreams", she said lightly.

The next day Francesca went to have a look at it herself. On the way back, she and the Sister with her, instead of taking the crowded trolley, quite openly thumbed a ride. A lady got her chauffeur to stop.

When they had got in the car, Francesca explained, "We have been out seeing a place I want to buy for an orphanage."

"Are you going to buy it?"

"I will if I can afford it."

"Where is it, Sister?"

Francesca told her.

The lady stared at her. Was this simple-looking nun joking? Apparently not, though she did smile a good deal.

"Well, Sister," said the lady, "I may be able to help you a bit. That place happens to belong to my husband."

That helped very much. The owners, interested in Mother Cabrini and her orphans, offered the property at a low price. The wife's argument with her husband, when he objected that they were almost giving it away, was, "You know you bought it only for me. Now we so very seldom go there at all. So why not let the Sisters have it? Then it will do some good."

An anonymous benefactor came forward with the hundred thousand dollars needed. It almost seemed as though God and Francesca were at this time playing a kind of game with one another.

❧ ❧ ❧

The same summer, Francesca was back in New York. She wanted to establish an orphanage nearer the city than was West Park, and to find this she went on long drives. One day she passed a large house in wooded grounds at Dobbs Ferry. It was, however, obviously not for sale, for as they drove in they saw that it was being used as a boys' school that had every mark of prosperity.

Nevertheless, Francesca asked to see the owner. It was his son who came into the parlor.

She opened with, "I should like to buy this place."

He smiled with polite indulgence and answered, "I'm sorry, but it's not for sale, Sister."

"But if you *did* sell it?" she persisted.

"Well, perhaps my father would let it go for a hundred thousand dollars."

"I couldn't think of that", Francesca told him. "Though at a lower price I would consider it."

The young man invited her to look over the place. It already had a chapel—one easily convertible to Catholic uses—a gymnasium and a swimming pool. It was exactly what she wanted.

As they said goodbye, the young man told her again, "I'm afraid you'll have to try somewhere else, Sister. My father is not wanting to sell."

"But you will take my card? If you change your mind ..."

"I don't think my father is likely to change his mind."

On their way out, Francesca managed to bury a medal of Saint Joseph in a flower bed. It needed only an instant as she bent down, apparently to tie her shoelace, to slip the medal into the soft mold. When they were in their car, Francesca turned to her companion and said, "You will see; Saint Joseph will drive those boys away."

A few days later the owner wrote asking her to make an offer.

❦ ❦ ❦

Again Francesca supervised the making of such alterations as were needed. And it was she who undertook to wash the outside walls. Wearing a straw hat, and with her skirt pinned back and her sleeves rolled up, she seemed to exult in what she was doing. How wonderful a home this would be for her orphans!

But every now and then, her strength would fail. Then a nun would run up and expostulate, "Mother, this is beyond you! Look, that heavy brush has slipped from your fingers, and your habit is all wet. You must stop and come down from that ladder."

Francesca merely smiled. "Oh, that's my clumsiness, Sister. I'm getting a lot of fun doing this. Please hand me up that brush."

And she would start all over again.

Nothing much needed to be done. The children were soon in that fine house and playing in its beautiful grounds. There they would cluster around Francesca as she sat under a tree. If she did not have some candy for them, they were at least sure of a funny story. It made her very happy to see how happy they were.

✿ ✿ ✿

The outbreak of the war brought this much change in her Rules: the superior of the house in Paris was instructed to give preference to daughters of killed or wounded soldiers; and, for the first time, because of war needs, an orphanage for small boys was opened there. In London, part of the school was turned into a military hospital.

Heavily the war lay upon Francesca's spirits, and she was often unable to sleep. When in 1915 Italy was drawn in, her anxieties increased, for although she was an American citizen now, she had not ceased to love the land of her birth. But in one way the war had a good effect upon her work; it gave her a chance to consolidate what she already had in hand, without having at the same time to cope with an unceasing deluge of newly arrived immigrants.

This, however, did not prevent her from initiating new plans and on a grand scale. Ignoring the fact that she was ill, she set out from New York for Seattle in August 1915, remaining ill throughout the long, hot, fatiguing journey. "I was not thinking of making this trip at all," she told her traveling companion, "but Our Lord has made me understand that He wants me to begin some new work, and so I said, 'If God wants it, He will give me the strength for it.' So here we are on our way." At night, when she thought she could not be heard, she was often moaning softly. Yet when they arrived five days later at Seattle at eleven in the morning, she went early in the afternoon to call on Bishop O'Dea. She wanted to ask his approval for the establishment of another orphanage there.

Upon obtaining his permission, she looked around for a place suitable for her purpose. After some search, she decided to buy the Perry Hotel, if possible, as it was for sale. When it turned out that the chief stockholder was a Mr. Clarke and that he lived in New York, she sent a telegram to the Sisters there telling them to get in touch with him at once. That was all she told them; she did not send Mr. Clarke's address, because she was afraid that if she asked for it in Seattle the local stockholders would discover what was in the wind and create difficulties. And well they might have objected—for her first instructions to the Sisters were that they should ask Mr. Clarke to *give* them the hotel; they were to try to buy it only if he refused to give.

Staggered by such an order, the Sisters nevertheless set themselves to obey it to the letter. But how were they to discover the right Mr. Clarke in New York? The only thing they could do was to ring up in turn all the hundreds of Clarkes listed in the telephone book, or all who seemed likely. The conversation ran:

"Are you Mr. Clarke?"

"Yes, I'm Mr. Clarke."

"Do you own a hotel in Seattle?"

"Say, what's this? Do I what?"

"Are you the Mr. Clarke who owns a hotel in Seattle?"

After hearing "No" a score of times, the Sister on the telephone at last heard, "Yes, I do own a hotel in Seattle. What of it?"

"Then may I come to see you?"

"Would you mind telling me who you are?"

"I'm one of the Missionary Sisters of the Sacred Heart."

The businessman was very indignant when he received the cool suggestion that he should give them his hotel. He wondered whether the Sisters who had called upon him were quite sane. All that they could do after that was to wire Mother Cabrini in Seattle for further instructions. They came by wire: "Go and offer Mr. Clarke the smallest sum of money he will take."

The smallest sum turned out to be immense; it was a hundred and fifty thousand dollars. But Bishop O'Dea told Francesca, "Even at two hundred thousand dollars, the Perry Hotel would be a bargain. You must not lose your chance of getting it for your orphanage." In order to keep the deal open, Francesca scraped together ten thousand dollars and then cast about for means to obtain the rest.

As soon as the affair became known in Seattle, there was the kind of uproar to which Francesca was by now accustomed. The other stockholders were angry that Mr. Clarke was letting the hotel go so cheap. On the other hand, there was opposition to the idea of the place becoming an Italian orphanage. If that happened, it was argued, property values in the neighborhood would drop. As those affected were influential men, they determined to prevent the completion of the transaction by seeing to it that Mother Cabrini secured no loan from any local bank. For five months—from November to April—the struggle went on, and during that time Francesca had to dispatch about a hundred telegrams of instructions. Her friends began to tell her that she was being obstinate and that the opposition was too strong for her. But she held on, set upon getting the hotel.

The question boiled down to this in the end: Where was she going to obtain the enormous sum of money she needed? In her other house in Seattle, there was a statue of Saint Anne teaching the Blessed Virgin to read. On Our Lady's book Francesca wrote, "A hundred and twenty thousand dollars", remarking, "There! Now she can't help seeing it." She had by this time contrived to gather thirty thousand dollars, but unless heaven helped her, she had exhausted her sources of supply. Then at the very last moment, the president of the Scandinavian Bank offered to lend Francesca what she had to have. On April 21, 1916, the Perry Hotel passed into her possession. It was the last of her many big business deals.

It also seemed to be, after all, a very bad piece of business. For after she had bought the hotel, Francesca decided that it was not suitable for an orphanage but that it would do admirably for a new Columbus Hospital. At this point, Bishop O'Dea intervened; he told her that he had given his permission for the founding of an orphanage, but so far from approving of a hospital, he forbade it. His prohibition reached Francesca on the Feast of the Sacred Heart. "On this day of all days!" was her only comment. Indeed it did seem, as on the same day in Brazil a few years previously, that the Lord was showing a strange sense of humor in the gifts He sent her. Now she had bought the building, with a huge mortgage, and had it useless on her hands. Coming at the end of negotiations that had worn her out, the decision of the bishop overwhelmed her. Francesca left Seattle for Los Angeles in November defeated and broken.

But she had always trusted in God, and God did not fail her. The bishop of Seattle relented a little later—that is, he relented to some extent. The Perry Hotel might be used for physiotherapy and electrotherapy treatments, though he still refused to permit the establishment of a general hospital. This concession, however, opened the door. By degrees, the special treatments faded into the treatment of all physical ailments. Before she died, Francesca was to learn that she had made no mistake in buying the Perry Hotel.

Chapter Nineteen

DEATH IN CHICAGO

When Francesca arrived in Los Angeles, the Sisters there were shocked to see how shattered she looked. Though they were accustomed to her being ill and in pain, they were hardly prepared for the worn, weary woman who tottered into the convent. They realized, however, that she had gone through a period of cruel strain in Seattle and that this had been followed by the crushing disappointment of Bishop O'Dea's refusal to allow her to open the Perry Hotel as a hospital. And they knew her recuperative power; after a little rest, she would of course get well again.

Yet they remained disturbed about her. She was not a woman who allowed herself to be depressed when things did not go her way. It was even impossible to tell from her countenance whether she had cause for worry or not; indeed, adversity, so far from making her downcast, made her lift up her heart to God all the more. When they remembered all this, they understood that her condition must be one of serious physical sickness.

Looking back upon her visit, they thought that she must have recognized how ill she was. There was an inexpressible tenderness about her; she had shown them more than her ordinary kindness. This could only have meant that she was saying goodbye, that she was aware that she was soon to depart from mortal life.

But that was reading in a significance when everything was over. For after a while, Francesca seemed to be a good deal better. Every day she was out doing a little gardening or feeding the birds for whom she had always had such an affection. And when on Christmas night she assisted at High Mass with the community, she sang the *Te Deum* with so glowing a face, so joyous a voice, that many of the nuns muted their own voices to hear hers. When she went up to the crib to kiss the Bambino, she struck them as being like an angel from heaven. They laid aside their forebodings. She was not very old, after all—only sixty-six—and she would recover, as she had done so many times before.

During that spring, there occurred what Sister Euphemia, who testified to the matter at the process for Francesca's beatification, considered a miracle. She related the incident with charming simplicity, even with a certain quaintness; but her account does not leave out Francesca's humor and common sense. It seems that Sister Euphemia had suffered for some years from varicose veins. After other doctors had been able to do her no good, she had consulted local Chinese and Japanese specialists, but the steam baths and ointments they prescribed left her as before. Now Francesca, aware of the pain Sister Euphemia was suffering, suggested that she should wear silk stockings, as they might be more soothing to the skin. But the Sister had a better idea than that; she purloined a pair of Mother Cabrini's cotton stockings and wore them—and was instantly and permanently cured. When Francesca saw her the next day walking about very briskly, she asked, "What has happened to you? You are all right now." When she was told about her stockings, she laughed; then with a serious face she said, "I hope you are not going to be so foolish as to say that my stockings cured you. It was your faith that did it."

Francesca was unable, however, to cure herself. She had benefited from the rest, but she was still far from well. So she said she would go to Chicago to consult the doctors in the Columbus Hospital. Actually she went because she was needed there on business. Though she was hardly able to stand, she insisted upon being put on the train.

While she was saying farewell she murmured, "Those birds, those birds...."

"What about the birds, Mother?" she was asked.

"Who will look after them now?"

❧ ❧ ❧

When she arrived in Chicago on the morning of April 18, 1917, some of the Sisters wept on seeing the change that had come over her. Yet so as to hide the real condition of her health, that same morning she went about her work. When they begged her to go to bed, she answered, "No, I have things to attend to. Besides, a little exercise will do me good."

But the nuns were watching her closely. Among them were Mother Antonietta della Casa, who was then superior at the Columbus Hospital and who succeeded her as General, and Mother Grace, now head of the institute in the United States. Francesca had always been amenable to her daughters when they felt that they really had to take her in hand. She had even asked that any of them who observed a fault in her should tell her about it. So now Mother Grace, when she thought things had gone far enough, used to say, "Mother General, you know that I always obey you. Tonight please obey me and go to bed at once." When Francesca was spoken to like that, she did obey, glad of an opportunity for practicing obedience.

The Chicago doctors told her—what she already knew—that she was suffering from malaria. Under the vigorous treatment they applied her fever diminished, but she was left with a weakness of the pulmonary veins. Yet it caused no special alarm. She was soon behaving as though there were nothing the matter with her. The nuns saw as usual, only perhaps more clearly than in the past, that light suffused her countenance and made her appear to be a being of another world. Somehow that made them feel that she belonged to them forever. It was hard to imagine that so radiant a creature would die. It was impossible for them to imagine what it would be like without her.

❧ ❧ ❧

By June, Francesca was flinging herself with immense energy into the preparations going on for several grand receptions. At conventual institutions no trouble is spared over such events. The apostolic delegate to the United States, Archbishop Bonzano, visited the hospital, and with him came Bonaventure Cerretti, the apostolic delegate to Australia, and Archbishop Mundelein—all three men who were destined to become cardinals. The thousand details necessary—or thought to be necessary—for giving them a sufficiently splendid welcome Francesca supervised herself, and the end of the day found her quite exhausted.

Shortly afterward there came another grand reception of a different kind. Francesco Saverio Nitti, the head of the Italian economic mission to the United States and afterward prime minister, visited Francesca with his colleagues. From that kind of official recognition much might be hoped. Some of the politicians who made up the party were perhaps not conspicuous for their practice of religion, but it was only politic to receive them ceremoniously. Again it was all very exhausting for poor Francesca.

Yet the excitement appears upon the whole to have done her good—at any rate to have done her no harm.

On July the 4th, when the spiritual exercises opened, she never missed any of the community devotions and was always the first to arrive in the chapel at five-thirty in the morning. On the closing day, she delivered an address to the assembled Sisters with such vivacity and in so clear a voice that they all thought her quite rejuvenated.

She was, however, very far from well. Though she refused to resign herself to inactivity, she followed the doctors' advice to the extent of going out into the country every afternoon for a drive. Then in the fields she gathered wildflowers and ferns for the hospital chapel. It was a kind of compromise retirement, if only of a temporary nature.

But even these little excursions were made of practical use to the community. On her drives, Francesca got the idea of buying a farm from which her hospitals in Chicago could obtain a supply of milk and eggs and chickens. She did buy just such a farm at Parkridge in October, even supervising the purchase of the cows. Francesca was not a farmer's daughter for nothing.

At the end of October, there began that Austro-German push that resulted in the great Italian defeat at Caporetto. All through November, things went from bad to worse, and it was not until Christmas Day that, by showing a desperate valor, the Italian army was at last able to hold its lines against the German thrusts. But by that time, Francesca Cabrini was dead. She could of course hardly have made a permanent recovery, but it is not too much to say that she was among the casualties of Caporetto. Her heart was broken with sorrow over her beloved native land.

All through November, she was failing. On the 21st, she went as usual to the chapel for the morning meditation, but when she went up to the altar rail for Communion at the end of Mass, she was seen to sway as though about to fall. Upon returning to her place, she fainted and was carried to her room. When the Sisters reproached her for having got up when she was so ill, her reply was: "Would you have had me miss Holy Communion today, the Holy Father's birthday? I admit it was a struggle to get up, but we must pray so much for the pope." Later, even on that day, Francesca went about her ordinary business.

So it dragged on for several weeks. Never would she miss the community recreations, and when Mother Antonietta begged her to spare herself, at least to that extent, Francesca said, "No, no; this is the only time I have with the Sisters. They look forward to seeing me, and it would make them unhappy if I did not go." When she walked into the recreation room, it was with such a joyous face that all except the two or three who really knew how ill she was were quite taken in. They were delighted that their Mother was looking so well and had no suspicion what an effort it cost her.

On the Feast of the Immaculate Conception, December 8, she had them play a kind of pious game at recreation. Each of the Sisters was to write a few lines about the Blessed Virgin—in verse if possible, something not too difficult to do in a language so rich in rhyme as Italian. But those who could not manage verse wrote in prose, and there were some Sisters whose tongue was English. To all their little effusions, Francesca listened with pleasure. Innocent praise and laughter made them all very happy.

That, however, was the last time she was able to go to their recreation. Even so, she by no means gave up her own fight for life, nor did she allow anybody to know what a fight was going on. If she withdrew now, it was

not mainly on account of her health but rather in order to
prepare herself in quiet for the approach of Christmas, a
feast specially dear to her.

For a Christmas present, she gave orders that each
member of the community was to have a new habit. As
she included herself in this, the Sisters inferred that she
could not have any forebodings that her end was near.
Afterward, they saw that she had meant her new dress to
be for her *dies natalis*. Even at the time, they wondered at
the words she selected to be printed on her Christmas card
that year. These were from the Psalm 42: *Emitte lucem tuam
et veritatem tuam: ipsa me deduxerunt et adduxerunt in montem
sanctum tuum et in tabernacula tua.* When one of the nuns
protested, "But Mother, *that's* not a Christmas greeting;
it's about the glory of paradise", Francesca merely said,
"Leave it as it is."

For the doctors and nurses at the hospital she prepared
little gifts, and when she heard that the five hundred children at the Italian school on Erie Street would have to go
without candy because of the difficult times, she exclaimed,
"Oh no, they must have their candy! Christmas would not
be Christmas for them without it." She instructed the Sisters to buy it at her expense.

It was now Friday, December 21, 1917. On that day,
she rose at her customary early hour and assisted at Mass
and also spent an hour in adoration of the Blessed Sacrament, as the Missionary Sisters do every Friday. The rest
of the day was given over to the doing up of the candy
in parcels. She worked feverishly, as though she knew
that this was to be her last day on earth, and kept saying
to those helping her, "Hurry, hurry!" The last parcel of
all that she wrapped up was a Christmas present for Archbishop Mundelein; it was a desk set in hammered brass
made by one of the Sisters.

The next morning, Francesca was too ill to rise, but nobody was alarmed; this was something that had been frequent with Francesca all through her life. As was also frequent with her at such times, she received several Sisters in her room and, still lying in bed, attended to some questions of business. Later in the morning, Mother Antonietta, the superior, came in and remained with her until 11:40.

As soon as Mother Antonietta had left, a young Sister went in and asked Francesca what she would like for lunch. Her answer was vague, but when pressed she said, "Bring me anything you like. If I don't take it I may take something else." She had remained fasting all the morning in the hope of being able to go to the chapel to receive Holy Communion. She was undoubtedly still hoping, late as it was, to get up for this purpose.

The Sister went into the passage and waited there for the food wagon. Just then Mother Antonietta returned; there was something she had forgotten to ask. When she pushed gently at the door and found it locked, she concluded that Francesca was dressing. She also knew that Francesca had a way of locking the door when she wanted to make sure that nobody broke in upon her contemplation of the Divine. That hint was enough: without knocking, she stole away.

A moment later, the Sister in the passage heard the key click in the lock; it was being unturned. Hanging on the frame of the door outside there was a bell; Francesca's hand went outside and pulled at the cord. The waiting Sister went in quickly with the tray still in her hand to see what was wanted and found Francesca fallen back in a wicker chair. Her nightgown was stained with blood, and blood was on the handkerchief she held to her lips.

Very frightened now, the young nun ran to the refectory in the basement, white of face and stammering,

"Our Mother! Our Mother!" Followed by the other nuns,
Mother Antonietta went with her at once to Francesca's
room, after sending for the priest and the doctor. Francesca's eyes were open and her lips slightly parted, but
she was already unconscious. There was nothing that the
doctor could do, nor could the priest do anything except
administer Extreme Unction and give her conditional absolution. Leaning her head against the arm of Mother
Antonietta, Francesca turned a last look on her daughters
and peacefully died.

It was a death in loneliness, but a death for which she
had always been prepared. She had long made it her custom to receive Holy Communion as though for her Via-
ticum. And though her dereliction was not so absolute
as that of her patron, Saint Francis Xavier, abandoned on
Sanchian Island, her case nevertheless reminds one of his.
She was Francesca Saverio in her death.

But in dying, she was also the Francesca she had always
been in life. Her first confessor, when as a child she took
to him her small problems, used to say, "Go and tell that to
Jesus." She was little Cecchina even in those last moments,
depending directly on her Lord.

Just what took place during them, when she was alone
in her room, we do not know, and any surmise would be
impertinent. But we may at least see here a final reserve in
a life that had been all reserve, the keeping of the *Arcanum
Regis*. While she was trying to get ready to receive Christ,
Christ had come for her.

Her secret had been preserved to the end, and no
attempt should be made to penetrate behind the veil she
held before her spiritual life. But we do get occasional
glimpses of this in the notebook from which quotation
has frequently been made in these pages. Only by accident was it discovered; only by accident did it escape the

destruction she made of all the other records of her deepest feelings. From it a final quotation may be drawn: "I wish to die of love after a life of total surrender to God.... Oh Jesus, I love You so much, so much! I am being consumed by Your love; for You I languish and die; but in spite of such intense ardor, I see—I feel—that it is only a pale shadow compared to the fire of love with which You surround me. Give me a heart as large as the universe, so that I may love You, if not as much as You deserve, at least as much as I am capable of.... I am Your victim, ready to be sacrificed; do with me as You will."

EPILOGUE

The Aureole

Francesca Cabrini, even while she was alive, privately received a kind of aureole from all the popes of her time. Leo XIII actually did call her a saint. Benedict XV, who as Monsignor Della Chiesa had drawn the brief she carried to America in 1889, described her as full of the spirit of God. And Pius X—who himself has been canonized—called her a true apostle of the Gospel. But such opinions were, of course, merely personal; Francesca's cause for beatification had to be introduced in the ordinary way.

The rules governing this matter have grown increasingly strict. There was a time when saints were made by popular acclaim. In fact, the first instance of canonization on the part of the pope was the one when John XV in 993 declared Ulric of Augsburg a saint. Yet for a long while after that date, the local bishops acted largely on their own initiative, until Alexander III forbade the introduction of a *cultus* without the permission of the Holy See. Throughout the thirteenth century, the method of canonization was often extremely summary and rapid, so that the aureole was often conferred within a year or two of the saint's death; nor was there any great practical difference between beatification and canonization.

With the decrees of Urban VIII in 1625 and 1634, the modern practice of long and close scrutiny did not actually begin, but it was from that time insisted upon under severe penalties. Canonization now frequently follows almost as a matter of course upon a pronouncement of beatification, for those whose causes have been introduced under the present legal forms. But because these forms are exceedingly rigid, many a cause is introduced that makes slow if any progress, and even after that it is hard to get beyond the preliminary stage of having one's virtues pronounced heroic.

The rules now call for at least fifty years to elapse between death and the opening of what is called the process, the most intricate and deliberate—and also the most expensive—of lawsuits. It is expensive because of the exhaustive enquiry demanded by the Church. For this reason, it might seem that nobody (however holy) has much chance of being canonized today who does not belong to a religious order prepared to pay the costs, unless he can arouse such popular enthusiasm as to have his devotees subscribe the necessary funds. Even then, however, there is no assurance that the process—the suit in law—will be successful. Though the expense of this suit does undoubtedly prohibit many saints from obtaining the formal honor of canonization, all the money in the world cannot obtain this unless sanctity has been established before the exacting tribunal of the Congregation of Rites.

In the case of Francesca Cabrini, the rule about fifty years was waived, as any such rule can be, by the direct action of the pope. The preliminary, or what is called the Ordinary Process, was begun ten years after her death— something almost without precedent in modern times. That her personal friendship with several popes had something to do with this may possibly be true, but can be only a minor factor. Papal policy with regard to canonizations is to proceed first with the causes that appear to be most likely to be of benefit to the Church as a whole. But the main factor must always be a glowing conviction as to

the personal sanctity of the Servant of God whose cause
is under consideration. Everything in Francesca Cabrini's
story contributed to that conviction; it had only to be told
to bring her the aureole.

All through Francesca's life there had been strange happenings. And those who knew of these regarded them as
miracles, though some of them, as is true of many of the
miracles related of other saints, may be susceptible of a natural explanation. A case in point is her telling the gardeners
at West Park to replant a fig tree they had cut down—and
its growing again. When the Promotor of the Faith—who
is pleasantly known as the Devil's Advocate—heard that
an inscription had been put up commemorating the circumstances, he incautiously jumped to the conclusion that
this had been done with Francesca's consent and so ques-
tioned her humility. His objection fell to the ground when
it came out that the inscription had been put up in 1928.
In any event, we are not obliged to believe that there was
anything miraculous here. And many similar things related
of Francesca during her lifetime may be accounted for,
as she accounted for them, on the ground that they were
brought about by the faith of others and not by any powers
with which she was endowed. It is not such things that the
investigating tribunal accepts as miracles in its own strin-
gent sense.

But when there is a physical cure—not a gradual improvement but a cure that is instantaneous and complete
and that competent medical judgment says could not possibly have occurred by natural means, and when such a
cure comes through intercession to the supposedly saintly
person after his death—*then* there is the kind of evidence
demanded. It was this kind of evidence that was supplied
as corroborative of Francesca's sanctity.

About noon on March 14, 1921, Peter Smith was born in the Columbus Hospital Extension in New York. As a matter of routine, the nurse put a solution of nitrate of silver into the child's eyes. She was in a hurry at the time. When she put down the bottle she stared at it, dumbfounded with dismay. She saw that she had used a fifty percent solution instead of a one percent solution, and she knew that that meant the baby's eyes had been destroyed.

Desperately she tried to wipe the solution away, but it was no use. The damage had been done. Without waiting to lay the child in his crib, she rushed with him in her arms to the nun in charge of the floor. "Sister, Sister!" she screamed. "Come and do something. I've done a dreadful thing. Get a doctor."

Two doctors were brought. They looked at the child's eyes, and they looked at the bottle of solution. It was as the nurse had said. She had stayed around hoping that there was some mistake in the labelling of the bottle, that it might not be as bad as she thought. When she saw their faces, she collapsed, weeping hysterically.

An eye specialist was sent for. He of course agreed with the other doctors.

"The cornea has gone", he pronounced briefly. "Nobody can do anything."

The superior hurried in. She thought that there was something that might be done after all. With her she brought a relic of Mother Cabrini and put it to little Peter's eyes before pinning it to his nightgown.

That night, she and the Sisters spent the entire night in prayer in the chapel. The nurse had already gone there and was begging frantically, "Please Lord, please Lord! Don't let that baby get blind. Mother Cabrini, won't you work a miracle!" She was not thinking of herself. She took it for granted that she would be discharged for gross negligence.

But that poor baby, to have this happen to him almost the moment he was born!

The next morning the doctors came again. One of them swung toward the other after he had bent down to the baby and asked his colleague, "Am I seeing things?"

The other doctor bent down now and looked into Peter's eyes with a light. "No, *you* are not seeing things; but *he* is. Those eyes are intact and perfectly normal."

In this case, a second miracle occurred immediately. That very day, Peter Smith got double pneumonia. His temperature was taken; it was a hundred and eight.

The Sisters sent for the doctors again. "Well," they said, "a degree less than that is invariably fatal." One of them turned to the superior and said, "Mother, you'll have to do some more praying. Even though those burns have not harmed the baby, this fever will burn him to death."

"Doctor," she returned, "Mother Cabrini has not cured his eyes just to let him die of pneumonia."

They prayed again, thankful for the first miracle, which had spared their hospital from a scandal, but pleading for a second. By morning, all symptoms of the pneumonia had gone. When the doctors came, one said, "I never knew of such a thing. Why, that child is perfectly all right. Not a trace of high temperature!"

"Look how he's sleeping", said the other. "Mother, your Mother Cabrini certainly can do extraordinary things."

Ten days after his birth, Peter Smith went home with his mother. Later a soldier in the army, all that he had to show for his mishap were two small scars caused by the silver nitrate as it ran down from his eyes.

Sister Delfina Grazioli had been more or less ill since 1915. In 1921, an X-ray examination showed her to have adhesions involving the gallbladder, colon, duodenum, and pylorus. There was an operation that year and another the next. But still she did not get better, so that she had two more operations, ten months apart, in 1925. She continued to waste painfully away.

By the end of the year, the doctors gave up all hope. Sister Delfina was sinking. Out from skull-like sockets gazed great dull eyes. She was too weak to eat or to talk, except in an occasional faltering whisper. Those who went into her room thought they could already catch the smell of death.

As the poor Sister was given only a day or two longer to live, the children at the Seattle orphanage were already rehearsing for her requiem. And on the morning of December 17, a Sister who had to go to the business section was stopped by the superior on the way out. "Oh, Sister," she was told, "while you're downtown you had better drop into the undertaker's and arrange for Sister Delfina's funeral. That will save you a trip tomorrow."

This Sister found she had to ring up the superior about something, and then heard: "You need not bother about the undertaker; Sister Delfina is better."

"What do you mean by 'better', Mother? You know what the doctor said."

"You come home. Sister is all right now."

And she *was* all right—not merely better, but perfectly cured. The night before, after praying to Francesca, she had seen her in a dream. She was still too weak to speak much or get out of bed, but she had simply announced that she was cured. Nearly twenty years later, she is still alive and has never had the slightest recurrence of her disease.

These are the miracles that were officially accepted for Francesca's beatification. The doctors in the cases wrote out all the details under oath, and these were sent to Rome, where each case was examined by two specialists appointed for that purpose. Their opinion was that in each instance there was something quite beyond all medical aid; that a cure under any circumstances would have been impossible, and that the instantaneous cure could only be pronounced as miraculous.

And Francesca's miracles are still occurring, though there is now no need to subject them to the same sort of technical scrutiny. Many of them are, however, attested to by the attending physicians. A doctor on the staff of the Columbus Hospital at Seattle is given up—and gives himself up—as incurable. Nevertheless, he gets well. So does a nun suffering from a heart complaint in New York. A young woman is cured of meningitis at Lodi in 1938; a child dying of peritonitis is cured at Chicago; an American nightclub singer, making her debut in London, is seized by laryngitis, puts a picture of Francesca to her throat and prays, and recovers her voice; a marine at Guadalcanal swims all night, after his ship had been sunk, praying to Mother Cabrini, whose relic he carries, and in the morning finds himself safe on shore. A relic is not involved in all these cases, but prayer always is. And though not every one of these happenings would be accepted as first-class miracles according to the definition of the Congregation of Rites, they may be miracles nonetheless. The two miracles accepted by the Holy See for the beatification of Francesca Cabrini are those of Peter Smith and Sister Delfina Grazioli. They were selected for presentation out of a number of others that might have served the purpose equally as well.

The first steps toward beatification were taken in 1928, when witnesses were examined under oath at Chicago, Lodi, and Rome. This, the Ordinary Process, was followed five years later by the Apostolic Process, which went over much the same ground. The medical evidence for the miracles was examined by the doctors appointed by the Congregation of Rites on March 15 and again on June 14, 1938. Then on July 31, Pope Pius XI issued the decree of *Tuto*, permitting Francesca's beatification. The ceremony of beatification itself took place on Sunday, November 13. The day was well chosen, as the following day is the birthday of the institute. Equally well chosen was the day for Francesca's feast; it was December 22, the day on which she died.

The ceremonies need not be described here, as they were in accordance with the standard pattern. It is enough to say that all the splendor of ritual at the Church's command is displayed on such occasions. To the ringing of bells and the peal of silver trumpets, Francesca's portrait was unveiled over the Throne Altar that is Bernini's masterpiece—and she was formally beatified.

Of the Missionary Sisters present, those from the United States made up the largest contingent, but there were ten Chinese postulants there—the China of which Francesca had dreamed as a child being at last open to the work of her daughters. Cardinal Mundelein sang the pontifical high Mass, and at the radio broadcast that evening he said he believed he could claim to be the first cardinal in the history of the Church to celebrate both the funeral services and the beatification ceremonies for the same person. Touchingly he concluded: "It is with the hope as well as the prayer that, having said the last blessing over her lifeless remains as well as the first prayer at Saint Peter's at her beatification, I may find her great soul to welcome me when the doors of eternity open for me."

At the same broadcast, Peter Smith, by then a youth of seventeen, also spoke, telling of his cure. "I for one", he said, "know for certain that the age of miracles has not passed."

INDEX